HOW
WE
LIVE
NOW

redefining home and family
in the 21st century

HOW
WE
LIVE
NOW

Bella DePaulo, PhD

ATRIA BOOKS
New York London Toronto Sydney New Delhi

BEYOND WORDS
Hillsboro, Oregon

ATRIA BOOKS

An Imprint of Simon & Schuster, Inc.
1230 Avenue of the Americas
New York, NY 10020

BEYOND WORDS

20827 N.W. Cornell Road, Suite 500
Hillsboro, Oregon 97124-9808
503-531-8700 / 503-531-8773 fax
www.beyondword.com

Managing editor: Lindsay S. Brown
Editors: Henry Covey, Emily Han
Copyeditors: Kristin Thiel, Emmalisa Sparrow
Proofreader: Jennifer Weaver-Neist
Design: Devon Smith
Composition: William H. Brunson Typography Services

First Atria Books/Beyond Words hardcover edition August 2015

ATRIA BOOKS and colophon are trademarks of Simon & Schuster, Inc. Beyond Words Publishing is an imprint of Simon & Schuster Inc., and the Beyond Words logo is a registered trademark of Beyond Words Publishing, Inc.

For more information about special discounts for bulk purchases, please contact Simon & Schuster Special Sales at 1-866-506-1949 or business@simonandschuster.com.

The Simon & Schuster Speakers Bureau can bring authors to your live event. For more information or to book an event, contact the Simon & Schuster Speakers Bureau at 1-866-248-3049 or visit our website at www.simonspeakers.com.

Manufactured in the United States of America

10 9 8 7 6 5 4 3 2 1

Library of Congress Cataloging-in-Publication Data

DePaulo, Bella M.
  How we live now : redefining home and family in the 21st century / Bella DePaulo.
     pages   cm
  Includes bibliographical references.
     1. Families—United States.   2. Dwellings—Social aspects—United States.   3. Lifestyles—United States.   I. Title.
  HQ536.D4297   2015
  306.850973—dc23

                                                                    2015004194

ISBN 978-1-58270-479-1
ISBN 978-1-4767-6300-2 (ebook)

The corporate mission of Beyond Words Publishing, Inc.: *Inspire to Integrity*

To my siblings, Peter, Lisa, and Joseph

And to lifespace pioneers everywhere, finding their place, their space, and their people, and inspiring us all

CONTENTS

NOT GOING NUCLEAR
So Many Ways to Live and Love

I've been writing about single life for many years, in academic articles, in my book *Singled Out*, and in blogs such as *Living Single* at Psychology Today.com. I take on just about every aspect of single life that is of interest to people who want to live their single lives fully and joyfully. In 2010, I wrote a blog post, "Not Going Nuclear: So Many Ways to Live and Love," with the tagline, "Increasingly, households and personal communities are not anchored by couples." Right away, readers began to share stories of their own non-nuclear ways of living that they had found magical. They talked about their communities of friends from their young adult lives and the extended families of their childhood. They lovingly described people who were not relatives yet had been invited into their homes and their lives. They admitted to their envy of couples who are truly committed to being with each other for the long term but not to living together. Rather than attracting trolls, the discussion generated reactions such as, "Your comment brings tears to my eyes."

Other readers emailed their stories to me rather than posting them online. That continued long after the post was published. The topic had captured their imagination and their emotions. Still, I may not have pursued the matter any further if I hadn't noticed something else—lots of people were talking about this beyond my one little blog post. Within just a few years, stories about imaginative living arrangements appeared in major newspapers and news services such as the *New York Times*, the *Washington Post*, the *Wall Street Journal*, *USA Today*, and Reuters, in sections ranging from garden and homes to aging, to the national and regional pages and the opinion pages. Magazines such as the *Atlantic*, *Time*, *Newsweek/Daily Beast*, *More*, *SmartMoney*, *Elle*, and *Dwell* all described innovations in living. Segments aired on ABC, CBS, NBC, and CNN. Regional media highlighted local examples, and bloggers of many stripes swapped stories and shared fantasies.

It was time to take the topic seriously. I wanted to learn more about the creative ways of living that today's adults are fashioning. I wanted to go beyond the mostly brief sketches that had been published and explore in greater depth the psychology of the choices people are making. I wanted to know how people living in different ways get help when they need it and companionship when they want it. I wondered what "home" means to people who are not living with family. I wanted to hear about the different arrangements people tried, what worked for them and what didn't, and what they learned about themselves along the way.

So, I spent a few years traveling from coast to coast, interviewing Americans in their homes. Men and women ranging in age from nineteen to ninety-one told their stories. More than four hundred others described their places, their spaces, and their people in a survey I posted online; their observations also shaped my understandings.

Some of the innovations I learned about in my research were contemporary inflections of longstanding traditions. Living with a group of friends under one roof, for example, is no longer just a young-adult way of living. That arrangement has become so popular among "women of a certain age" that there is an organization devoted to making it happen; it is, of course, called Golden Girl Homes. Multigenerational homes might sound old-fashioned, but they, too, have become increasingly popular over the past decades. The twenty-first-century versions accommodate more generations and more diverse sets of relatives than ever before.

I don't think I fully appreciated, before starting this project, the depth of some Americans' yearning for the communal experiences of village life. I had never heard of cohousing communities, in which people create neighborhoods with homes arranged around an open, green space. The special twenty-first-century adaptation of village life is that autonomy matters as much as interconnectedness. Cohousing residents share a common house, where they typically meet a few times a week to share meals, but they have their own private homes or apartments as well.

The cherishing of autonomy and independence among today's adults is reflected in the record number of people who live alone—in the United States and around the world. It was news to me—of the very best kind—that there is a modern-day innovation dedicated to fulfilling the lifestyle wishes of people like me. At sixty-one, as I look ahead to my later years, what I want most is to stay in my own place, on my own, as long as possible. Thanks to the national Village movement, that is more attainable now than it has ever been before.

Some of the ways of living that I discovered are utterly contemporary. I had not known that there is a nationwide registry, called CoAbode, of tens of thousands of single mothers looking to live with other single mothers and their kids. Even more radical are the parenting partnership registries for single people who want to have kids without raising them singlehandedly. People who sign up are looking for a lifelong commitment to parent together; romance and marriage are not part of the package.

Lifespace Literature

Until now, there has been no unifying concept or name to tie together the stories that have been written about the ways we currently live.

I'll call the topic *lifespace literature*. It is about the lives we envision and then build around our places, our spaces, and our people. It taps into Americans' obsession with real estate and with the popular best-places-to-live features, but goes beyond that relatively narrow focus to incorporate the people who are important to us and our own psychological relationships to places and spaces and people. It recognizes that a place to live is also a way to live, and we have never had as many choices as we do now.

In this book, I pull together many media accounts of contemporary experiments in living and put them in the context of the changing demographics and values of American society. I also draw from social-science research, some of it my own, to make sense of how we are living now. Why are our choices so different than they were in the past, and why, in some instances, are they so very similar? Many of the studies I describe were based on representative national samples, so they transcend any of the idiosyncrasies of the particular set of people I interviewed.

The heart and soul of this book are the people who let me into their homes and their lives. I didn't know what to expect when I sent out tentative feelers. Years later, I am still blown away by the graciousness and openness of the people who responded. They told me their stories, warts and all, knowing that they would be released like balloons into the publishing air and not knowing into whose backyard they might land.

The people I interviewed do not make up a very large group, and they do not capture the experiences of all Americans. Their lifespaces are just a sampling of the many creative ways that people are living in twenty-first-century America. Still, I hope their stories will help readers realize how many attractive options they have now and inspire them to think up some new ones.

Some of the people I interviewed asked me to use a pseudonym. I use the real names of the other people—either their first names or their full names, as requested. The ages I report are from the time of the interviews.

When I ask people what matters to them in deciding how and with whom to live, they mention everything from dealing with the tasks of everyday life to existential concerns about who will care for them in later life. On a psychological level, there are two things that just about everyone wants, though in vastly different proportions. You won't find them mentioned in real-estate circulars, in reports from demographers about the ways we live, or (with rare exceptions) in the writings of architects, builders, or city planners. They want time with other people and time to themselves.

Everyone is seeking just the right mix of sociability and solitude, with both easy to come by. Sarah Stokes, who lives on her own, sometimes has so many social invitations that she stops answering her phone. Other times, though, her social circle is too quiet, and she is disheartened by having to be the one to initiate.

By living in cohousing, Karen Hester has found a way to have a place of her own and easy sociability too. Just steps outside her door, she finds neighbors in the courtyard or in the common house. There are community dinners several times a week, and a day now and then when the group comes together to keep the grounds in good shape. Anja Woltman and Tricia Hoffman live at opposite ends of a duplex, so each has a home of her own as well as a friend right next door. Robert Jones lives with his brother and sister-in-law in a big old Southern house in a charming small town. He finds his easy sociability, though, with his poker buddies and his theater group, and the neighbors he sees every day as he walks to work.

In choosing a way to live, people are also regulating access to themselves in ways that are both profound and mundane. Whether they end up satisfied with their situations depends on the fit between what they want psychologically and what their living arrangements afford. The important questions include:

- To what extent do you want to know other people and be known by them?
- How much control do you want over the depth to which you are known by other people?
- Do you like the sense of presence of other people?
- Is solitude something you enjoy now and then or something you crave?

People who want to know other people and be known to them are happy to engage in the day-to-day exchanges of pleasantries, but they don't want their contacts with their fellow humans to end there. They want to be friends and not just acquaintances.

A *New York Times* story captured the essence of the conditions conducive to the development of close friendships, as documented in social-science research: "proximity, repeated and unplanned interactions, and a setting that encourages people to let their guard down and confide in each other."[1] The rhythms of cohousing, with regular or semi-regular dinners, meetings, and the occasional workdays—together with the spontaneous chats along the pathways of neighborly spaces—offer magnificent opportunities to develop relationships with breadth and depth. In cohousing, relationships can grow in their own good time. The more deliberative versions of house-sharing, which go beyond mere roommate mentalities, are also rich with the potential for forming close, personal bonds.

Maria Hall, who lives in a home of her own, is happy to cede some control over the access that people have to her and her house. "I don't have a 'you have to call me before you come over' policy," she tells me. "If the truck is in the back, just come on in. If there's something on the floor, step over it." When I visit Diane Dew, who lives on the first floor of a two-story building, I notice that the people on the top story across the way could probably see into her windows. That might make some people feel observed and self-conscious. Diane, though, tells me that she loves opening her shades in the morning and waving to the children eating breakfast near their kitchen window; they, in turn, blow kisses to her.

Not everyone wants closeness from the people around them. That's what Lucy Whitworth learned from her community of women, who live in a house and two duplexes arranged around a generous stretch of gardens and fruit trees. Telling me about the kinds of people who have fit into their group well over the years, Lucy said that it was important that "you don't mind if people know about who you are."

The sense of the presence of other people, though distracting to some, can be reassuring to others. One of two widows who live next door to each other told me that in the evenings, when she looks outside, she is comforted by the sight of the light on in the home of her friend. Marianne Kilkenny, who shares a house with four other people, likes the privacy she has in her own suite. At the same time, she enjoys hearing the soft sounds of her housemates going about their daily routines outside her door. She missed that when she lived alone.

Just about everyone I interview wants at least *some* private time. I thought for a moment that I had found one person who doesn't, Danica Meek, a twenty-one-year-old who lives in a tiny room in a big house that she shares with one other woman and three men. When I ask Danica what she likes to do by herself, she can't think of anything at first. Then she says she might like to do some writing but has not done any yet. As we continue to talk, though, she mentions how much she enjoys being the first one up in the morning and starting her day in peaceful solitude. Len, a ninety-one-year-old widower who opened his home to his daughters and grandsons, does not see the appeal of living alone. But he also shares with me what he remembers of a quote from Einstein: "Being alone can be painful in youth but sweet in old age."

For some, solitude feels more like a need or a craving than a mere desire. Arlia, who has a committed relationship but insists on living on her own, explains that she "requires" time alone "to get centered and balanced, to feel solid."

How We Live Now opens, in chapter 1, with a sneak peek of some of the innovative lifespaces that anchor the subsequent chapters. That chapter is also the place where I offer a nod of appreciation to some of the dreamy lifespaces of the past, including some of the better-known ones (the hippie communes) and a few that are less well-known but had so very much to offer (such as a city that was built to cater to single parents). I'll also spoil the ending and tell you what I've concluded, after years of research, about the relationship that I think is the most significant one in twenty-first-century American life: it is friendship.

The book begins with lifespaces involving the most togetherness and then proceeds to the ones offering the most privacy and solitude. Chapter 2 is about a way of living that is not so new but has been newly embraced in the past few decades: sharing a home with two or three or even four generations of family, or with extended family or adult siblings. Chapter 3 is also about people who live under the same roof with other people; but this time the housemates are friends or acquaintances who soon became friends, rather than family. The people featured in chapter 4 all have their own private residences where they may be living alone, with friends, in a nuclear family or other family, or some combination. What makes them special is that they and the other people who live near them have decided that they want to live in a genuine community, where they get to know and care about each other, and become part of one another's everyday lives. Toward the end of the book, in chapters 6 and 8, I share the stories of people who live alone. The people in chapter 6 are all in committed, long-term, coupled relationships, but they have chosen to live in places of their own. Chapter 8 is dedicated to single people who live alone.

Two groups of people—parents who are not couples (chapter 5) and seniors (chapter 7)—get special chapters. Some of the most innovative lifespaces have been created by people who are solo parents, or who are single and want to be parents but do not want to raise children on their own. Also remarkable are the many creative lifespaces imagined by today's seniors, who looked at the too-frequent institutionalization of their elders and vowed not to let that happen to them.

Many of the people I profile could have fit in more than one chapter. There are, for example, single parents who live in cohousing, whose stories I tell in the chapter on living in community (chapter 4) rather than the chapter on single parenting (chapter 5). There are also seniors who are sharing a home with other seniors or living apart from the love of their life, whose stories I tell in chapters 3 and 6 rather than in the chapter on living arrangements for the new old age (chapter 7).

In my interviews, I talked to people who are not looking for the one perfect living situation. Instead, they believe that different arrangements suit them best at different times in their lives. Others simply crave novelty. Even if they like the way they are currently living, before long, they are itching to move on.

Then there are the people who really do want to find their ideal living situation and settle in to live their best, most authentic, and most meaningful life. Over the course of the interviews, I'd sometimes get a sense that I was talking to people who have found their place, their space, and their people. Then I knew just how that person would answer three of the last questions I asked.

Q: When you have been away for a while, how does it feel to come home?

A: I love it.

Q: What has been the most contented time in your life?

A: Right now.

Q: How long will you stay here?

A: They'll carry me out of here.

1

HOW WE LIVE NOW
Finding Our Place, Our Space, and Our People

In the fall of 2012, an article in the "Great Homes and Destinations" section of the *New York Times* began like this:

> In a slowly gentrifying section of Bushwick, Brooklyn, where gunshots are no longer heard and the local brothel has been turned into a family home, five friends made a 10-year commitment.
>
> The group—two architectural designers, two fashion designers and one advertising executive, all in their 20s—rented 2,700 square feet of raw space and agreed to fix it up and live there for a decade. Two years into that commitment, it seems to be going pretty well.[1]

In just a few understated sentences, the *Times* captured a way of living that would have been nearly unthinkable not so very long ago. A confluence of cultural, demographic, and economic factors have turned the opening decades of the twenty-first century into a time of unprecedented innovation and experimentation as Americans search for their places, their spaces, and their people.

The choices of the five twentysomethings are remarkable in a number of ways:

- **Demographics and relationships:** The five men and women in their twenties are making a ten-year commitment, and it is not to a spouse or even to the goal of finding a spouse, though that is not out of the question. It is a commitment to one another; as friends. In 1956, the median age at which Americans first married was as young as it has ever been—22.5 for men and 20.1 for women. By 2013, though, the respective ages had jumped to 29.0 and 26.6—and that's just for those who *do* marry.[2] Today, the twenties can be devoted to all manner of pursuits; marriage and children, while still an aspiration for many, no longer dominate.
- **Geography:** They are staying in the city and not looking toward the suburbs. That's new too. For the first time in at least two decades, cities and surrounding suburbs are growing faster than the regions beyond the suburbs.[3]
- **Architecture and design:** A century ago, many Americans were selecting houses from a Sears catalog. Now, adults can step into a big hunk of raw space that stretches beyond a space fit for a couple or a nuclear family, and envision a place they will call home.[4]

The friends have separate bedrooms. They share showers, a bathroom, and space for entertaining. They are also sharing their lives; they consider themselves family.

These five people could have followed a more familiar script. Instead, they dreamed. They designed their own lives, with their own place, their own space, and their own people.

Another group of young New Yorkers, all heterosexual single men, began living together just after they graduated from New York University. That was eighteen years before they were interviewed about their experiences by the *New York Times*.[5] When the rent for their loft in Chelsea doubled after fourteen years, they could have gone their separate ways. But they are close friends, and they chose to look for another place they could share instead.

The four men, all approaching forty, found two stories of a concrete building in Queens that they affectionately call Fortress Astoria. The men have their own rooms (more like tiny apartments) and share a kitchen, living room, and garden. None of the bedrooms are adjoining, so the men have privacy when they want to bring dates home.

"We are really close and care about each other deeply," one of the men said. "And yet we give each other lots of space . . . We've got all the benefits of a family with very little of the craziness that normally comes along with them."

Not one of the men is a parent, but that doesn't make them all that unusual. In 2012, the birthrate in the United States fell to the lowest level since 1920, when reliable records first became available.[6]

The ease and comfort they feel with one another is clearly one of the main attractions of the way the men live, but so is the money they save by splitting the rent and utilities four ways. Without the pressure of a pricier housing tab, the men can pursue circuitous, risky, and exhilarating career paths that the company men of eras past could not imagine. One of the friends tried an office job for a while. The health insurance was nice, but the work wasn't. He is now a personal trainer. His roommates are in filmmaking, acting, and the design of role-playing fantasy games.

In a vibrant Seattle neighborhood, complete with markets, cultural venues, and convenient public transportation, a group of artists longed to find affordable housing. There wasn't any. There was, though, an old hotel that captured the fancy of their dreamy minds. With help from the city, they converted the hotel into a cooperative home with twenty-one living spaces, including doubles, triples, and solo "Zen" units.[7]

The housemates—who range in age from nineteen to fifty—share kitchens, bathrooms, lounges, laundry facilities, and a roof deck. It is their responsibility to keep the building in good shape, but they throw work parties to get that done—so it doesn't feel like a chore. They have potlucks at home and organize outings to local stomping grounds.

The Brooklyn, Queens, and Seattle stories are all examples of one of the newly fashionable ways of living in twenty-first-century America: under the same roof with people who are not your spouse or family. The bond that unites the housemates is not blood or marriage but friendship.

The trend, however, is not confined to urban areas, to young adults, or to "artistic types." All across the nation, unrelated people who once went their separate ways (often with a spouse and kids in tow) are now living together.

Older people have proven themselves remarkable innovators. Americans are not just living longer than ever before, they are also staying healthy longer.[8] They may need some help as they age, and the growing numbers who are divorced, widowed, or have always been single may want companionship, but most prefer to find those resources and people outside of institutional settings.[9]

And so they fantasize and make things happen. After AARP surveyed twelve hundred women forty-five and older about how they would like to live, the published report highlighted this quote from a fifty-seven-year-old: "I keep telling my friends that we all need to buy a big house with a common area downstairs and live together—not like a nursing home but truly a place where we have communal living."[10]

That's just what three women from Mount Lebanon, Pennsylvania, did. They were all divorced, living on their own, working full-time, and in great shape. They were in their fifties and concerned that maintaining their independence may not always be so easy. So, they set out to find a place they could share. It has now been about a decade that they have been living happily ever after in a charming five-bedroom brick Colonial on a tree-shaded corner lot.[11]

Just outside of Indianapolis, two single women, best friends for decades and accustomed to living on their own, also decided to live together. They were fifty-five and fifty-nine when they found a small three-bedroom home in a cozy community known as a pocket neighborhood.[12] In Saratoga Springs, New York, another pair of longtime friends—one retired and the other on the cusp of retirement—sold the homes they owned and bought one together. In the single-level home, they each have their own bedroom, study, and bathroom down a long hallway from a big kitchen, dining room, and family room.

Grown Kids and Their Parents Staying Together

Another group of Americans is also, in growing numbers, living with people other than a spouse. They are young adults who are heading back home to live with their parents—or who never left. They are not just the youngest of the grown children but also those hugging the thirty-year-old milestone.

In 1980, hardly anyone in the twenty-five- to thirty-four-year-old demographic wanted to live with their parents, and only 11 percent actually did. That was the lowest percentage on record. By 2012, the rate had climbed to 23.6 percent. The recession of 2007 to 2009 provided part of the impetus for the homeward trek, but not all; the trendlines had been creeping up continuously since 1980.[13]

Some grown children, such as twenty-two-year-old Georgetown University graduate Aodhan Beirne, head back to their childhood bedrooms to sleep under their dinosaur blankets.[14] Others find fresh ways to live at home while still maintaining a space of their own. Ella Jenkins, twenty-three, lives in her parents' backyard in Frazier Park, California, in one of those undersize homes attracting outsize media attention. She built her mobile 130-square-foot house with the help of her stepfather. It may seem tiny to others, but it is welcoming and bright. "I just feel this wonderful feeling of peace," she said. "I just walk in and feel it's huge."[15]

The sizeable number of young adults moving back in with their parents has caused a bit of a kerfuffle among the punditry. The kids are called the boomerang generation, the go-nowhere generation, and generation stuck. The moms and dads who take them in are called helicopter parents and worse. The critics, though, may be appraising this new trend through twentieth-century glasses.

Today's young adults and their parents are not the same as the ones from the generation-gap years of the 1960s and 1970s, when many parents just could not fathom what their kids were thinking. They have more in common now: "the invisible line between parent and child is dissolving."[16]

In a 2012 generations survey, the AARP asked young adults about their relationship with their parents, and they also asked boomers to describe their bonds with their parents when they were in their early twenties. In every way, the younger generation reported more connectedness with their parents than did the boomer generation. They said they talk with their parents more often and more deeply, see each other more often, and are more approving of young adults living with their parents.[17]

The close connections continue after the young adults move out. In fifteen countries, social scientists tracked the lives of people who had lived with their parents during their early adult years. They found that those who had lived with their parents longer remained in closer touch with their parents after they left than siblings who headed out on their own at an earlier age. Years later, they still helped each other a bit more too.[18]

There is little to suggest that young adults living at home are just mooching off their parents. About 90 percent help with household expenses and nearly 50 percent pay rent.[19] They do build their savings by living at home instead of in a place of their own. And that, claimed family scholar Steven Mintz, is a good thing. Spending early-adult years with parents, he suggested, "is the best preparation for success in an economy that rewards ambition, risk taking, entrepreneurship, and adaptability."[20]

Many Relatives and Ages, All Under One Roof

The boomer parents and their own parents may not have been very close during the boomers' young adult years, but increasing numbers of them are living together now. As in the past, aging parents sometimes live in granny flats or mother-in-law apartments; but today's multigenerational home-sharers are dreaming up new arrangements. In British Columbia, for example, Ann and Gord Baird and Ann's parents built a place together that straddles the line between one home and two. Each residence has its own kitchen, but the two kitchens are connected with a pass-through. The two semi-independent houses share plumbing, heating, electricity, and the washing machine.[21] In Port Orchard, Washington, Kathy Peck and her husband live separately from Kathy's mother—but the two houses are right across the driveway from each other.[22]

Dramatic increases in longevity over the past century have profound implications for the ways we live. A twenty-year-old in 2000 was more likely to have a living grandmother than a twenty-year-old in 1900 was to have a living mother.[23] That makes it increasingly possible for three or more generations to live under the same roof. In the past decade or so, people have been doing just that.

The first decade of the twenty-first century was also a time of increasing home-sharing by other combinations of family members. They included pairs of siblings, skipped generations (for example, grandparents and their grandchildren), and various assortments of cousins, aunts and uncles, nieces and nephews, and others.

So Many Ways to Live Alone

Add together all of the categories of people now sharing a home—the unrelated adults, young adults who have returned to live with their parents, aging parents who are living with their middle-aged offspring, siblings who move in together, and other sets of relatives sharing a home—and you have a trend that is as formidable as a better-known one: the increase in living alone. In 2013, nearly thirty-four million American adults lived alone.[24] Another 41.2 million adults shared a home with one or more adults who were not a spouse or romantic partner.[25]

Official Census Bureau counts of people living alone are based on a straightforward criterion: just one person occupies the dwelling unit. The bureau is only looking at the residence and who is inside it. Broaden the view, though, and now this matter of living alone has many textures. Consider two longtime friends with homes right next door. They see each other nearly every day and often go to dinner or shows together. They each count as living alone. So do two friends who live on separate sides of a duplex. Even some who live in places of their own in what may look like an anonymous apartment building have friends nearby—maybe even the same floor of the same building—because they chose to be close to one another. Pull back even further, and the person living solo may be part of a neighborhood deliberately created by people who want to live as a community—with homes of their own but who regularly get together for activities such as dinners, gardening, discussions, and outings.

Others who live alone are connected to another person in a more surprising way—they are in long-term, coupled relationships. Some are married; some are even married with kids. These are not (just) the couples constrained to live apart because of job demands; such commuter marriages have been part of our lexicon for some time. They are the couples who could live together but choose not to. They prefer to have their own places and spaces. We know about dual-dwelling duos from Hollywood, such as Tim Burton and Helena Bonham Carter, Woody Allen and Mia Farrow, and some dignitaries from the past, such as Mary Wollstonecraft and William Godwin. Ordinary people live this way too. In the United States, about 7 percent of women and 6 percent of men do so.[26]

Some dual-dwelling duos live very near each other. Laura Ann Jacobs and Robert Pardo, for example, each live in a tiny bungalow, one behind the other, in Lake Worth, Florida.[27] In San Francisco, Juliana Grenzback and Joshua Brody live across the street from each other—one in a house, the other in an apartment.[28] In White Pines, California, Dave Wallace lives in the home that he owns an hour down the mountain from the home Donna Guadagni owns.[29]

The City Built to Cater to Single Parents

Among the Americans who may be especially open to creative ways of living are single parents. In the contemporary political landscape, single mothers are too often scapegoated as the cause of the nation's ills. There was a time, though, when professionals thought deeply and creatively about how to seamlessly integrate places for living with ways of making a living, especially for single parents and working wives.

One model was a city built around a shipyard. Both housing and child-care were affordable, public transportation was convenient, and on-the-job training was readily available. The childcare centers were

> open twenty-four hours a day, seven days a week (just like the shipyards), complete with infirmaries for sick children, child-sized bathtubs so that mothers [did] not need to bathe children at home, cooked food services so that mothers [could] pick up hot casseroles along with their children, and . . . large windows with views of the river, so that children [could] watch the launchings at the yards.[30]

The place was Vanport City, Oregon, the real location of women represented by the celebrated icon Rosie the Riveter. Vanport City was designed to support the wartime productivity of adults who were not at war, including single people, single mothers, and wives whose husbands were overseas. When World War II was over, however, so was Vanport City.

This is an example of the industrial model of housing that places a premium on efficiency.[31] It was replaced by the model of home-as-haven, the one we have come to regard as traditional. Each nuclear family owned a home of its own—perhaps an iconic Cape Cod—on a lot of its own, out in the suburbs. Maybe men returning from the war welcomed the privacy and intimacy their havens afforded them after years of bunking with fellow soldiers. Not all of their wives were delighted to step away from their jobs as riveters and welders, but many of them did, staying home to raise the kids while their husbands went off to work.

The development of suburbs dotted with single-family homes continued apace, even as the number of single parents, singles without kids, and couples without kids continued to grow, and as more of the mothers in nuclear families worked outside of the home.

For the new demographics, the realities of suburban life did not match the idyllic images splashed across the pages of glossy magazines. Commutes were costly and time consuming. Daycare was expensive and inconveniently located. The adults who stayed home felt increasingly isolated, and they were not just imagining their disconnection.[32] A national survey ongoing since 1974 has shown that Americans have never been less likely to be friends with their neighbors as they are now. The lowest levels of neighborliness were recorded in the suburbs.[33]

In earlier times, mothers could find people within their own homes to help with the children. The birthrate was higher, and extended-family living was more commonplace, so both young girls and grown women were available to pitch in. Demographers studying changes in households between 1880 and 2000 found that over that time period, fewer and fewer females were residing in each household, and more of those who were in the home were preoccupied with jobs or school.[34]

Creating the Contemporary Village

For all the conveniences and efficiencies of the industrial model of living exemplified by Vanport City, it has not become an attractive alternative to the home-as-haven model. The stark housing structures had no aesthetic appeal. The teams of interchangeable childcare workers who fed and bathed the children and then handed them off to their mothers at the end of the work shift lacked the warmth and personal involvement that Americans prize. Now that fast-food restaurants, laundromats and dry cleaners, and 24/7 convenience stores are ubiquitous, there is less unique value to residents (and less potential profit for merchants) of the on-site services that Vanport City provided. The industrial model is also unlikely to foster a sense of community or neighborliness.

An alternative to both the industrial and the home-as-haven models of housing is the neighborhood strategy, in which people create a community that really is neighborly. When these intentional neighborhoods are successful, they are a boon not only to single parents but people of any marital or parental status—or any other characteristic, for that matter—who want to live in a real community.

Some groups try to create a community from a neighborhood that already exists. Cul-de-sacs, in which a relatively small number of houses are already arranged around a circumscribed space, may be particularly amenable to neighborliness. Interested participants can initiate regular neighborly events (such as potlucks or coffee klatches) or organize the sharing of resources (such as lawn equipment) or services (such as childcare).[35]

In Boulder, Colorado, an architect and a builder with years of collaborative experience created a unique arrangement of three flat-roofed, modernist townhomes. Two of the townhomes are separated by just a narrow walkway. The third sits atop one of the other two. All three feature glass corners and showcase the spectacular mountain views. The builder and his wife live in one of the homes, the head of a graphic design studio and his spouse are in another, and a single woman, who is an internet entrepreneur, has the home on top. Both couples are in their sixties. The single woman is forty-six. The *New York Times* called the community a semicommune—the residents' experience is not all about togetherness; they have ample privacy too.[36]

People interested in recapturing the small-town neighborly ethos in modern American society no longer need to improvise. There is a model for doing so that has been implemented successfully across the United States. It is called cohousing. In 2012, I traveled to Oakland, California, to attend the annual Conference of the Cohousing Association of the United States to learn about the phenomenon firsthand.

I was especially eager to hear visionary architect Charles Durrett, who introduced the concept of cohousing to Americans and went on to design dozens of U.S. cohousing communities. In a darkened room illuminated only by his slides, he perched informally on a chair and told his stories.

In 1980, when he was attending the University of Copenhagen, he walked to and from the train station each day. On the way, he passed numerous sets of homes and apartment buildings devoid of any social interactions. One cluster of houses, though, was different:

I saw a lot of activity between the houses. People were stopping with their laundry basket in hand to talk to their neighbors. In the evening, there might be three or five people sitting around a table with a cup of tea or a beer. On the weekends, two or three people were in a parking area, looking under the hood of a car.[37]

Durrett learned that the group had created their own neighborhood. They found the land and recruited architects and planners willing to let them take the lead in designing their neighborhood and residences. Each decision was designed to foster community. Houses were turned toward each other, around a courtyard, where children could play and adults could stop and chat. Cars were kept on the periphery, out of the way.

Once cohousing communities are built, the residents are still in charge; the communities are entirely self-governing. Residents attend regular meetings to make decisions and aim for consensus. They also do not pay others to maintain their neighborhood. Everyone pitches in, usually on designated workdays, which residents describe as adding to the camaraderie. In cohousing communities, everyone has a personal apartment or house and a second house that everyone shares. The common house always includes a kitchen and a dining area, and often other rooms too. The community members typically have dinner together several times a week, and people take turns cooking and cleaning up.[38]

Each cohousing community incorporates elements that matter to the residents. The common house might include a library, a shop, a playroom for the kids, or a band room for the teens. Guest rooms and laundry facilities are often added too. That way, individual houses no longer need to dedicate space for those functions, homes can then be more compact, and both living expenses and individual footprints can be reduced.

On several days at the conference, attendees had the opportunity to board buses and visit various cohousing communities around Oakland and Berkeley. In each community, residents opened their homes to us, letting us walk through. One of the guides was a teenage boy. In the grassy areas at the center of the communities, kids ran around and so did their dogs. There were chicken coops and rabbit cages, gardens and barbecue pits. Photovoltaic panels on some of the buildings occasionally generated more power than the community used.

Exciting Times for Lifespace Professionals

Lifespace pioneers, who are creating new ways to live and love, include many ordinary people trying to solve the puzzles of their own lives. Increasingly, the professionals are getting involved too. I suppose planners, builders, architects, scholars, and policymakers must have longed for such opportunities to indulge their imaginations after decades pre-dominated by detached single-family homes on suburban lots.

Now, they are eager to tout the new trends in housing and development. John McIlwain, a senior fellow at the Urban Land Institute in Washington, has said that the standard ways of thinking have been upended by nonstandard ways of living. Instead of typecasting home seekers as first-time buyers and move-up buyers, for example, builders are recognizing the significance of life-cycle categories, such as single people with no children, single parents, multigenerational families, empty nesters, older baby boomers, and all sorts of people "who have little in common with the old notion of 'a family equals two parents with two kids.'"[39]

Many homeowners have been improvising as, for instance, when an empty nest leaves them with rooms to rent or to share, or when the nest that seemed to be emptying refills with grown children and aging parents. They look at their garage or attic or a room that doesn't get much use and transform it into a living space. And with zoning laws that institutionalize prejudices against multiunit dwellings in the suburbs, many do so illegally.

In a time of new interests and demands, laws are slowly changing, and so are the housing options on offer from the nation's largest home-builders. A Coldwell Banker survey of more than one thousand real-estate professionals found that more and more new homes are designed to include features such as second master bedrooms, separate kitchens, and separate entrances.[40] Pulte Homes offers layouts with big "flex rooms" and markets what they call the "Grand Retreat"—an apartment above a garage.[41] KB Homes has an Open Series, with up to six bedrooms.[42] Lennar boasts of "Next Gen—the Home within a Home."[43]

The professionals surveyed by Coldwell Banker also underscored a different trend: a growing number of boomers want to downsize. Some cite money as the main reason, but many point to a wish to live a simpler life. "After decades of living large—mini-mansions in subdivisions the size of cities—some Americans are retrenching and showing a new appreciation for the small, cozy, and neighborly."[44]

"Small" can sometimes mean super small. In New York City in 2012, Mayor Michael Bloomberg launched a competition for the design of apartment buildings with micro-units; the winning architects touted amenity-packed modular units from 250 to 370 square feet.[45] In a city with 1.8 million households of just one or two people but only a million studios and one-bedroom apartments, the need seems pressing. Seattle, San Francisco, and Boston have also forged ahead with their "apodment" buildings. The Seattle micro-units, for example, have drawn residents ranging in age from eighteen to seventy-two, including grandparents and young singles, scientists and truck drivers.[46]

Forward-looking thinkers have been joining forces to reimagine ways of living. In the fall of 2012, for instance, a group of builders, urban designers, architects, remodelers, policymakers, and real-estate professionals met in Portland, Oregon, for a one-day summit, "Build Small / Live Large." This was not a meeting of the National Association of Realtors, the industry behemoth that has been organizing annual conferences for more than a century and now flaunts an attendance of more than twenty thousand at each one. The three hundred or so Portland attendees gathered for "an intensive day of inspiration." On their docket were cutting-edge topics such as microhouses, pocket neighborhoods, innovations in accessory dwelling units, and designs that transcend Peter Pan homes (built on the assumption that everyone is able bodied and no one ever grows old).[47]

The Way We Used to Live

Experiments in living are not a new thing in the United States, however. The Shakers, for example, came to America in 1774, bringing with them the belief that all of the adults in their community were brothers and sisters. In the early years of the following century, one of the newly established communes was the Oneida Community in New Harmony,

Indiana. Their ideology discouraged any special attachments between particular men and women because all of the adults were considered to be married to one another.[48]

In the purest form of communal living, everything is shared—the land, the living spaces, the food, and even the clothes. Few such communities have survived into the twenty-first century. In Israel, even *kibbutz* life, now more than a century old, has adapted to contemporary mores and welcomes some privatization and privacy.[49]

To modern-day Americans, the best-known experimental communities are the hippie communes that proliferated in the 1960s and early 1970s. Hippies' countercultural ideology and love of sex, drugs, and rock and roll got the most press, but their quest for connection and community may have been even more important.

The commune from the countercultural era that has endured the longest without interruption is Twin Oaks, in Louisa, Virginia.[50] That's the one based on B. F. Skinner's popular novel, *Walden Two*—required reading when I was in college, but not when I got to graduate school and Skinner was still walking the halls of Harvard. Today's Twin Oaks members still try to sustain the community economically by making and selling products such as hammocks and tofu. Each resident works more than forty hours a week. (Tasks such as caring for children, milking cows, and doing other domestic chores all count as work.) In return, they receive food, housing, healthcare, and a small sum of personal spending money. Many large group houses have been built over the years; and in a nod to the valuing of solitude, members now have private rooms (but no televisions) within the group houses.

Twin Oaks boasts of no *one* central leader and no *one* religion practiced by all. The residents believe in egalitarianism, pacifism, and sharing, and strive for a small environmental footprint. Newly formed intentional communities often claim similar values.

Many contemporary innovations in living still retain the reverence for community that was at the core of communes past. Now, however, an emphasis solely on community appeals to very few. Americans—even those who want to live in a place that feels like a community—increasingly want their own spaces, whether that is a home of their own or a small apartment in a shared house. They prefer more autonomy, too, especially with regard to income. They do not want to be assigned jobs or told how much spending money they are allowed.

Historically, communes were often located in remote areas. Their geographical withdrawal was an expression of their ideological critique of society.[51] Today, Americans drawn to pocket neighborhoods and cohousing communities enjoy the "we" feeling that their spatial clustering inspires, but they also want to be a part of the larger society and not apart from it.

The Undervalued Relationship with an Oversized Place in Our Lives

In this nation of ever-shrinking families, sometimes geographically dispersed, there is a claim that people like to make when they have found a group of non-kin who have a special place in their hearts: "We're like family." Family has that rock-solid there-for-you sheen that no other kind of relationship has ever achieved. Despite decades of cynicism on all sorts of other matters, family is still sentimentalized. Yet it may be friendship, more so than family, that captures the essence of twenty-first-century life.

Friendship is chosen, not ascribed. It is voluntary. No, actually, it is double voluntary: you choose your friends, but you only get to have them as friends if they choose you back. You can have as many friends as you wish—as long as they want you too. The places of particular people in our lives can change as we become closer or more distant, emotionally or geographically, and as our interests and life circumstances evolve. That's the nature of contemporary life. The fluidity and elasticity are more akin to friendship than to kinship. Family shifts much more slowly, with marquee events such as birth, adoption, marriage, divorce, and death, rather than everyday life changes.

Friendship is not a comprehensive relationship. Romantic partners can fall for love songs proclaiming "you are my everything," but that's not what friendship is made of. Ever since Aristotle described three different kinds of friends—friends of utility, of pleasure, and of virtue—we have known that a set of friends can be a diverse lot. We can have friends we only see at basketball games or book club, friends we see nearly every day at work, and friends who are our confidants. Specialization is fine—we do not expect to like all of our friends in the same way or for the same reasons.

At the heart of friendship is fondness. Friends spend time together because they enjoy each other's company. Unlike spouses, they have not signed legal documents, and they less often extend invitations out of the feelings of obligation that sometimes govern family relationships. It's that double-voluntary quality once again.

The voluntary part of friendship is sweet. People hang out with you because they want to and not because they have to. The dark underside, though, is insecurity. If your friends do not have to be there when you are seriously ill or otherwise in need of help, can you really count on them? I think we like to say that the most important non-kin in our lives are "like family" because it feels more reassuring than to think of them as what they are—our friends.

Maybe we have that wrong. Maybe a network of friends can provide more resilient and flexible care than a spouse or small number of immediate family members.

Consider Lucy Whitworth, whom I mentioned earlier. In her early seventies (when I interviewed her), Lucy has always been single and has no children. The Census Bureau would classify her as living alone. According to the conventional wisdom, we should feel sorry for Lucy because she "doesn't have anyone."

About ten years ago, Lucy faced a diagnosis of breast cancer, with surgery and chemo to follow. When word of her grim news spread, forty-nine people stepped forward and asked how they could help. They became known as Lucy's Angels. An organizational strategy was developed, with a point person to coordinate. Each of the Angels could offer the kinds of help that person wanted to give, when available to give it. No one felt overwhelmed or burdened by the stress of caregiving. Lucy maintained control. She could tell the point person what she needed; and when she wanted time to herself, she could have that too.

Although the Angels created their own network of care, the process has now been systematized on websites such as Lotsa Helping Hands.[52] It is not just single people who participate; the friendship model that characterizes the way we live now is beneficial even to someone who has a spouse or nearby family members. Helping hands pitch in to help other caregivers as well as the person most in need.

Do-It-Yourself Lifespaces

This book is not just about living with friends or with family or in a place of your own. It isn't just about fashioning your own space or creating the community you've always dreamed of. It is about all of those options and so many more. Most of all, it is about choice.

In so many domains of our lives, choice is more available and more valued than it ever was before. To the youngest generation of adults, it is taken for granted. Children who grew up choosing their own TV shows rather than gathering around the living room with Mom, Dad, and the sibs to watch the same show; who chose their own music and sometimes their own food; who often had rooms, and even phones, of their own, are not going to lead Stepford lives as adults.

Already, the millennials are making choices that were predicted by almost no one. That exuberant anticipation of becoming old enough to drive has morphed, for some, into a shrug. The proportion of teens with a driver's license dropped 28 percent between 1998 and 2008. Adults under thirty-five own fewer cars and drive fewer miles. The "ownership society" is not their thing—not even home ownership. This rate for the under-thirty-five demographic fell by 12 percent between 2006 and 2011. The recession played a role, but so did preferences. Millennials are telling real-estate consultants that they like living in city centers and surrounding metropolitan areas, where residences are small and modes of transportation are accessible and plentiful.[53]

Adults of all ages can now turn on the television and see a vast array of ways to arrange a life. Gone are the days when television brought us little more than the nuclear-family land of *Ozzie and Harriet* and *Leave It to Beaver*. Twenty-first-century television has been a candy store of ways to live, some played for laughs and others utterly serious. Step onto the sets of shows such as *Parenthood*, *Modern Family*, *Six Feet Under*, *Brothers and Sisters*, and *Blue Bloods*, and you will find at least two generations sharing the same home. *Big Love* showcased an unapologetic portrayal of polygamist living. On *Grey's Anatomy*, many of the high-powered interns of the fictitious Seattle Grace Hospital, who started out as strangers, lived together in one big house; nine seasons later, most are now surgeons, but some are still living together in the same home. The early years of *Grey's* also featured a brain surgeon who savored his solitude in his old Airstream camper parked under the sky, apart from the rest of the world. On *Private Practice*, some of the doctors had places of their own, but two of them were right next door to one another.

Sweeping pronouncements about the state of society have long been topics of great fascination. Are we becoming a nation of loners, "bowling alone"?[54] Or are we so hyperconnected that we have lost touch with our true selves and are now living in an age marred by "the end of solitude"?[55] Such questions remain significant, but as psychologists step to the forefront of our cultural conversations, we are reminded of the uniqueness of each individual. Those who love their solitude are not troubled by the prospect of bowling alone or living alone, while those who relish their ties to other people may be cheering the demise of solitude.

Mobility is like that too. Whether it is something to be embraced or avoided depends on the person. To extraverts, for example, whether they move around a lot or mostly stay put does not matter much. For introverts, though, it is a whole different story. A study of more than seven thousand adults showed that introverts who had moved frequently when they were growing up, compared to those who rarely moved, had more difficulty developing strong personal relationships and maintaining them over time; and those difficulties seemed to undermine their happiness and satisfaction with their lives. There was even a hint that introverts who had moved around a lot did not live as long as introverts who were less mobile.[56]

A 2011 article in *Yes! Magazine* was titled "The Roommate Revolution: Why Living Alone Is Overrated."[57] I am not going to argue that any way of living is overrated; overrated is in the eye of the beholder. Instead, I want to describe a variety of lifespaces, all of which have worked well for some people and would be unfathomable to others. We all face constraints on the kinds of living arrangements we can pursue. Scarce financial resources, for example, can be limiting, though in these pages you will find some very creative and fulfilling lifespaces fashioned by people of little means.

There are two kinds of constraints that can be overcome, however, and I hope this book will help us all surmount them: the limits to our imagination when it comes to thinking about ways to live, and our misgivings about living in ways that are deemed too old fashioned or too out there or too anything else.

2

ONE BIG, HAPPY FAMILY
Relatives Sharing and Caring

She's just a little thing, a beautiful, slender, mocha-skinned girl with big brown eyes and a winsome smile. She's Mari, eight years old and the youngest of the four generations of women in the Lewis household. Her mom, Brianna, is twenty-six; her grandmother, Rebecca, fifty-four; and her great-grandmother, Virginia, eighty-three. They live in a semi-detached townhouse in a Twin Cities suburb. Virginia heads south when winter approaches; I arrive for my visit just after she leaves.

Mari is the emotional center of the family. All three adults take care of her. During the school year, her grandmother drops her off at the bus and her mother picks her up at the end of the day. Her great-grandmother often watches her during the summers. She has hardly ever had a babysitter.

Rebecca's favorite thing about being a part of this multigenerational household is clear: she loves getting to see her granddaughter every day. Brianna, though still in that stage of life that scholars have dubbed "emerging adulthood," has already tried out different paths in her quest to find her niche. Now she's sure she's found it: "I think my genuine happiness is being a mother. Yeah, I like to go out and have my fun, but I get high off life just making sure [Mari's] ready for school."

Mari, her mom tells me, is "so genuinely happy. And even through my roughest times, that girl completes me. I know you shouldn't let other people complete [you], but she does . . . I couldn't ask for a more perfect child."

Mari wears all that affection lightly. As her mom and grandmother and I talk, she busies herself in the kitchen, occasionally emerging to hang out with us in the living room. She has a quiet voice and the soft step of the dancer that she is. When I ask to take a picture of all of them, she positions herself between her mom and grandmother with one knee bent and her head resting adorably on her own shoulder. Her arms are around her mom's waist, and her grandmother has one arm around her daughter and the other around Mari. It is a picture of love.

It is also a picture of diversity. This is a multicultural family as well as a multigenerational one. Grandma Rebecca is European American and Native American; she describes her skin tone as peach. The lithe Brianna, also a dancer (and a passionate one at that), has an African American father. Her complexion is caramel colored, perhaps a bit lighter than Mari's. All three have the same big, warm smile. They even look coordinated, though I doubt they planned it that way. Brianna is in stylish pink sweats and wears them like a model. Rebecca, who has strawberry highlights in her blond hair, is wearing a soft-pink jersey under a pretty-patterned white sweater and a casually draped pink-and-white scarf. Mari has on a comfy top and a sparkly pink skirt over black leggings.

The Lewis household is welcoming and fluid. When I visit, every door to every room is open, except for Brianna's bedroom—she doesn't want me to see what a mess it is. (I know mess. I doubt it qualified.) It mostly stays that way, except when Rebecca or Brianna have a male friend over or when Rebecca needs time to herself. Then she goes into her room and shuts the door—"that's my oasis." Not Brianna. "I'm not the type of person [who] needs alone time."

Despite their distinctive looks, Rebecca and Brianna have some similar tastes, and when they have designs on each other's stuff, "there are no boundaries." Brianna mentions that when they want to borrow each other's things, they ask first whether the other person is planning to wear it. Otherwise, Rebecca offers, "it's a free-for-all with the jewelry, the perfume, the shoes."

Learning More from the Lewises: Meanings of *Home* and *Alone*

Rebecca shows me two of the bedrooms upstairs. Mari's is a Hello Kitty–festooned nest of stuffed animals, books, cute wall art, and a pink dresser. Rebecca is artistic. Her bedroom—and just about every other room—flaunts one or two of her hand-crafted designs of colorful jewels, stones, or shells, sometimes arranged in squares or rectangles, other times more free flowing.

We talk downstairs in the bright and open living room. Brianna curls into the arm of the beige leather couch in front of the picture window. Rebecca is in a matching chair, in front of a fireplace. The turquoise drapes and coordinated décor are there for the long run; the creepy paper spiders and cobwebs will fold up and slink away after Halloween.

Brianna loves getting to live in this house. She could live on her own if she wanted to, but then she would be in a small apartment. "I always said that if I had to make an apartment my home, that would be fine. I guess I'm spoiled that I never had to experience that." Rebecca is proud of transforming the dwelling into a place that draws compliments from the people who visit. But to her, "a house is just a house. The . . . people in it is what makes that home." Over the years, she has lived in different kinds of places with different configurations of people. The living arrangement she has now, she says, with four generations all under the same roof, really suits her. It best captures who she really is.

The four-generational Lewis household was not always all women. Rebecca's son, Brianna's brother, used to live with them too. The time just after he moved out, at age twenty-one, was one of the loneliest stretches of Rebecca's life, even though he stayed in the area. The whole family has dinner together several times a week, sometimes meeting at a restaurant after Brianna's or Mari's dance rehearsal. On Sundays, Rebecca's son and his girlfriend often join them.

Rebecca also feels lonely each time her mom leaves for the winter; that first week particularly, she really misses her. Brianna is very attached too. Describing her grandmother to me, she says, "She's like my best friend."

For a while, all of Rebecca's and Brianna's friends were mutual friends. That felt too enmeshed, especially to Brianna, and some uncharacteristic dissension festered between the two. It was hard on both of them. Now, each has friends of her own, as well as a few friends they still have in common. They are bonded again, in a more sophisticated way. "It is more like a peer relationship now that [Brianna] has gotten older," Rebecca tells me.

Rebecca does not have a best friend. She always thought she wanted one, but "I have learned that's not really necessary. I have a select group of friends, and each one of them has a purpose in my life."

Occasionally, both Rebecca and her mother are away, leaving Mari and Brianna in the house by themselves. The first time it happened, Brianna loved the first few days. She had "this exciting feeling," almost like she was a rebel.

> And then after that, I'm like, this is lame. It's stupid. Mari would be gone at a friend's house, and I was like, what am I going to do? . . . I don't want to live on my own. I don't want to do it to pretend to show somebody that I'm independent. I can afford to go live on my own; I don't want to. It's not fun to me . . . It's very lonely.

When I ask Brianna if she can think of any attraction to living alone, she talks about the possibility of meeting someone and moving out.

That's what *alone* means to Brianna—living with a husband and child but not with her mom.

Rebecca was once engaged, and when Brianna was away, her fiancé moved in. After a few days, Rebecca developed a severe viral infection. This is the moment they all talk about—those people who love having a spouse to share a home and a life with. This, they say, is when people who live alone get their comeuppance: sure, it may seem fine when you are well, but wait until you see what it is like when you are sick. Rebecca saw what it was like to have a partner under the same roof when she needed care: he mostly ignored her. By the time Brianna returned, the engagement was off and the guy was out.

Brianna had Mari when she was eighteen years old. She needed a lot of help, and her mother was there for her. Over time, Brianna grew more confident in her parenting. Now, she sets the rules, and everyone else follows them. For all the intensity of Brianna's love for Mari and her talk of Mari "completing" her, she does not want her daughter to be too focused only on her.

> I don't ever want Mari to think that I'm just the end-all or be-all or that I have all the answers, because guess what—I don't. I have a close network of people that I want her to trust. If she feels like she can't come and say something to me but she needs to get it out there, I want her to go say it.

Brianna used to think she could not be happy unless she had a man. "I was shopping for a marriage." But then she realized she had been making herself lonely by thinking that way. "I look at my girlfriends that do have marriages and I'm like, holy crap! I have to go now. I'm going to sit in my peaceful home. You go deal with that."

Rebecca, too, probably has a less stigmatized view of single life and a less romanticized view of married life than she once did. Still, both she and her daughter are open to the possibility of meeting someone and marrying; and they expect that they would move out of their family home if they did. They have discussed this at length and agreed that there would be no hard feelings should that happen. They would still be very much a part of each other's lives.

"Just because I were to get married or to live with somebody doesn't mean that I'm going to forget who my mom is," Brianna tells me. "I need my mom in my life every day . . . My daughter does not know any different than [seeing] my mom every day."

The way the Lewises live has something in common with the person who may be the most powerful man in the world. President Barack Obama also lives in a multigenerational home. And he does so by choice.

When Barack and Michelle Obama first moved from their Chicago home to the White House, they did not want to do so without Michelle's mother, Marian Robinson. She had to be persuaded—she was settled in her bungalow outside of Chicago, where she had friends and family, favorite places to visit, and things to do. She had never lived anyplace other than Chicago, but she agreed to go along to help with the children, thinking it might be temporary. Now the president is in his second term, and she has never left. Not since Harry Truman was in the Oval Office has a mother-in-law lived in the White House full-time.[1]

Often, it is Marian Robinson who shuttles granddaughters Malia and Sasha to school and back, and helps them with their homework. Like many others who are part of flourishing multigenerational households, though, she has found a balance between the time she spends with the other generations and the time she spends with her own friends, pursuing her own interests.[2]

The whole family has developed comfortable routines. Michelle told Oprah Winfrey, "There are many times when she drops off the kids, we hang out and talk and catch up, and then she's like, 'I'm going home.' And she walks upstairs."[3]

Introducing her mother to a gathering in the East Room of the White House in 2010, the First Lady said, "The opportunity to have three generations living in the White House, it's beautiful."[4]

The Way We Used to Live

In the iconic Norman Rockwell painting *Freedom from Want*, Grandpa and Grandma stand at the head of the Thanksgiving table, their beaming children and grandchildren gathered around. The year is 1943. In our cultural imaginations, that's how Americans lived in the first half of the twentieth century and in the decades before—in multigenerational families.

And in fact, the clear majority of Americans from those times who *could* live in multigenerational households did choose to do so.[5] But here's where our fanciful notions of the way we were go wrong:

- Most of those people could not live in a household spanning the generations, even if they wanted to. Life spans were short; on the average, a person born in 1900 could only expect to live about forty-seven years.[6] That meant that the lives of most grandparents and their grandchildren did not overlap for long, if at all.
- In places such as central Italy in the late eighteenth century and Russia in the early nineteenth century, married siblings sometimes lived together in joint families.[7] Americans almost never do that and almost never have.

♠ Another constraint on the potential number of multigenerational households in the United States was that Grandma and Grandpa, even if they did live long enough to share a home with their grown children and grandchildren, could only live in *one* household; their other adult children could not have them at their hearths.

♠ Consider, too, that women had more children than they do today, in part because they had far less control over their own fertility.

Combine the short life spans with the parents who had lots of children but could only live with one of them, and you end up with startlingly low numbers of households that included people sixty-five or older. As a slice of all households, that number never topped 12 percent.[8]

Although historical records are not as definitive as we might like, indications are that most older people in the late nineteenth and early twentieth centuries were not "taken in" by their adult children. Instead, they stayed in their own homes.[9] One by one, their children may have married and left to set up households of their own, but usually one grown child stayed right there with them. The offspring who stayed in the family home even after marrying had incentives beyond filial devotion—they often stood to inherit the family farm or business.

Before the days of wage labor drew young men out from under the control of their fathers in their family homes and into the towns and cities, the older generations held all the economic cards. They owned the farm, the business, the home. Until the middle of the twentieth century, it was the better-off elders who were more likely to live with kin. The poorer old people often lived as boarders or servants or, literally, in the poor house. Not until 1960 did the financial equation reverse, with the less-well-off coming together to live with their older or younger kin in greater numbers than the more economically secure.[10]

The racial equation has flipped too. Until at least 1940, the percentage of households that included a relative sixty-five or older was greater among whites than nonwhites. Since then, whites have been the least likely to live with several generations of kin.[11] In 2008, for example, compared to only 13 percent of whites, 25 percent of Asian adults, 23 percent of blacks, and 22 percent of Hispanics, lived in multigenerational households.[12]

The middle of the twentieth century marked the beginning of the end of the popularity of multigenerational living. Before then, living with relatives was normative; it was the default choice. You needed a reason *not* to do it. The suburbanization of America, though, was on the horizon. Adults increasingly preferred to live with just their own nuclear families. With the advent of Social Security, more older people had the financial wherewithal to live on their own if they so desired, and improvements in health made it possible for them to take care of themselves for longer periods of their lives.[13]

The forces that lured the younger generation out of the family home continued apace. For example, the number of family farms continued to decrease, and jobs continued to be available that were not tied to family economies. The rise in educational opportunities, especially after the passage of the GI Bill, probably contributed to the demise of multigenerational living in several ways. Many young people left home to pursue degrees, and once they got to college, they may have been exposed to ways of thinking that encouraged individualism more than traditionalism.

All of these factors contributed to the downslide in multigenerational living that eventually thudded to an all-time low in 1980. Once again, however, the tides have turned. A 2011 Pew Report opened with these observations:

> Without public debate or fanfare, large numbers of Americans enacted their own anti-poverty program in the depths of the Great Recession: they moved in with relatives. This helped fuel the largest increase in the number of Americans living in multi-generational

households in modern history. From 2007 to 2009, the total spiked from 46.5 million to 51.4 million.[14]

Many Americans have been battered by job losses, underemployment, growing housing costs and foreclosures, and surging healthcare costs. Living with relatives helps. Household income (adjusting for the number of people) is lower in multigenerational households than in other household types, but rates of poverty are lower too. In a national survey of Americans in 2011, more than half of those living in a multigenerational household said that their living arrangement had made it possible for at least one family member to continue their schooling or enroll in job training. More than 70 percent said that it had improved the financial well-being of one or more of the people in the household.[15]

Economic factors, though, are not the entire story. The reemergence of multigenerational living started long before the recession of 2007–2009. Ever since 1980, the numbers have been ticking up.[16]

Fortunately, the 2011 survey didn't stop at the questions about finances. The researchers also asked about interpersonal dynamics. Most people living in multigenerational households said that their living arrangements made it easier to provide care to the people who needed it, whether they were aging relatives or little kids. Although more than three quarters of those living in such households said that the arrangement sometimes added to their stress, an even greater number said that it had made their relationships better than they were before.[17]

Len and His Daughters and Grandsons: Sharing Music, Meals, and Kayaking

When Lena, Len's wife of forty-nine years, died at age eighty, Len had their white-brick ranch house to himself—all three bedrooms, basement, kitchen, dining room, living room, and music room. That lasted ten days. Then his daughter Lauren (whose much older husband would soon need to be cared for in a facility for Alzheimer's patients) packed up her nearby rural home and returned with her two sons, six and nine, to the mid-Atlantic college town where she grew up.

Len had been using one of the rooms as a study, but he soon transformed it into a bedroom for his younger grandson. When even that arrangement seemed too crowded, he had an addition built to the house.

Len's other daughter, Sally, has always been single. She had been teaching in a boarding school in the South. Once the new addition was built, her old bedroom was available again. She retired early and moved back in.

When I visit, Len is ninety, Lauren sixty, Sally fifty-eight, and the grandsons twenty-three and twenty. (The twenty-year-old is away at college.) The older grandson finished college the year before and then, like his mom and aunt before him, he returned home. When I arrive, he had just left with his Aunt Sally to spend the summer in Nantucket, where he would work on the same farm where his mom had worked every summer when she was in college.

I interview Lauren, then Len, in the room that best captures the spirit of this family—the music room. The grand piano is the centerpiece. There are stacks of sheet music (Bach on top), a coffee table and end tables and music stands. Louvered windows on three sides offer views of the lush gardens maintained by Len and his daughters. At one end of the yard are three kayaks protected by tarps, a splash of turquoise visible from under one and orange from another.

Outdoor adventures, music and books, gardening, and farming have bonded this family through the generations. Len taught Sally how to sail when she was little, and she, in turn, taught Lauren's sons. Len and his daughters still like to load those colorful kayaks on the top of their battered truck; then off they all go, up the mountain and down the river. Sometimes they go to the mountains to hike. That's something Len also did with his grandsons before they went to college. As for music, Lauren and Len like to play tunes Len has already memorized; he is at the piano, and she favors her recorder. Len and his daughters sometimes go to concerts together. They are also in the same book club—they call it the Geriatric Book Club.

Holidays are family times for all three generations. No matter where the grandsons may be, when Thanksgiving or Christmas comes along, they want to be home.

The activities the family members share, though, take up the smaller part of their social lives. Most of the time, they live fairly independently, pursuing their own interests with their own friends. Len, for instance, walks two miles a day to see the nearly ninety-one-year-old he calls his girlfriend.

At home, days begin quietly. Len is the first one up, at 4:45 AM. That's a good part of the day for him, "but that doesn't mean I mind the others coming in. I love it, I really do." Everyone is on his or her own for breakfast and lunch. At precisely 6:00 every evening, Len, Lauren, and Sally gather for dinner. The two daughters take turns cooking what Len describes as "gourmet dinners." The grandson living at home joins them if he likes what they are having. Whoever cooks also cleans up. Len empties the dishwasher when he gets up in the morning.

Both Lauren and Len tell me story after story about this wonderfully happy home. But is this three-generational household really as congenial as they make it sound? I asked Len and Lauren about tensions, and they offer the same answer. Lauren and Sally get along, but sometimes it takes special effort. Lauren admits that they used to "fight like cats and dogs" when they were little, but they do better now. "For two women in the same house," Len says, "I think they really do very well, and it's certainly good for [his two grandsons to have] their aunt in the same house."

Really, I ask—they actually liked that? "Oh, yes, I think they liked it tremendously."

There could have been conflicts about child-rearing, but that never happened. Speaking of her dad, Lauren says, "He doesn't lecture. He told me once a long time ago he decided not to be the mean old grandpa and interfere in how I brought up the children." She loves how he teaches quietly, by example.

They have a custom in the family of telling each other when they are heading out, where they are going, and when they are coming back. Neither Len nor Lauren complains about a lack of privacy or solitude. Len says that if he wants more time to himself, he can go in his room and shut the door, but he only does that when he's playing the French horn and wants to spare the others the noise. Lauren says she is flexible—she's happy spending time alone and also happy to be with other people. A few days after the interview, I receive a follow-up email from her. "I always welcome a quiet spell," she says, when everyone else is out of the house. She also has a sanctuary, "the place to which I look forward to escaping every day, where nobody can get to me." That is her bathroom, where she treats herself to "a nice, relaxing, hot bath."

With Len, it is well over an hour into our conversation before I get to a question for which he has no ready answer. "Is there anything you don't like about the way you are living now?" He just can't think of anything.

Lauren has an instant answer to my question about what she likes best about her current living situation. "My dad's a really great person. I mean, obviously, I love him to death."

Two-Generation Households: The Disappearing Generation Gap

Not all multigenerational homes include three or more generations. Of those households including just two generations, the most common are the ones in which aging parents and their adult children live together, and those in which young adults move back in with their parents—or never leave. (Skipped-generation households, in which grandparents live only with their grandchildren, are less numerous.) Feelings about aging parents living with their grown children have evolved over the years. Most of today's angst, though, is directed not at that familiar way of living but at the young people who are living at home when, in the past, so many of them had already left.

By 2012, more than one out of every three Americans between the ages of eighteen and thirty-one were living with their parents.[18] The numbers were high even for the upper end of the young-adult age range. Among the twenty-five- to thirty-four-year-olds, 23.6 percent were living with their parents in 2012, more than double the percentage who were doing so in 1980, when that living arrangement was as uncommon as it has ever been before or since.[19]

A crescendo of studies, opinion pieces, and personal essays grappled with the question of why this was happening. The most popular answers involved economics, education, and singlehood.[20]

Millennials have gotten the short end of the economic stick. Their wages are low, and their rates of unemployment are high. Those without jobs are especially likely to be living with their parents. In a 2006 survey, more than half of the young adults who moved back into their parents' homes said that they did so because they couldn't support themselves (57 percent) or they wanted to save money (69 percent). More than 90 percent of the young adults who had never left home said that they were saving money by living with their parents.[21] (That didn't mean they were contributing nothing, though. Nearly 50 percent paid rent and nearly 90 percent helped with household expenses.)[22]

Contemporary young Americans are also more likely to be single than same-aged peers in decades past. In 1980, the median age at which Americans first married—among those who did marry—was 22 for women and 24.7 for men. By 2013, marrying in your early twenties was unusual. First-time newlywed women were 26.6, and men were 29.[23] The numbers who stayed single were growing too. Young Americans who are not married are much more likely than their married peers to be living with their parents.

Millennials also differ from the young adults of the past in their dedication to higher education. In 1980, 17 percent of adults twenty-five and older had completed four years of college. By 2013, 32 percent had.[24] Young people still pursuing their education are more likely to be living with their parents (and they are classified as living with their parents even when they are in the dorms).

As important as the economy, education, and single life are, they do not tell the whole story of the rise of young adults living with their parents. The trend was gaining strength long before the Great Recession. Plus, even within the three categories—the unemployed, the students, and the single—the number living with their parents has been increasing over time.

The story that many want to tell is one of damnation and blame. Today's young adults, according to the derisive narrative, have been coddled by their helicopter parents, have "failed to launch," and have turned into generation stuck, the go-nowhere generation. They have been called "basement kids" and "nest dwellers." Psychotherapist Brooke Donatone incensed a whole swath of millennials by proclaiming that they have been so overhelped by their parents that they are incapable of studying and doing their own laundry on the same night.[25]

There really are parents who, out of anxiety, help too much, and in doing so, undermine the development of coping skills in their children.[26] As a blanket explanation of the growing number of young adults living with their parents, though, it misses all the good stuff.

The best of the good stuff is the relationship that many of today's young adults and their parents have with each other. In a 2013 poll of parents of eighteen- to twenty-nine-year-olds, about three quarters said their relationship with their adult child was mostly positive, and only 2 percent said it was mostly negative. Even more strikingly, when asked about the sources of enjoyment in their lives, more of the parents mentioned their relationships with their grown children (86 percent) than their relationship with their spouses or partners (75 percent).[27]

The positive feelings between the generations seem to be grounded in the intimacy that comes with frequent interactions and knowledge of the little ups and downs of everyday life. More than half of eighteen-to twenty-nine-year-olds and more than half of the mothers—and even the fathers—of grown kids that age have contact with each other every day or almost every day.[28]

Scholars Karen Fingerman and Frank Furstenberg underscore how different today's rate of connecting is from the past:

> In 1986, about half of parents reported that they had spoken with a grown child in the past week. In 2008, 87 percent said they had. In 1988, less than half of parents gave advice to a grown child in the past month, and fewer than one in three had provided any hands-on help. Recent data show that nearly 90 percent of parents give advice and 70 percent provide some type of practical assistance.[29]

The new closeness is not just a side effect of a bad economy, and it is not even something that can be pinned solely on the relatively recent ubiquity of cell phones:

> We first observed a shift in this relationship [between parents and young adult children] in 1999, when the economy was booming. Even before the cellphone era, many 20-something women talked with their mothers several times a week.[30]

But what if parents are in touch with their grown kids constantly, giving them advice and help several times a week? Wouldn't that be bad for the kids, and maybe the parents too? Fingerman and her colleagues studied about four hundred parents of nearly six hundred grown kids. They asked about all sorts of support, including emotional, practical, and financial, as well as giving advice, socializing, and talking about the events of everyday life. Then they zeroed in on the grown children who had received several of these kinds of support several times a week.

That's what they considered "intense support." More than a fifth of the grown children got this intense support from their parents, and more than a quarter of the parents said that they gave intense support to at least one of their grown kids. As the authors noted, those rates are similar to those found in studies of help given to older parents: between a fifth and a quarter of middle-aged American adults provide intense support to an aging parent.[31]

Both the young adults who had received intense support and the parents who had given it thought that the amount of support was excessive. (The others in the study, who were not helped so much, thought that the amount of support they received was about right.) But here's the *wow* point: the grown kids who received intense support were more satisfied with their lives and more likely to have a strong and secure sense of what is important to them than those who were not helped intensively. We can't know from this study alone whether the young adults were more satisfied and focused on goals because they were helped so much; the study is only suggestive. But what it suggests bucks our intuitions about meddling parents creating infantilized adults. The problem, as Fingerman and Furstenberg suggested, "isn't with the help, per se, but with viewing that support as abnormal and worrying that it could cause harm."[32]

Parents have a very different place in the lives of today's young adults than they did in decades past. I like writer Jennifer Wright's observation about how two popular television shows capture that difference:

> *Sex and the City*, a show that dealt with Gen-Xers, barely touched on a single protagonist's parents. Miranda's mother died, and the back of the head of Charlotte's father seemed to appear at her wedding, but it's hard to say whether Carrie Bradshaw even had parents. In *Girls*, a show about millennials, relationships with parents prove as important as romantic relationships. Entire episodes are dedicated to them.[33]

That was Fingerman and Furstenberg's conclusion too. The twentieth century, they note, was all about marriage and romance. (I call that attitude *matrimania*.) In the twenty-first century, though, when so many people are single for so much longer—sometimes for life—relationships with parents may have surpassed relationships with romantic partners in their significance for young adults.[34]

In the surveys of millennials and their parents, most were not living together. Perhaps that makes it easier for them to feel mostly positive about each other. But many young adults living with their parents also describe very fond feelings about their parents as well as their living situations. In a survey of eighteen- to twenty-four-year-olds who had never left their parents' home, four out of five said that they never left because they enjoy living with their parents, and even more said that their parents make it easy for them to stay.[35] Move up to the next oldest group of grown children, twenty-five-year-olds through thirty-four-year-olds, and include those who returned home as well as those who never left, and the sentiment is still overwhelmingly accepting. More than three-quarters say they are satisfied with their living arrangement.[36]

Compared to parents whose grown kids have left the nest and never returned, parents whose kids have come back to live with them are just as satisfied with their family lives and their housing situations. They feel emotionally closer to their grown children than they did when the kids were away, and they enjoy more companionship with them too.

It is not 1980 anymore—or 1970 or 1960. So many of the differences that separated the young adults from their parents in those decades—their politics, their taste in music, the way they dressed, the way they talked, the way they looked at the world—have radically diminished. The generation gap is gone.

Randye Hoder gave this nod to the new normal as she described her relationship with her twenty-one-year-old daughter, who lives at home:

My daughter and I shop together and sometimes share clothing. My husband has gone to concerts with both of our children, and I've worked on political campaigns with them. We share book recommendations, hike together, and all enjoy going to the gym.[37]

Her family's experiences fit the national profile. A survey of adults in 2012 found that only 28 percent of them believed there were strong conflicts between younger and older people. In fact, when they were given a list of potential points of contention in American society—including, for example, conflicts between races or political parties, between the rich and the poor, or between immigrants and nonimmigrants—generational conflict was rated dead last.[38]

Frank Shyong, twenty-five, was unenthusiastic when his immigrant mother wanted to move in with him after her job search took her from the family home in Tennessee to Los Angeles. She had different opinions about decorating, air-conditioning, the arrangement of the kitchen, and the wisdom of his choice to pursue a career in journalism. Yet they, too, settled into comfortable and comforting routines:

When there's friction in the hospital where she works, I help her rehearse her English phrases that convey professionalism and demand respect. She reads Chinese newspapers, suggests articles for my beat, and tells me stories about our distant family in Taiwan . . . And sometimes, after a day of getting doors slammed in my face, there's a plate of homemade, pan-fried dumplings waiting at home. As a child, I took little gestures like that for granted. As an adult, I can translate her actions into words—she's telling me, every day, "I love you."[39]

Every year that young adults live with their parents seems to add to the strength and lastingness of their connections to their parents. In a wide-ranging study of about fifteen thousand parents and their grown children from fifteen nations, young adults were contacted five years after they had moved out of their parents' homes. The longer they had stayed with their parents, the more often they stayed in touch with them. They also lived closer to their parents than the kids who moved out sooner. They helped their parents a bit more too (even after taking into consideration their greater proximity), and their parents helped them more as well.[40]

I'm not suggesting that all young adults and their parents benefit when they live together, becoming closer and more supportive. Some grown children really *are* backed into their lot by circumstances—often economic—and would rather be living some other way. Dave, for example, loved living alone when he had a job as a computer technician. He savored the solitude and the peacefulness. But he got laid off. He then tried to support himself by accepting a job at a call center, but in his thirties, he got laid off again. That's when he moved back in with his parents in a comfortable, small-town home at the foot of the Rocky Mountains. He went back to school to earn a new degree and is now looking for work in that field as a ticket to a place of his own. In the meantime, he picks up a bit of money doing photography. When I ask him about living with his parents, he says things like, "It puts a roof over my head," and, "It is what it is." He pays some rent, does some household chores, and occasionally goes out to dinner with his parents, but most nights he takes his dinner back to his room and eats there. He talks to his parents every day but liked it better when he only talked to them every other week.

Dave's lifespace is not the one he would design for himself. He is, temporarily, stuck with it. With a better economy, people with Dave's profile of interests and preferences move out of their parents' homes. More telling are the choices of people such as Brianna, who are secure, happy, and grateful to be living in a multigenerational home. As more of them share their stories, with much pride and little defensiveness, they open up the multigenerational lifespace to others who also love living that way but have been less sure about saying so.

We tend to think of the experiences of today's young adults as uniquely American and uniquely twenty-first century. Jon Grinspan, a scholar at the Smithsonian Institute, disagreed: "The idea that millennials are uniquely 'stuck' is nonsense." During the Industrial Revolution in America, young adults often settled for jobs that were just temporary or beneath their capacities. That was also a time when the age at which adults first married climbed to twenty-six, an especially stunning figure for people whose life expectancy had not quite reached fifty. The young adults of the time and their parents and pundits all wrung their hands. But they needn't have. "Those who did best tended to accept change, not to berate themselves for breaking with tradition."[41]

Fast-forward to the much-celebrated GI generation (born between 1901 and 1924), and again, there was much consternation about kids these days. As the authors of *Millennial Momentum* noted:

> Like the Millennial Generation, the GI Generation was raised in a protected manner by its parents and even tended to stay with their parents well into adulthood . . . Early in World War II, Army psychiatrists even fretted about "how badly Army recruits had been over-mothered in the years before the war."[42]

The American experience, even by contemporary standards, is not so exceptional when considered in the context of the whole world. The international competition that has come with globalization has slashed jobs and wages far and wide, leaving young adults with less attractive and less secure jobs and job prospects. In countries with strong government supports, like Sweden and Denmark, young people can still march on, undeterred, pursuing their education while living in places of their own. But in less generous nations, such as Japan, Spain, Italy, and the United

States, the young are often at home. In Italy, for example, 37 percent of thirty-year-old men are living in the same place they always have: at home with their parents.[43]

Horizontal Family Households: Siblings Sticking Together

I once did an informal survey of scholars who study personal relationships. (There is a whole field of relationship science, spanning multiple disciplines.) I asked them to name the relationship that is likely to last the longest. They all had to think about it. Some said it was the marital relationship, one or two said it was the relationship between a parent and a child. Neither answer is correct. Most spouses do not meet their partners until they are already adults. Parents and their children typically have at least those first few decades together, but then parents usually die long before their children do. No, the relationships that are likely to last the longest are those between siblings.[44]

The Jones Household: Small Town, Big Heart

In the picture, the four Jones brothers are standing in front of their home in the small town of Salisbury, North Carolina, Easter baskets in hand. They have on matching white dress shirts under their Easter jackets. All of them are wearing long pants and dress shoes except for youngest and littlest, Robert. He's probably about five years old and is endearing in his short pants and sneakers. They are all smiling but not too broadly.

It is now a half century later, and I'm interviewing Robert in the home just down the street from the one in the picture. The family moved there when he was sixteen. His father died three years later. One of Robert's brothers, Randy, never left.

Robert went away to college and then spent fifteen years exploring different lifespaces and jobs. He lived in a dorm room, a small house, a duplex, a garage apartment in a big house, and a little farmhouse on a huge estate where cattle used to wake him up every morning, mooing outside his window. He lived in Virginia and Colorado, as well as various towns in North Carolina. With his friend Carol, who grew up in the house next door to him, he traveled out West and to the New England states, as well as to Canada. He worked as a residential counselor for boys with learning disabilities, on a farm with a man who made hammer dulcimers, and in bars and restaurants. He always wanted to live at the beach, so in 1989, he packed up his car—"I had the bike in it, the futon on top, all of my belongings"—and was on his way to the North Carolina coastal town of Wilmington. On the way, though, his car broke down, and it took every penny he had to repair it. He turned around and headed to Salisbury, to the home where Randy and his mother were still living. Now, he thinks of that "little car that couldn't" as fate.

Really, though, it wasn't just about the broken-down car. "You know, my mother was getting older then, and at some point, I knew I was going to have to be the one." Robert and Randy had three more years with her after Robert moved back, before she died of pancreatic cancer. Afterward, Randy met Ruth, and their relationship grew serious. Ruth moved in with the brothers, and she and Randy married. They did not move out, and neither did Robert. The three of them still share the home. As for the future, Robert tells me, "Oh, I'm not going anywhere." He is now as rooted as the majestic trees that soar above the roof of his old Southern home.

My friend Susan, who lives in Salisbury, has driven me to Robert's. We are early, so we think we'll just sit in the car for a while and take in the view. Robert, though, soon shows up on his big, inviting, wraparound porch; spots us; and welcomes us in. (Tofu, the cat, is a little less sure about us.)

The two-story stucco home, with dormer bedrooms upstairs and a sunroom and sleeping porch out back, has character. Like the other homes up and down the street, it sits close to the street, with a small, grassy yard in front. A white lamppost stands to one side of the path connecting the sidewalk to the stone steps leading up to the porch. A huge, pink magnolia tree reaches across the yard from the other side. The white picket fence is relegated to the backyard.

Inside the front door, the hallway leading to the stairs to the second floor is big enough to comfortably fit a sofa, table, chair, and grandfather clock. On the right side of the house is a living room, bedroom, and bathroom with a claw-footed tub—all used mostly by Randy and Ruth. On the other side is a mustard-colored sitting room with magnificent bay windows, a traditional dining room in moss green, and a kitchen. Robert's bedroom and bathroom are upstairs. Just about every room is filled with the photos, timepieces, lamps, vases, and other markers of a home in which the same people have been living for forty years. We settle into the sitting room—Robert's second favorite part of the house, after the front porch—and Robert serves us iced tea and resumes the story he has already started to tell.

Ruth talked to Robert before joining the household. Robert told her he had no problem with her moving in. "I don't mind change," he cautioned, "but I'll only change so much." He never did need to change much. He still has his own bedroom, bathroom, and living room; and Randy and Ruth have theirs. They all share the kitchen, dining room, and sunroom. Robert favors the front porch; Randy and Ruth like the backyard better.

Ruth brought her own sense of style to the home. She picked out the colors for each of the rooms, enlarged the tiny closets, remodeled here and there, and in many other ways, "Ruthinized" the home. Robert appreciated that. He was even more grateful when she took over the organization of the finances. Before, it was Robert who made sure that the bills got paid. Randy contributed his share, but sometimes

Robert would have to remind him four or five times before he finally got around to it. Around the house, they split the chores. Robert takes care of the front yard; Randy and Ruth cover the back. Though Randy doesn't care much about tidiness, if Robert wakes up to dishes in the morning, he will wash them while he waits for his coffee to brew. (They don't have a dishwasher.)

The old home is often begging for this repair or that, and occasionally, it absconds with an item the way dryers do with socks. (Robert has been searching for his camera for days.) Other than that, Robert comes up with only one answer to my question of what he doesn't like about his living arrangement: now and then, he walks in on Randy and Ruth when they are in the middle of a conversation that they would probably prefer to keep private. But that's probably more of an issue for them than for him.

Toward the end of the interview, I try again to see how much he really does like the way he lives by asking my fantasy question: how would he live if he had all the money in the world? He admits he'd like to have the house to himself. But he would build a home for Randy and Ruth right next door.

"Mother," Robert says, "held the family together." The brothers never made much of an effort themselves. Robert was grief stricken when she died, but he now thinks that one of the most wonderful things happened afterward. He calls it his mother's legacy: the siblings took their mother's love and made it their own. Every week, an email goes out to the whole family, including Robert's nieces and nephew, and a flurry of responses ensues. Randy has been scanning pictures of the brothers from their childhood and posting them on Facebook. (The Easter photo is one of them.) They all organize family vacations. Beach Week happens every single year, no exceptions. Until the nephew and nieces graduated from college, the whole group gathered for the week between Christmas and New Year's. Robert remembers watching his twenty-year-old nephew mixing a drink one New Year's Eve, then looking at his brother and marveling, "Your son is with you on New Year's Eve." Most twenty-year-olds would want to be with their friends to celebrate the New Year, but in the Jones tribe, the young adults want to be with family.

In their everyday lives in the same house, though, Robert and Randy have little interaction with each other. "As I jokingly say, we grunt at each other." Randy works at the local paper and comes home early in the morning as Robert is getting ready to leave for his job. They almost never have dinner together. Robert's job involves donning funny hats, gathering children all around him, and telling stories. He works at the local library.

The street where Robert lives is in a historical district of a small town with a small-town feel. He loves sitting on his front porch, where friends and neighbors drop by and chat. He can accommodate quite a few of them: I count four rocking chairs, two wicker chairs, a straight-back chair, a wicker couch, and a smattering of plants, planters, and tables.

Friends who are driving through the neighborhood will sometimes stop in the middle of the road and banter. Day and night, there are joggers and people walking their dogs. Robert's dog is so familiar with Robert's friends that he recognizes their footsteps; when the dog barks, Robert knows that he's not going to find someone he knows at his doorstep.

Robert bristles when anyone dares to question his decision to live in a small town. "I can read the *New York Times* just like you can," he tells them. He walks to work—it is just two blocks away—and to the downtown area, also just a few blocks away, with its shops, restaurants, and the theater he and a group of like-minded souls envisioned in a series of meetings in the very room where I am interviewing him now. "I don't like to be hassled," he explains. "I like getting to Lowe's in five minutes. I like being five minutes away from Harris Teeter [a local supermarket]. I don't want to be sitting in traffic."

When I ask him what he likes best about the place where he lives, Robert replies, "I love the location." It is a cliché about real estate—what matters most is location, location, location. I thought I knew what that meant, but I spent some time checking online. I found lots of articles with answers (for example, a good location is one with a good school district, good views, or good resale values for the homes), but not one of them mentioned what Robert says: "Friends are very important to me."

Robert loves where he lives for many reasons, but one of the most important is that most of his good friends live within two blocks, and many are single. He begins to list them and gets up to five names when he starts adding people by the group instead of one by one. There's the theater group, of course. For birthdays, a gang gathers for potluck dinners. And once a month, he plays cards "with a bunch of men—it was our rebellion against book clubs."

Do Robert's and Randy's rootedness make you feel nostalgic for a bygone era? Robert returned to his hometown at thirty-three, and he doesn't plan to leave. Randy never left home at all. Isn't that how Americans used to be, before we became so mobile and so rootless?

That's the story we tell ourselves. Maybe we were securely ensconced among family and neighbors and friends in the 1950s, but ever since, we have become ever more itinerant and restless.

There's only one problem with that story—it is wrong.

A recent report found that more than half of all American adults (57 percent) had never lived outside of the state where they were born. Nearly 40 percent had never left their hometown.[45]

What's more, Americans' inclination to move has been decreasing over time. The Census Bureau has kept track of that since 1948, and trendlines have clearly been heading down, down, down. In 2011, the percentage of Americans who had moved within the past year hit an all-time low of 11.6 percent. That's for *all* moves.[46] Most often, when Americans move, they don't go far. The percent who had moved out of state was under 2 percent.[47]

Although data from earlier centuries are sketchier, indications are that American mobility has mostly been decreasing since the nineteenth century. Sociologist Claude Fischer, who has studied mobility for many years, pointed out that "the great majority of Americans were more *settled* at the end of the twentieth century than at its middle, and indeed, probably more settled than at any earlier time in American history."[48] When people who have never left their hometowns are asked why they stay, most of them (74 percent) point to the tug of family ties.[49]

American Triumphalism: Our Misplaced Faith in Just One Way of Raising Children

When it comes to the well-being of children, Americans engage in nuclear family triumphalism. They are convinced that children who are raised by two married heterosexual parents are going to be happier, healthier, better educated, less likely to get in trouble, and better off in just about every conceivable way than kids who are brought up any other way. I was raised in that sort of household myself, along with my three siblings, so I suppose I could have put on my victor's T-shirt and waved my self-celebratory flag. The social scientist in me, though, wanted to know whether the children of nuclear families actually deserved their special status.

When I was writing *Singled Out*, I pored over stacks of relevant studies. I was stunned to find how small some of the differences were between, for example, the children of single parents and the children of married parents. Even when there were real differences favoring the children of married parents, the interpretation was not always as straightforward as media reports suggested. Studies following children over time, as their living situations changed or stayed the same, sometimes showed that children of divorced parents who seemed to be doing worse than children of married parents were already having problems before their parents split. Apparently, it isn't single parenting that is the problem but a home filled with conflict and rancor.[50]

Most studies of the children of single parents did not distinguish between those who are living just with their parent and those like Mari from chapter 1, who are living with others as well, such as grandparents or great-grandparents. Does that matter? In what is perhaps the most comprehensive study ever conducted, more than eleven thousand adolescents from a representative national sample were studied. They were raised in ten different kinds of households, including different kinds of one-parent, two-parent, and multigenerational households.[51]

Conventional wisdom would predict that the children raised by married parents in nuclear family households would do especially well. And they did do well. But the children of divorced single parents raised in multigenerational homes did just as well: they were no more likely to smoke or drink and no more likely to initiate sex at an early age; and they were just as likely to graduate from high school and enroll in college.[52]

There were other adolescents, though, who did even better—they were the children of parents who had always been single who were raised in multigenerational households. Compared to the children of married parents in nuclear family homes, those teens were less likely to smoke or drink, more likely to graduate from high school, and more likely to enroll in college. (The age at which they started having sex was no different.)[53]

When I hear politicians, pundits, and (sadly) even some academics *tut-tut* about single parents and their children, I think about those results. I also think about Brianna, Mari's mom. To those who do not know her, she fits into all of their boxes of blame. She was a teenager when she had Mari. She never married. She's black. She has only a high school education. She is also a remarkably thoughtful, level-headed, and devoted mother; and she is raising a delightful child who is the love of the lives of all of the adults who surround her.

The results of research studies tell us how particular groups compare to others on the average. There are always exceptions. Not all teenage children of never-married single mothers in multigenerational households are going to refrain from smoking and drinking, and choose to go to college. Also, there can be inconsistencies across studies. For example, smaller and less carefully controlled studies of the children from multigenerational households have sometimes uncovered less encouraging results. When that has happened, though, there is a typical culprit—there is conflict within the household about how to raise the children.[54] Len's determination not to be the "mean old grandpa" who interferes with his daughter Lauren's parenting was probably one of the important contributors to the success of his household. Rebecca and Brianna's commitment to working through their different approaches to parenting probably contributed to the success of their household.

The flip side of America's nuclear family triumphalism is the nation's obliviousness to the importance of kin other than nuclear family members. It is not just in cultural conversations and political rhetoric where extended kin are neglected; scholars are just as bad. In the premier journal for research on family, the *Journal of Marriage and Family*, only about 12 percent of all articles are about relatives other than nuclear family members.[55]

Yet such relatives are often important to us, even when we don't live with them. Robert cherishes those holidays and Beach Weeks with his nieces and nephew. The summer before I met her, Brianna wanted to visit her father but needed help with the airfare; she turned to one of her uncles. Nearby relatives are sometimes integrated into family routines and rituals—like when Brianna's brother joins the women of the Lewis household for dinner so many Sunday evenings.

Individuals who are less well-off financially are more likely to live near kin. They are also more likely to be there for the relatives who need them, doing errands, giving rides, and offering help with childcare and household chores.[56]

Other countries—Asia, for example—have stronger traditions of valuing extended family members. There are also some hints that such practices may be of special significance to children of single parents. In a cross-cultural study, the reading skills of fifteen-year-olds in five Asian nations and the United States were assessed. They key question was whether the children of single parents differed from the children of married parents. In the United States and Japan, the children of married parents did better. In Hong Kong and Korea, the differences were negligible. In Thailand and Indonesia, the children of single parents were better readers than the children of married parents. The author suggested that in many Asian countries, extended family members step in to help when needed, providing money and time, as well as social and emotional support.[57]

When I ask Brianna if she has any advice for people contemplating their own multigenerational possibilities, she says, "Anyone who thinks about doing this needs to realize that there are going to be . . . challenges. It's not going to be this perfect world . . . It takes effort [from everyone involved] to make it work." Still, when her friends say that they envy her and her relationships up and down the Lewis family tree, she does not try to dissuade them: "I wouldn't change it for the world."

3

ONE BIG, HAPPY FRIENDSHIP
Housemates Go Long and Deep

The house where Marianne Kilkenny and her husband had been liv-ing for the past few years was huge. When they moved in, it was brand new. Maybe Marianne should have loved it. Priscilla, the cat, knew better. Giving expression to Marianne's unhappiness in a way that only a beloved pet can, she strutted into the closet of the master bedroom and peed all over it.

That's when Marianne realized it was time to leave.

Living in a cul-de-sac alongside the seventh hole of the Silver Lake Country Club was Marianne's husband's dream, not hers. Marianne was approaching fifty and had no children. The giant houses on her street, set off by sprawling lawns, were filled with young families. Marianne craved connection, but the neighborhood didn't feel like a community; and it didn't feel like home.

But what was Marianne's dream? While she was working eighty hours a week at her high-tech job in Silicon Valley, she didn't spend much time pondering the possibilities. In fact, except for the part about not having kids, Marianne had simply lived the life that she thought she was supposed to live: "You get married, you buy a house, you have a family. You go to work and you come back and you have dinner together; you have the pool in the backyard, and the neighbors come over." Marianne did not give up on the prescribed path when it did not lead her to the promised land the first time around. Her current husband was her third.

She also knew how her living arrangements were supposed to evolve over time, and she followed that script too: "bigger house, bigger house, bigger house."

That didn't work. Now what?

She hired her gardener to help her pack her car and tie some furniture to the top; then she and Priscilla headed down the 101 to San Jose, where Marianne would live in a small rented cottage behind a house. She thought they must have looked like a scene from *The Grapes of Wrath*, with tables sliding off the roof and onto the highway. (Her ex remarried and stayed in the house on the golf course.)

She had hoped for a time of calm, but that was not to be. Her mother became seriously ill and died within three years. Her father died fifty-one weeks later.

Something had to give. It wasn't just the emotional exhaustion of being there for her parents through the last years of their lives—then grieving their deaths—that had gotten to Marianne. She was also feeling apprehensive about her future. She did not have a child of her own. She did not have a spouse. Who would be there for her in her later years?

She took a year off. It was a time for reflection and reading and searching and experimenting. That time-out would set her life on a whole new course, in which her own quest for the most meaningful way to live would grow into a passion to help others find their ways too.

Before she did any research at all, Marianne already had a special place in her heart for one particular way of living. She always did love the Golden Girls, those four feisty women who shared a home in the long-running television hit. She was riveted by the rhythms of their relationships—the way they traded stories and quips, year after year, coffee cups in hand. The little linkages of their everyday lives seemed to add up to a big, strong bulwark against whatever life threw at them.

Then Marianne met another group of older women who shared a house and made it their home. They were not real either. This time, they were the protagonists of a beloved series of Joan Medlicott novels, the Ladies of Covington.[1] Women pressed copies into the hands of their friends with such zeal that sales eventually reached three quarters of a million. The Ladies of Covington—cautious Grace, outspoken Hannah, and fragile Amelia—were widows who first met each other at a dreary Pennsylvania boardinghouse. Two had been deposited there by their children; the other arrived on her own. When one unexpectedly inherited a ramshackle farmhouse in North Carolina, the three cajoled each other to do what no one ever thought they would: drive away from the place where they were warehoused, renovate the farmhouse, and build a life together.

The conviction that later life was not meant to be lived in an institution leaped from television screens and novels into the imaginations of a generation of Americans who set out to find a different way. Some came together to share ideas and experiment with new models of living. Marianne found herself on the same quest.

Then she discovered Second Journey, the group that would influence her the most. Fundamental to the mission of the organization is a call for community. Seniors would do best, the group claims, to live interdependently. They should set their sights beyond card games and shuffle board, and instead, aspire to goals such as service, mentoring, and their own personal growth and deepening spirituality. A number of ways of living are amenable to such active, meaningful, and interconnected lives, including sharing housing and living in intentional neighborhoods and communities.

When Marianne learned that Second Journey was organizing a visioning council, a democratic think tank featuring the leading innovators of new ways of living in later life, she was there. And she felt comfortable enough to speak out about her own dreams for living her best life.

Just one year later, Marianne took the leap from wide-eyed student at the visioning council to the next trailblazer in the living-in-community movement. She moved to Asheville, North Carolina, a funky Southern town nestled between the Smoky Mountains and the Blue Ridge Mountains. Small in size at about eighty-three thousand, it is big in innovations in living. Shared houses, ecovillages, and cohousing communities are all in or around the town. Asheville is also less than a half hour away from Barnardsville, home of Joan Medlicott, author of the Ladies of Covington series, and probably the inspiration for the fictional town of Covington. Marianne was in Asheville for less than a month when she first called Joan and invited her to lunch.

In 2007, Marianne organized the conference "Women Living in Community: From Dreaming to Doing." She approached the leaders she so admired, and one after another, they agreed to speak. Ninety women from the United States and Canada traveled to Asheville for the two-day event.

After that, there was no stopping Marianne. She organized other conferences, led workshops, spearheaded meet-ups, and coached individuals to find their own most meaningful ways of living. In turn, people she inspired found like-minded souls and began hatching plans.

Meanwhile, Marianne conducted her own personal experiments in living in community. She had a wonderful experience sharing a house with another woman who even had the same first name. The other Marianne became a shared-housing convert, and continues to live under the same roof with other non-kin. Marianne also lived in a home on her own—in a tiny community of one other woman living in her own home and a couple living in the third home. But the new arrangement did not lead to all the spontaneous socializing and deepening friendships she had envisioned. She kept searching.

When Don and Gloria, a couple from Madison, Wisconsin, sent out feelers about their interest in moving to Asheville and living in community there, three different people referred them to Marianne. She invited them to visit and offered her place as their home base. The three of them lived together for a few weeks. They felt comfortable with one another and discovered they shared values about how to live. They even discussed the details of how they would make decisions and manage any conflicts if they did decide to share a home. Marianne, though, still owned the home she was in, which was not suitable for a shared-housing arrangement with individual rooms or apartments.

Don and Gloria's scouting turned up a big, roomy home, well cared for, in a verdant neighborhood in West Asheville. The owner was open to renting the home to a group of adults who wanted to share the house, as long as Don was willing to maintain the home and collect the rent checks. Don and Gloria were in. Linda and Kath, two women who had met in Marianne's workshops, were interested too. Even with separate spaces for Linda and Kath, there was still room for Marianne. She already knew she liked those two women, but she still had her house to sell.

On Christmas day of 2010, Marianne was in a festive mood. A friend was going to come by later in the day to pick her up and head to the stately Grove Park Inn for a celebratory holiday dinner. The inn offered fresh, local food and dreamy mountain views. It was a real treat. Headed down the stairs of her home with her arms full, Marianne slipped on the last four steps and landed on her rear. Coffee was splashed on the wall, her backside was throbbing, and there was no one else in the house. The experience was, she would later say, her "literal kick in the butt." For years she had been nudging the people she coached with leading questions like "What are you waiting for?" So what was *she* waiting for? Don

59

and Gloria asked her the same thing. There was still room for her in their beautiful shared home.

Marianne did it. She moved into the home where she had a suite of her own and the companionship of Linda, Kath, Gloria, and Don.

"The first morning that I got up here, Linda and Kath were sitting at that table, drinking coffee in their bathrobes. I brought my coffee and I said, 'It's *The Golden Girls*! We're here!'"

A short circular driveway leads up to the front of the shared home where Marianne and her housemates live. Looking down as I step out of the car, a white sun symbol painted on the asphalt seems a tad out of place, but the rest of the scene is an iconic image of Southern hospitality. The house is a two-story Colonial featuring a generous wraparound front porch with white picket railings and ceiling fans.

Marianne and her housemates have invited friends, neighbors, and community members interested in innovative ways of living to gather inside their gracious home. They have hosted Meetups, potlucks, educational events, and holiday parties. I discovered something similar in my visits to other shared houses and intentional communities—people who have made proactive decisions to lead more interconnected lives often have open hearts and open homes.

In everyday life, when just the housemates are around, I imagine the living arrangement is conducive to easy sociability. Don't they see each other in the hallways and common spaces, make spontaneous plans to go for walks or see movies, and perhaps sit down to break bread fairly often? That's what Marianne had hoped for, but at first, it didn't happen as routinely as she had wished. When she raised the issue, the group decided to gather for dinner on Monday evenings, with all the housemates bringing their own food. Not everyone shows up every time, but it is on the calendar.

I wonder about the day-to-day issues. Who cleans the common spaces? What if one housemate has much higher standards for cleanliness than the others? What about guests? Who mows the lawn?

There are the inevitable frictions, Marianne concedes, but she sees them as opportunities to learn and grow. She believes that the people who fare best in shared housing "are willing to face controversy and don't look at conflict as bad." She told me about a time when something was bothering her about one of her housemates. It would have been easy to just ignore the problem, and that option was tempting. Instead, though, she asked to talk with the housemate, knowing that "when I get to the other side of this, the relationship will be bigger and deeper, and that's why I'm here."

In another instance, Marianne learned that a housemate was dissatisfied with how Marianne had carried out her task of keeping the hallways clean and had complained to another person about it. Marianne had a different suggestion for the unhappy housemate as to how the matter could have been handled: "Tell me about it. That'd be fine."

Marianne and her housemates make deliberate efforts to stay attuned to one another and address potential issues before bad feelings have a chance to fester. In fact, this thoughtful and systematic approach to potential conflicts strikes me as one of the most significant differences between this household and groups of people who come together as roommates merely as a matter of convenience or finances.

Every Monday morning, they meet in the common living- and dining-room area. They begin with a brief meditation. Next, each person takes a turn describing current feelings or concerns. The others listen. They do not try immediately to fix any problem.

Marianne's typical reaction afterward: "Wow, someone really heard me." She finds great joy and fulfillment in the meetings. "Eating together, you can have a bond, but this is beyond that."

Practical matters are handled straightforwardly. With regard to chores, for instance, the housemates divvy up tasks such as mowing the lawn and cleaning the common areas according to individual preferences. Marianne worried about noise before moving in, but that has never been a problem. They are all familiar with each other's routines, and they maintain a respectful quiet and refrain from doing things such as laundry when they know someone is sleeping.

Media stories on shared housing have often focused on the financial advantages. Considering the challenging economic times, that's not surprising. Compared to when she was living alone, Marianne pays far less to live in a much more comfortable home, in a more attractive neighborhood. The lower rent is the biggest difference, but her share of the utilities is smaller too. Task sharing also helps. If one housemate does the gardening and another the mowing, then no one needs to hire a gardener or a person to mow the lawn. If each person lived alone, that one person would be responsible for mowing, gardening, and cleaning. Together, they are able to split the chores and each has more free time.

Marianne patiently answers all of my questions about conflicts and hassles and finances, just as she does when she responds to media inquiries, but what she most wants to talk about is the good stuff. Everyday life in her home is filled with small acts of kindness and unexpected joys.

She takes pleasure in the most mundane conversational exchanges. When someone asks how her day is going, even dull tasks like vacuuming seem less onerous. When a housemate tells her how nice she looks, she walks out the door "a little bit taller." She likes the sense of the presence of other people milling about the house. When she lived alone, she says she "could go for days only hearing the sound of my own voice." In one of her blog posts on her Women for Living in Community website, Marianne described the people in her house as "a chosen family who looks out for each other."

I think about the three marriages Marianne has had and ask if her love of sharing space was part of the attraction.

"I've never been a great proponent of sharing my own space."

Really?

When she walks into her suite in the house and closes the door, she wants the space to herself. She dates and invites men in, but adds, "I love sleeping by myself and always have. The last guy I dated, [on] our second date I said, 'I don't want someone 24/7. The fact that you live an hour and a half away is cool.'"

Like almost everyone else I interviewed, Marianne values her privacy, her time alone, and her own personal space as well as her time with other people.

Months after Marianne moved into the shared house, she was taking stuff out of the trunk of her car when she stumbled over a root growing out of the driveway. Once again, she was on the ground, hurting, with the wind knocked out of her. This time, though, Gloria heard her gasp of pain from upstairs and rushed down to see if she was okay.

It was a meaningful moment. Later, Marianne got out a can of white paint, and where the root once tripped her up, she painted a symbol of the sun.

The Way We Used to Live

In the nineteenth century, house sharing was commonplace, but it had an entirely different sensibility. Boardinghouses were not places where people came together as friends to share their lives. Instead, the houses were run by a landlady, often with the help of servants, who provided laundry service and three meals a day to people who rented rooms. Boardinghouses were usually in urban areas. Historians estimate that up to half of nineteenth-century city residents were either boarding or maintaining a boardinghouse.[2]

Single men who had come to the city to find work, single women with teaching jobs, and young married couples not yet ready to live on their own all found their way to boardinghouses. A boarder slept in a small room—sometimes private and sometimes shared with strangers—and joined the landlady, her family, and the other boarders for meals in the dining room.

Among the reform movements that marked the turn of the twentieth century was a protest against overcrowding. House sharing became stigmatized, and new zoning regulations added teeth to the bite of moral approbation.

By the middle of the twentieth century, suburban life had become fashionable, and few cared to share their homes with anyone other than nuclear family members and perhaps some extended family. In 1950, only 1.1 percent of all households comprised two or more unrelated people.[3] For nearly two decades, this remained the status quo. But then house-sharing numbers started to tick up.

In the life story of the esteemed activist and iconoclast Maggie Kuhn, 1970 was a very big year.[4] Forced into retirement from a job she loved simply because she had reached the age of sixty-five, Kuhn issued her *cri de coeur*: "Don't agonize, organize." The group she founded and led was the Gray Panthers, and old age hasn't been the same since.

Less well-known is that 1970 was also when Maggie Kuhn began inviting other people to live with her in the two adjoining homes she owned in the Germantown section of Philadelphia. By 1981, she had seven housemates ranging in age from twenty-one to thirty-nine—two single women, three single men, and one couple—as well as six cats, a dog, and a tank of fish. She called them her "family of choice."

Sharing a home was Maggie Kuhn's answer to the retirement communities that she dismissed as "glorified playpens where wrinkled babies can be safe and out of the way."[5] At Kuhn's place, the couple and each of the single people had a private apartment that included a kitchen. Solitude was theirs when they wanted it, but they also shared meals frequently, sometimes celebrated holidays together, and cared for each other during illnesses.

"We've grown to have very close and loving friendships that endure," Kuhn offered. "We depend on each other, without being sentimental about it."[6]

In front of a fireplace in Kuhn's home, the couple got married. At the ceremony, Kuhn gave voice to her philosophy of living: "I said families and couples could not live unto themselves alone, and that two people being just internally involved are not going to make it."[7] Maggie Kuhn never did marry and had an answer for anyone who asked why: "sheer luck."[8]

In 1980, at a White House miniconference on older women, Kuhn told the delegates about her family of choice. She won them over. In their conference report, they included the recommendation that older women should consider sharing homes with unrelated people of all ages.[9] Not one to wait for others to act, Kuhn founded the Shared Housing Resource Center in 1981 and ran it out of the first floor of her home.

Maggie Kuhn died in 1995, but her vision of shared housing lives on. Today's National Shared Housing Resource Center (NSHRC) is a clearinghouse of information for people looking to share their homes, to find homes to share with others, or to start their own home-sharing organizations.[10] State and regional home-sharing programs are listed in a directory. Housing professionals, researchers, government officials, and the media have all found useful resources at NSHRC. Maggie Kuhn would be proud.

Sharing a Home and Life in
Twenty-First-Century America

In 1980, the year before Maggie Kuhn created the Shared Housing Resource Center, the Census Bureau still counted only 3.3 million households of unrelated people; that was 4.1 percent of all households. By the turn of the twenty-first century, the numbers had nearly doubled to 6.5 million, or 6.1 percent.[11]

Today, all across the nation, Americans are living the new happily ever after. They are living with people they care about, sharing meals, indulging in the comforting ritual of how-was-your-day exchanges, and spending holidays together. The "new" part is that the people with whom they are sharing homes and lives are not just spouses or romantic partners.

Some people already have the foundation of friendship to anchor the home that they share. They knew each other for some time before they decided to live together. Others find their own way to suitable housemates. If they are familiar with an organization such as the Golden Girl Homes in Minnesota, they walk through a six-step process. It begins with attending a free information and orientation session, proceeds through a series of classes and networking events, and continues with follow-up events after a successful match is achieved.

Seekers of house-sharing experiences who know about NSHRC can use those resources to find home-share groups in the place where they are dreaming of living. Some people have no idea that resources such as NSHRC or Golden Girl Homes exist.[12] They try Craigslist; they hear about a promising Meetup; or they spread the word through their friends and family, church groups or book clubs, or social and professional networks.

More of the people seeking shared housing are women than men. More women than men stay single, and women live longer than men; so in the later years of life, there are more women than men. Of course, many men as well as women face widowhood and divorce in later life. In fact, people sixty-five and older are the one group for whom the rate of divorce is still increasing. There is a big sex difference, though, in reactions to the end of a marriage. Men are much more likely than women to marry again.[13]

Women who have spent much of their adult lives living with other people, such as those who were previously married, are especially intrigued by the possibility of living with their female friends. (Women who have lived alone are less enthusiastic.) When the AARP asked women aged forty-five and older to explain the appeal of sharing a home with friends, nearly 90 percent said that it was the companionship that was most attractive. More than 80 percent noted that affordability and safety mattered too.[14]

Maria Hall: Lots of Different Rooms for Lots of Different People

All I knew about Maria Hall before I met her is that she opened her house to kids with nowhere else to go and made it their home. That sent me into full stereotype mode, and I expected to meet a wispy woman, with delicate, flowing hair, wearing one of those soft Indian-print skirts that were popular in the '60s.

My friend Susan, who put me in touch with Maria, drives us past the front of the two-story Southern saltbox—where a white rocking chair sits on the porch, and ivy meanders over the railings and around the posts—to the driveway in the back, where we park next to Maria's black pickup truck; then we walk past a shed and a cobalt-blue bottle tree, and knock on the back door.

The sixty-five-year-old woman who greets Susan and me from her kitchen is wearing stone-white canvas pants, a black T-shirt, and glasses. "I've always been plump, with not much hair," she quipped. The house is as surprising to me as Maria is. Every room is distinctive. The first floor sports a "Jimmy Carter room" (Maria's office, filled with whimsical political memorabilia), an elegant Asian-themed sitting room, and a rustic dining room. Upstairs, there's an impressively equipped music room and a fun-filled crafts room—Maria calls it her "woman cave." Maria's bedroom is there, too, with its blue-cloud wallpaper and two cats sprawled on the bed like they own it. In another bedroom are pictures of Michael, the guitar-playing teen living there now.

Homages to the people Maria loves are all over the home. Dozens of framed photos are arrayed around stenciled letters spelling out *family* on the landing at the top of the stairs. On the refrigerator door, on tabletops, and in bookshelves are photos, mementos, and works of art created by the children who have lived with her. On the back of the chair at the head of the dining room table is a gray sweater. It belonged to a man, now deceased, who was like a brother to Maria. In keeping with a tradition of Zimbabwe, the country he was from, the sweater will stay there always.

Twenty-five years ago, Maria bought the house for eighteen thousand dollars. Since then, twenty-one people have lived there, and not all have been children. When a professor at the local college died suddenly, a scholar from Costa Rica was hired to take his place. The school asked Maria if she could put up the man, his wife, and their two kids for a few days until they found a place to live. They stayed for four years. A Costa Rican friend of the professor wanted to study in the States; he stayed for a few years too. The local college used to have an international dorm but had to close it; a Japanese student moved in with Maria for two years. Other housemates included eighteen-year-old guys who had become just too much for their parents to handle.

Maria was born in South Carolina, but she doesn't know exactly when. She was adopted by a family with a home so small that she had to share a bed with her mother. Her papers, she tells me, had the word *bastard* stamped on them. Maria did not do well in school and was sure she was "dumber than a brick." The professionals at the junior college she attended realized she wasn't dumb—she was dyslexic. Maria loved the school and the people who took an interest in her. When her parents came to get her after the first year, thinking that she should quit college and work in a department store, she locked herself in a closet. Now she is forty-two days away from her second master's degree, and she already has a long history of successes at career counseling (which is what she is doing now), drug and alcohol counseling, and advising Veterans Affairs on civil rights.

When new people move in to the house, Maria encourages them to make it their home. Food, drinks, art supplies—all are there for the taking. For the teens and young adults, there are a few rules: no drinking, smoking, or sex in the house.

Regardless of how many people are living with her at the moment, Maria hosts supper on Thursdays and lunch on Sundays, to which those not living in the house are invited too. Typically, between two and fifteen show up. Sometimes Maria does all of the cooking; other times different people bring or prepare different dishes. Afterward, each person scrapes his or her own plate.

The night before my visit, a Saturday, Maria hosted eight people. She had studying to do, so she went upstairs after she finished her dinner. Hours later, she came back downstairs and found all eight of them still there, enjoying each other's company and the welcome feeling of being in Maria's home.

In between all of the scheduled events are plenty of informal visits. Maria has an open-door policy—her friends are welcome to show up without calling in advance. That's something she especially appreciates about her life as a single person: she doesn't have to apologize for having friends stop by, as she did when she was partnered.

When she was twenty-three, Maria tells me, "I did what every girl thinks she is supposed to do: I got married." She and her husband were not a great match. He loved Waterford crystal; she liked Lego bricks. He wanted her to learn to sew and gave her a book called *The Perfect Virginia Housewife*; she preferred to ride her bike. When her husband read an article about the huge number of children in the foster system, the two decided to adopt. After eighteen years, the marriage ended, and Maria turned to the relationships that seemed more natural to her all along: with other women. She lived with one of the women for more than a decade. It was the loneliest time of her life. For the past nine years, she has been single.

Maria's stories of connecting, socializing, and nurturing other people are punctuated with heartfelt odes to solitude. At age nineteen, by signing up to be a resident assistant in college, Maria had a room of her own for the first time in her life: "I could smell it, feel it, taste it." During the summers, even after she graduated, she returned to the college to work. "There was a little stream that ran by one of the buildings there. It was called 'the Prayer Room.' I used to stay out there for hours. Nobody knew where I was." When she was married, her husband recognized her need to have time and space to herself. "That shed out there—for many years, that was where I really lived." Nowadays, when no one else is at home, "I love it. I study at this [dining room] table. There's something warm and wonderful about every room. I like the freedom of being able to come down here and work on a paper for a while, [to] sit in the Jimmy Carter room."

Looking back over her life, especially the early years, Maria thinks she "had a lot to not recommend me." Yet,

At some point, I just decided that I'm going to have a good time. You have the power to write your own story. Most of us, even in our brokenness, can unbreak and stick ourselves back together, and have a good time.

Danica Meek: Loads of Young People, Loads of Fun

Although house sharing may be growing among those who can afford to live alone, it also continues to be popular among young people just starting out. One of the youthful home sharers I interviewed is Danica Meek (mentioned in the introduction).

Danica could have coasted indefinitely. At twenty-one, she was living amicably with her parents, who respected her privacy and never asked for rent. Her mother still did the cooking and cleaning. Danica, though, was restless. She had finished cosmetology school and had a job in a beauty salon. Her friends could not relate to her living situation, and she had grown weary of the long drive to work.

Her salary was modest, and the Southern California city where she worked was expensive. She didn't think she would ever want to live alone, but she still did not know that many people who lived close to her job. Finally, she saw her opportunity when she was visiting her friend Suzanne, whom she had met at beauty school. Suzanne was rooming with three guys and four dogs in a big house on a hill minutes away from the salon where Danica worked. Looking longingly at a room that appeared to be empty, Danica asked if anyone was staying in it. The room wasn't entirely empty—it was the laundry room. But it was big enough for a bed and a dresser. Suzanne and her roommates agreed to the plan, so Danica moved in.

Approached from the front, the low-slung house looks modest. Inside, though, there is a huge living room with big, comfy couches, built-in bookshelves, and sliding glass doors. A walk down a hallway adorned with *Pulp Fiction* and *Spiderman* posters and long-fanged masks leads to a kitchen-and-dining-room area with big bay windows. The unobstructed view takes in the Santa Ynez Mountains in the distance, and the rolling hills populated by palm trees and farmlands closer in. In the backyard is a patio with planters, a grill, lots of chairs, and side-by-side boards for a bean-bag toss, painted with menacing fang-filled faces.

The day-to-day life of Danica's situation will sound familiar to just about anyone who's lived with roommates in their young adult years. Roommate selection can be haphazard. Mealtime protocol is mostly fend-for-yourself. Cleanup is iffy.

Then there's your roommate's friend who shows up one night for a visit and stays the weekend on the couch in the living room; the burst of lusty music that jolts your day to a start long before you had planned; and the roommate who instructs you on the proper way of cooking chicken when you are perfectly happy with your own way, thank you very much. And if weekly gatherings for meditating, sharing feelings, or resolving issues are your thing, you're directed to the nearest yoga studio.

But there are moments of wonderment here too. In her room, when Danica looks away from the washing machine and out the window, she is treated to a peek of the Pacific Ocean. And when she and her roommates decide to put on a show, they go all in.

For Halloween, they invited 150 of their closest friends to the house for a zombie prom. They spent weeks preparing, creating eyeballs by sticking olives in hunks of cheese and fashioning other delicacies in the shape of brains. They hung thirty-five bags worth of simulated cobwebs. So delighted were they with the look of the house that they left the decorations up for months, until real spiders began to appear in the fake cobwebs.

After the Halloween party, Danica thought:

Oh my God, this is totally where I'm supposed to be when I'm twenty-one. I'm supposed to be in a house where there's fun happening all the time. And yeah, the house was disgusting afterward, but it was so worth the cleanup . . . I'm so happy I live here and have these opportunities to be in a place where we're allowed to be loud and make a mess. And it's *our* space; we don't have to apologize to people for it.

Danica does not expect to live in the big house on the hill for long, but living there now is part of the process of discovering the kinds of living arrangements that work for her.

Living with roommates has long been a routine experience for young adults on college campuses. But what is happening beyond the standard arrangement of sharing a room in a dorm?

I was in college when I first heard of the version of house sharing called cooperative living. After our first year, my roommate and I drew good-enough lottery numbers to move out of our dorm room. It was bittersweet for me—I liked the idea of moving into a room of my own—but my roommate and I were close, and I would miss seeing her all the time. Her choice was to move into Ferry House, which was Vassar's co-op. Several dozen students lived there, prepared meals together, maintained the house, and lived more frugally than the rest of us in the dorms.

Well, it was 1976. By then, hippie communities had been popular for more than a decade, so it wasn't too surprising that a college campus not much more than an hour away from the site of Woodstock would have its very own version of communal living. Unlike many of the hippie communities of that era, though, college co-ops did not die. In fact, Vassar now has two more: Beige Buddha for vegetarians and Meat House for carnivores. Many other colleges and universities have co-ops too.

Somewhere Around Thirty: The Overlooked House-Sharing Demographic

Annamarie Pluhar, who wrote a guidebook for finding housemates, had this to say about the kinds of people who might like to live with others who are not their partners: "Sharing housing is for adults of any age and all circumstances, those in graduate school or retirees, working people, empty nesters or single parents, professionals who have homes in one place and jobs elsewhere."[15]

The financial or logistical appeal of house sharing to the particular categories of people Pluhar mentioned is evident. Perhaps less obvious is that the particular demographic that showed the biggest increase from 2007 to 2010 in living with unrelated adults was the group of twenty-five-year-olds through thirty-four-year-olds. Home sharing also increased during that time for adults in younger and older age groups, but not as much.

Scholars in the United Kingdom have recognized that home sharing with unrelated adults has been on the rise there too. In 1998, they initiated the Single Young Adults and Shared Household Living project.[16] The researchers were not surprised to find that young adults accounted for much of the recent popularity of home sharing. That's what is expected of young people still in school or just getting started in the workplace. Often, they cannot afford places of their own, even if they do want to live alone.

The more striking finding was that many of the older twentysomething home sharers were not struggling financially. More than half were in Social Classes I and II (professional and managerial workers), and nearly half had at least one degree-level qualification.[17]

Researchers from the Shared Household Living project interviewed seventy-seven young adults from twenty-five peer-shared households in southern England. Their sample of eighteen- to thirty-five-year-olds purposefully included mostly people with managerial and professional jobs; students were excluded, except for a few unconventional ones who were not as young as the others in their programs.

Most of the interviewees told the researchers the same thing that Marianne Kilkenny told me: by sharing a home, they could live in a more appealing place than they could afford by living alone. Some noted that living with housemates freed up financial resources they could use to pursue other interests or goals.

Yet they, like Marianne and the vast majority of the women who participated in an AARP study of attitudes toward living with friends, said that money was not the most important factor. Most could have rented a place on their own, and some even considered buying a home of their own. Ultimately, though, that's not what they wanted. They chose to live with their peers.[18]

At the outset, thirty-six of the seventy-seven people interviewed had romantic partners, and within a year or so, eight moved to be with their partners. The others, though, wanted to maintain their romantic relationships while living with their friends. A twenty-four-year-old woman had moved to Southampton to be closer to her partner, but she did not want to live with him. "If I'd just moved in with him, I wouldn't have had any friends." She did not want the arrangement she described as, "that's it now—that's you living with him."[19]

The interviewers asked about bickering and blowups and heard about some, but their predominant sense was of "a strong commitment to the deliberate nurturing of friendship."[20] In some houses, residents already shared the connection of working in the same type of job or even the same company. In others, such as the home co-owned by two yoga instructors, the housemates shared a lifestyle or political perspective. All shared the rhythms of their everyday lives.

Residents often gathered for meals, group outings, and birthday celebrations. Some households also created rituals that underscored their identity as a cohesive group. One, for instance, had a housemates-only champagne breakfast every Christmas morning.

Sue Heath, the lead researcher on the project, believes that innovative ways of living change the way people think about intimacy: "Workmates may become best mates, strangers may become housemates; partners may be kept at a distance, friends may live together; family members may become like friends, friends may become like family."[21]

Marice: Many Nationalities, One Common Understanding

A few years ago, Marice, thirty-nine, moved from China to the United States with her teenage son. She had a good job in human resources in Washington, DC, but the transition was difficult. There were language differences and cultural differences, and she was raising her son on her own. Eventually, she realized how she wanted to live—in a big house with lots of other people who would be like family.

She rented a six-bedroom house in a tree-lined neighborhood just off the tangle of highways around DC. She and her son took one room each and then she set out to find housemates to rent the other four. She hoped that some of the people would be like her, newcomers who had come to the United States from other countries. She wanted to help them make the adjustment. When I visit, Diego, a young man from Mexico, is in one room and an Iranian couple in another. The remaining two went to Americans— Paul Godbout, a sixty-two-year-old single dad from DC, who shows me around the house, and his twenty-year-old son, who is planning to move into the other bedroom soon.

As the person who dreamed up the idea of creating this family of choice and then made it happen, Marice could have laid down the rules of the house. But that's not how chosen families work—especially when all of the family members are adults. Instead, they all get together periodically to craft the rules they will live by. Their current list includes the following:

- ♠ The common good trumps individual wants.
- ♠ All rules must be agreed upon by everyone.
- ♠ All rules are subject to change.
- ♠ Personal items stay in personal spaces.
- ♠ Each person is responsible for keeping his or her own room clean.

- ♠ Responsibility for the shared spaces is divided among the house-mates. (Paul and his son take care of the backyard.)
- ♠ When you leave a common space, it should look the same as it did when you entered it.
- ♠ Use utilities sparingly; turn off lights in rooms that are not in use.
- ♠ Use the washer and dryer only when the noise won't bother the others.
- ♠ No wearing shoes inside the house, and no feet on the furniture. (Those are Paul's least favorite rules. In a place of his own, he'd put his feet up on the coffee table while watching television. Still, he says he doesn't mind. "It's good for me.")
- ♠ Everyone buys his or her own food. There are designated shelves for items that people want to share.
- ♠ No food in the bedrooms.
- ♠ Anyone who breaks a rule places a quarter in the piggy bank.

Paul tells me that the piggy bank joined the household the first time someone broke one of the rules, and he admits that someone was him. He calls out to Diego in the other room, asking how many of the quarters are his, but in the ensuing banter, Diego cops to none of them.

Everything about Paul, from his blue jeans and tousled sandy-brown hair to his easygoing demeanor, suggests someone who is comfortable in his own skin, contented with his life and his lifespace. It wasn't always so. He struggled through divorce, depression, problems with alcohol, a fore-closure, and the dissolution of a once highly successful transportation business that he ran for thirty-five years with his twin brother.

Growing up, Paul was one of thirteen kids. He hopes he will always live with other people. He would like to be married again and have a place of his own—a home he "would open to somebody if they needed it." Paul enjoys performing random acts of kindness. Giving to others, he believes, is the most reliable road to happiness.

"What has been the happiest time of your life?" I ask.

"Right now."

A Home for Two, Twenty-First-Century Style

In 1977, Diane Dew was working in a small-town hospital and living alone. She felt isolated and lonely, so she decided to look for a roommate. (We first heard about Diane in the introduction, waving through her window to kids in the apartment across the way, and we'll learn more about her in the next chapter.) On an index card, she wrote, *Roommate wanted, male or female*, and posted it on the hospital bulletin board. The hospital staff considered the "male or female" part scandalous and made her take it down.

The kind of lifespace created by two people who live together as roommates has been around for about as long as anyone can remember. What is newer is the version in which one roommate is male and the other is female, and both want to live together not just as roommates but as (platonic) friends. The arrangement seems to be proliferating, and now the typical reaction from other people is interest or even envy, rather than outrage.

Diana Moghrabi, fifty-six, and Brad, thirty-seven, were first introduced to each other by a mutual friend in their small Southern town, and then they ran into each other again and started talking. Diana had been living alone for the previous ten years. Brad was in the process of moving from the Midwest and was renting a room in someone else's house. He was also on a spiritual journey and wanted to get rid of a lot of his stuff. Diana had been carrying the same boxes of mementos from her married days from one place to the next, and had yet to unpack them. The two decided to host a joint yard sale. Diana really liked Brad's couch and bought it before anyone else could get to it.

Their friendship developed effortlessly. They started a tradition of spending Sundays together at Diana's place. As soon as *CBS Sunday Morning* started, Brad was there.

A few years before, Diana had been interested in finding a new place, but then the economy tanked, and she hadn't had a raise in years. When a friend of a friend asked her to look at a house that was available to be leased, she agreed, just to be nice. Brad went with her.

They took one look at the place and were instantly smitten. It was a single-story home, pale yellow with white trim, set off by colorful flowers and bushes in the front and a generous yard out back. They both loved the lime-green accent wall in the big, white kitchen. The house looked modest in size from the outside, but inside, they found two bedrooms and three other bright, tasteful rooms, in addition to the kitchen.

Soon they were sharing the home. Diana was now paying less and getting more than she had before. They had each other's company, which was at least as important as the economics or the house itself.

They settled into compatible routines. On Sundays, they still watch CBS together—now in their bathrobes—with Brad stretched out on the couch that was once his own. Weekdays, they have a cup of coffee together before going to work. They usually cook together on Tuesdays and Thursdays. They take turns buying the items they both use, such as bread and milk, and sometimes they walk to the market together.

Brad does more of the work of keeping the kitchen neat; Diana usually keeps the bathroom clean. They hire someone to take care of the yard. When I visit, everything is immaculate.

Diana and Brad have gotten to know each other's friends and often have them over for social visits. Most of the time, when they close the door behind the last of the guests, they look at each other and say, "Oh, wasn't that nice!"

I try in a few different ways to find out what Diana does not like about living with Brad, but there doesn't seem to be much. There was a time when they were going their own way most of the time, and Diana did not enjoy that at all; once they reengaged, though, "the fun came back." Brad is a multitasker, who is often watching television, typing on his computer, and checking his phone while chatting with Diana; when

she grows weary of such divided attention, she goes to her computer and checks Facebook. Diana has moved Brad's shoes into his bedroom a few times, leaving her feeling like the mother to him that she does not want to be. Also, if left to her own decorative devices, she would not have a small replica of the statue of David in her hallway.

Because of their different schedules and interests, Diana and Brad routinely get time and space to themselves without having to plan for it. Diana works at a variety of jobs, including teaching word processing and other computer skills during the day and ballroom dancing at night. That keeps her away until late two nights a week. Brad likes to go off on adventures on the weekends; during my visit, he is kayaking. They each have their own independent relationships too. Diana loves having a core group of friends nearby. She is also close to her "baby girl," now thirty, who lives less than an hour away. The adolescent years were stormy; but now "we are friends, and I think that it is richer every time we are together."

Diana and Brad have fun together, and they have serious conversations too. Brad likes to talk about what it means to live an authentic life. Diana says this of her life previously:

> I felt like I was always trying to do what everybody else wanted to do on their timeline and [in] their way and [with] their potato salad recipe . . . I have learned from Brad that it is very different when somebody accepts you the way you are.

The Lifespace of the Future: What's Your Fantasy?

Maybe it is because Marianne was one of the very first people I interviewed for this project, or perhaps it is because she has thought so deeply about living in community; whatever the reason, when I have some burning question about twenty-first-century lifespaces, it is her ideas I am especially interested in hearing. The last question I asked her was

this: "How would you live if you could magically live any way at all? Pretend money is no object, and neither is anything else."

I have posed that question to many different people, and often they need to pause for a moment to think about it. Not Marianne. She has it all mapped out, from the look and feel of the community to the specifics of her own dwelling.

At the center of Marianne's fantasy community is a shared house. A variety of dwellings radiate out from the center—some small cottages, some bigger homes. People live in them solo or with others. The range of possibilities accommodate economic diversity. The community also allows people to stay in the idyllic neighborhood yet move to different kinds of places within it as their needs change, over the course of their lives.

The community includes gardens and other spaces where neighbors gather, and no one has to walk more than half a mile to visit anyone else. Individuals and families of all ages are welcome, and particular attention is paid to the needs of the community members as they age.

Several special people live among them. One is a person with medical training, who can lend a hand with everything from the colicky baby to the preschooler who just fell off his bike, to the older person trying to navigate the thicket of medicines and doctors and paperwork. Another is a general caretaker, available to provide a ride or a meal or to run an errand. These people are not strangers working for minimum wage; they are amply compensated neighbors and friends who have been part of the community for years.

For herself, Marianne envisions a two-story dwelling as her home, her workplace, and her showplace. She imagines waking up every morning in her personal space on the ground floor, meditating, and having breakfast. Later, her coworkers arrive, and they all head upstairs to gather in the office space. Personal life and work life feel less separate. And Marianne hosts an open house now and then, so others can see for themselves this new model for living.

4

LIVING IN A COMMUNITY
From Neighbors to Friends

Suburban living, so often the target of criticism and even disdain, once seemed magical. The esteemed urban strategist and planner Christopher Leinberger believes that the dream version of suburbia was inspired by the 1939 World's Fair "Futurama" exhibit, a wildly popular scale model of the America of the future:

> Visitors watched matchbox-sized cars zip down wide highways. Gone were the crowded tenements of the time; 1960s America would live in stand-alone houses with spacious yards and attached garages. The exhibit would not impress us today, but at the time, it inspired wonder.[1]

For the next sixty years, Americans made their way to the suburbs, pushing out farther and farther from the city.[2] They got their single-family homes, their attached garages, and their big yards set back from the streets in neighborhoods with nothing else but other similar houses. Work was elsewhere; so was shopping; so was entertainment. To get to any of those places, suburbanites needed to hop in their cars and drive. By 1960, 31 percent of the population lived in suburbs. By 2010, more than half did.[3]

Even as suburban growth continued (urban growth did not begin to surpass suburban growth until 2011), both residents and professionals were growing weary. Suburbanites were frustrated by the time they spent in their cars. When at home in their castles, they sometimes felt isolated and lonely. Architects and planners decried the soul-sucking sameness of the suburbs, and the wastefulness and alienation of the sprawl.[4]

In the 1980s, worried professionals began to come together to compare notes and create visions of new ways of living that would offer a better quality of life.[5] Although many of the professionals were architects, their focus was on people and human interactions, more than on buildings. They imagined neighborhoods where people would be out on the streets, walking to stores and school and work, running into each other, and stopping to chat. They envisioned streets that would be safe for joggers and bicyclists, and be visually interesting. They thought that communities should have a sense of place unique to their history and environs rather than a monotonous, prefabricated replicability.[6]

The architects also had some ideas about the kinds of features that would encourage the neighborliness and civic-mindedness to which they aspired. Homes, they thought, should be fronted by porches instead of garages. The houses should be close enough to the streets to invite conversations with passersby. Streets should be narrow enough to discourage drivers from speeding.

In 1993, a group calling itself the Congress for New Urbanism wrote a "Charter of the New Urbanism," spelling out their principles and goals.[7] The group has become increasingly popular and influential ever since, as have similarly motivated movements such as Smart Growth and Transit Oriented Development. Writing often in the pages of the *New York Times*, Allison Arieff is a powerful spokesperson. "Bring back the sidewalk!" she urged in one of her articles, explaining: "Community is born from social routine—running into neighbors at the mailbox or while walking down the street. Design for these serendipitous encounters."[8]

The authentic neighborly feel that so many professionals are trying so hard to create in new places (or re-create in old ones) is what many individuals I interviewed had already achieved by improvising and innovating on their own. Others discovered a model that was already established—cohousing—and put their own stamp on that.

The Cohousing Revolution

Many years ago, after Lynne Elizabeth finished college, her young family lived on an undistinguished street of row houses in Philadelphia. Each house had just a tiny stoop in front, not even a front porch. One evening, when several neighbors were sitting on their stoops, a man brought out some Maryland crabs he had prepared and shared them with the others. Another neighbor brought out some beer. There they all sat, newspapers in their laps, eating crabs and drinking beer. The kids joined in, too, minus the beer (and probably the crabs).

They all enjoyed it so much, they decided to get together again. They started celebrating birthdays, then holidays. They had become very fond of their place on the street—and protective of it. They didn't want cars speeding through, so they wrote petitions, gathered signatures, and got speed bumps installed. It was, Lynne tells me, their "public living room."

In a way that was totally organic and un-self-conscious, Lynne and her neighbors had created what so many people crave—a real community. In a way that may well be universal, the ritual of sharing food shaped and cemented their bonds. Kids and grown-ups and great-grown-ups all intermingled. Their neighborhood was a distinct space, and they all cared about it.

As much as they loved their time together, they also valued their privacy; their homes were their own. They had time alone as well as their time together, solitude as well as community.

Around the same time, twenty-seven families near Copenhagen, Denmark, were also pining for a way of living that would offer them a real sense of community without giving up the privacy of their own homes. They found a site where they could design and build the neighborhood of their dreams. They arranged their homes around a shared space in the center. Cars were kept out of the way. They also built a home they all owned—the common house with its own kitchen and dining room, where they would meet periodically to prepare and share meals. There were lots of kids in the community, so the common house also included playrooms. Laundry facilities were there, too, along with workshops and a few guest rooms. By design, the spatial arrangements encouraged neighborliness. The residents wanted to see each other over the course of their everyday lives, and be there for each other in ways large and small. They succeeded.[9]

That was in the early '70s. By 2010, there were more than seven hundred of these *bofoellesskaber*, or "living communities," in Denmark alone.[10] The idea caught on, making its way to countries such as Sweden and the Netherlands; Germany, France, Belgium, Austria, Italy, and Switzerland; Australia, New Zealand, and Canada.

Kathryn McCamant and Charles Durrett were American architecture students studying in Copenhagen in 1980 when they first discovered one such community. The impression stayed with them even after they were back in the States; and in 1984, they set out on a thirteen-month return trip to take a long, close look. They visited 185 communities. They had their mission: they would bring the concept back to the United States and call it cohousing. The first American cohousing community, Muir Commons, was built in Davis, California, in 1991.[11]

By now, the cohousing movement, though still relatively small, has enough cachet that some developers try to build their own clusters of homes and market them as cohousing communities. In so doing, they have outed themselves as inauthentic wannabes. Participation is definitional to cohousing. From the moment one "burning soul" or small group of similarly passionate people decide that cohousing is for them, deciding to make a new cohousing community happen, they are the driving force in planning and designing the community where they will live. Sure, they usually recruit plenty of professional help along the way, but those professionals are the listeners and the advisors, *not* the deciders.[12]

The participatory heart of cohousing keeps on beating even after the community has been established. At regular times—maybe once a month—residents come together to make decisions. This is true participatory democracy. The residents—not elected representatives—do the governing, and they try for consensus. There are no hierarchies in cohousing. Perhaps a few residents will receive training in leading consensus-based decision making, but their role is to make the meetings more effective and more efficient, and not to be crowned king or queen or president.

When a playing field needs some sod, a path needs to be cleared, or repairs need to be done—again, it is the residents who provide the person-power. Workdays are scheduled periodically—sometimes called work parties—and cohousers contribute what they can, whether that is labor or treats for the laborers. Common meals are participatory too. Every so often (the frequency varies with the community), residents come together to share a meal in the common house. People take turns as the chef and assistant chef who prepare the meals and clean up afterward. That means that for each turn in the kitchen, residents get many more dining experiences in which they sit back and enjoy the food and the company. Each individual home also has its own kitchen—cohousing is about community, but it is also about autonomy.

As essential as the participatory process is in defining cohousing, so is the deliberate design for community and autonomy. Cohousers are especially sensitive to the ways in which spatial arrangements can create or discourage conviviality. Take, for example, the arrangement of the homes. I like to think of dwellings as people: if a group of people wanted to get to know each other, they would not line up facing each other in two straight, rigid rows, too far apart to really see anyone else clearly. That's how houses are arranged on many conventional streets. Instead, a group of people at a small social event might gather around a table; or at larger events, they might cluster in small groups of different sizes. Cohousing dwellings are arranged like people who want to socialize. In smaller communities, they are often arranged around a courtyard or other grassy area. In larger ones, there are sometimes clusters of homes here and there.

Cohousing homes might include a small front porch and yard but no fences or garages. There are pathways and open spaces but no through streets. Cars are banished to the periphery. The common house is an easy walk from any residence and often in plain view. All of these features increase the odds that people will run across each other over the course of their everyday lives.

As in the original Danish cohousing community, the common house in American cohousing communities often includes laundry facilities, workshops, playrooms, and guest rooms. Most cohousing communities are not ideologically driven, but residents do tend to care about the environment. Sharing these specialized spaces is a way of living more lightly on the land. Each household does not need to include extra space for an infrequently used workshop or washing machine, for example. These design features, though, sustain friendships as much as they sustain the earth. Head to the little laundry room in your own private home, and there is probably no one else there. Make your way to the machines in a common house, and you will see your friends and neighbors when you get there—and also along the way.

Current cohousing communities have between seven and sixty-seven housing units (often duplexes, but there are houses and apartments too), with most in the twentysomething range. That's deliberate too. The numbers are meant to be small enough that community members can know each other and stay connected but large enough to ensure stability and continuity over time.

Residents garner a large measure of autonomy simply by having homes of their own. The placement of dwellings allows for privacy as well. The fronts of the houses face the paths, gardens, and shared open spaces—that's where the socializing happens. The backs are more private, and residents can head there when they want their solitude.

Temescal Commons: Sharing and Caring— and Solitude Too

When I met Lynne Elizabeth in 2012, decades after those heady days of the Philadelphia row-house neighborhood, there were more than 120 cohousing communities in the United States, and she was living in one of them. Her time in that Philly neighborhood lasted only as long as her husband's time in medical school. Their marriage did not last either. When I interviewed her, she was living on her own in her cohousing townhouse.

Cohousing communities can be in cities, suburbs, rural areas— really, anywhere. In the United States, they predominate on the coasts and near cities. Lynne's community, Temescal Commons, is in Oakland, California. That city is part of the East Bay, home to more cohousing communities than any other area in the nation. Before I left, I saw Mariposa Grove, Berkeley Cohousing, and Temescal Creek, as well as Temescal Commons.

Most cohousing communities are built from scratch on a wide-open piece of land. In cities, though, such possibilities are rarely available, so cohousers look for opportunities to reuse commercial or industrial buildings, or to adapt dwellings that already exist. Those communities tend to be on the small side. Temescal Commons began as an urban infill project with two lots, a farmhouse, and a barn. It now has nine residential units (including three duplexes and one triplex), housing nineteen adults and five kids, plus the common house and the multiuse barn. In addition to Lynne, there are (when I visit), two other single women, two single men, and six couples—three with kids, one with a first kid on the way, and two with no kids. Across the street from the community is a family that has known many of the community members a long time; they enjoy the cohousing community so much that they have become a satellite family, participating often in meals and events.

Every cohousing neighborhood is a sensual delight. Cohousers seem to have little tolerance for the bland or predictable. Dwellings come in playful hues; and in some communities, such as in Bellingham, Washington, the style of architecture is Northwest Scandinavian Craftsman. Shades of yellow, green, adobe, and brown alternate—one on the top level of the duplexes and another on the bottom. Mariposa Grove includes a yellow house with white trim and a white house with yellow trim, and violet stair railings. Temescal Creek sports a yellow house with royal-blue trim and a burnt-orange-and-yellow-stucco common house with avocado metal railings. Lynne's community, Temescal Commons, includes Scandinavian-inspired townhouses as well as a big yellow house with white trim.

When you step inside Lynne's two-story townhouse, you enter an open dining room and kitchen with tall blond cabinets. The stairs on the right lead up to the second floor where Lynne runs the small press she founded. We stay downstairs and settle into the comfortable living room in the back, where a beautiful L-shaped desk hugs the corner beneath three windows.

Having lots of people around is the story of Lynne's life. Growing up with her parents and two brothers, her next-door neighbors were her aunt, uncle, and some of her cousins. She had fifty cousins on her father's side. Every summer, they all gathered at her grandfather's farm. She has fond memories of all of her aunts convening in the kitchen, washing dishes and bantering. Before and after the days in the Philly row house, Lynne lived with groups of people under the same roof.

Now, during working hours, Lynne shares her home with the staff of her publishing company. After they leave, if it is one of the two days a week when dinner is served in the common house, that's where Lynne heads next. Sometimes she and others stay long after the last plates have been cleared, just to continue their conversations. The community also gardens together once a month. If Lynne wants company other times, the common house is again a good choice; people hang out there often. Lynne also has a social network beyond Temescal Commons. "Each of us living here has a constellation of friends and activities that are quite separate from cohousing."

When Lynne was married, she felt that her time with friends was curtailed by the preferences of her less sociable spouse. The loneliest times of her life occurred during those years. Not too long ago, Lynne had a sweetheart for a few years. It was a mixed experience. "I would spend weekend time with him hiking and doing the wonderful things we did, but that also meant that the circles of girlfriends and other friends would not get attended to."

To Lynne, the best thing about cohousing is "the shared caring for the neighborhood and each other." If someone needs help with childcare or dog care, neighbors are always available. If someone is hospitalized, cohousing friends are there to visit. When a cohouser is ailing at home, neighbors show up with chicken soup and the latest news from the community. "It makes me want to cry just thinking how much people really care for each other."

Lynne acknowledges that there are stresses, difficulties, and disagreements in cohousing. She gives the example of a tension she is currently carrying around and had not yet taken the time to resolve. Her neighbor recently got some puppies, and one seems none too fond of Lynne, barking at her every time she walks out her door. Maybe the dog knows that Lynne previously expressed concern about all the dog poop in the yard, but no matter.

I was sitting out there eating lunch the other day and the dog was going *yip, yip, yip, yip, yip,* and she [the neighbor] came out and

took her dog in. And I could tell that she was aggravated with the
dog . . . I think she was thinking I'm aggravated with her.

Lynne thinks she should have told her it is okay, and soon she will.
"I just want my neighbor to know that I understand, she's doing her best,
and didn't want her to feel bad."

When I ask Lynne if she got the amount of solitude and privacy that
she wanted, she says that is sometimes a challenge, but not because she
is living in cohousing. Instead, it is the industriousness of her staff that
occasionally becomes a problem, when they want to stay and work late.
"I just felt I needed private time to call friends or cook dinner, or just do
whatever I wanted to do and not have a staff person here."

When Lynne first moved into Temescal Commons, she was raising
her youngest son, then in middle school, on her own. (Two older children were already grown and on their own.) Twins his age were already
living in the community, and he saw them occasionally, but he was most
smitten by the six other kids who were younger than him. He had never
spent much time around little kids before, and he found that he loved
them. They, in turn, looked up to him and adored him. Seven children
all had each other as playmates and a whole big grassy area to play in,
without ever crossing a street.

A group of young adults became very fond of Lynne's son and made
him a part of their group. Through his middle school and teenage years,
they included him in game nights (Settlers of Catan was a favorite) and
outings to concerts. Sometimes he went to church with them too.

Lynne cherished the way her cohousing community embraced her
son. The other community members could elicit a side of him that she, as
a parent, was unlikely to see. She caught snippets of their conversations
at dinners at the common house sometimes, when he was sitting with
them and she was at another table, close enough to overhear a bit. They
might start out asking him how it was going lately, but then they would

go wider, and eventually he would end up telling them about his dreams for his life.

Cohousing with Children

Just about everyone I talked with about cohousing, regardless of status as single or coupled, parents or not parents, mentioned what a wonderful experience cohousing could be for kids, for people with kids, and for people who love kids.

Rachel, who lives in a rural cohousing community, was married with the first of her two children when a job offer in a new town left her grappling with the question of how to live. She could have headed to the nuclear-family land of suburbia, but that never did appeal to her. An established cohousing community was twenty minutes away from work. She and her husband and child visited now and then to check it out; the kid-friendliness appealed to them the most. With cars kept away from the copious green spaces in the center of the neighborhood, children could run out the door and play freely. With all the other kids around, there was never any need to set up play dates. Unobtrusive adult supervision was everywhere. All the adults knew all the kids, so someone was always looking out for them, wherever they were. Rachel and her family were sold, and when child number two arrived, they finally made the move.

When Marinus Van de Kamp moved from the Netherlands to the town of Bellingham, an hour or so north of Seattle, he got married, looked around, and saw that his neighbors were building big houses. So he did too. The standard American stand-alone house in a standard-issue neighborhood, though, just did not fit with who he really was or what he valued. He had grown up with his brother and his parents in an eight-hundred-square-foot home surrounded by farms. Five hundred people lived in his village, and they all knew each other. He missed that.

For his daughter who was on the way, he and his wife wanted a place for her to grow up where the neighbors would have a meaningful place in her life. "Fences and garage doors, we didn't like that." The couple visited cohousing communities to learn more about them and then gathered a small group of like-minded dreamers. A year or so and many meetings later, another group trying to develop an ecovillage joined them, and in 2000, Bellingham Cohousing was born.

Karen Hester, the burning soul who inspired the creation of Temescal Creek cohousing, just a few blocks from the Temescal Commons community where Lynne lives, is single and has no children. She needs her "kid fix," she tells me, and her cohousing neighborhood provides that.

In Temescal Creek, the parents of a fifteen-year-old boy divorced. His mother moved out of the community, and the son stayed there with his dad. I ask Karen if she thinks it helped the teen to be able to stay. "Oh, absolutely." He was surrounded by his friends, and lots of adults who cared about him and looked out for him. When his father started dating and expected to be home late, the teen stayed over at his friends' places.

Bill Hartzell has had a hand in developing three cohousing communities, including the first one in Pennsylvania. He's on the board of directors of the Cohousing Association of the United States. Asked to answer the question "What is cohousing?" for the organization's website, he told a story about his sister-in-law. Becca was a single mother to a two-year-old, living in N Street Cohousing in Davis, California, when she had a seizure while teaching her middle school science class. The cause was cancer, and the prognosis was grim. Her cohousing family and friends were there for her and her daughter every day for the rest of her life. They cooked for her, cleaned for her, brought her to medical appointments; and they offered companionship, support, and caregiving for her daughter. More and more often, her daughter stayed over with one of the couples in the community. Her mother's wish for her was that she could grow up in the N Street community. Within a year, Becca died. A toddler lost her mother, but she was adopted officially by the couple who had already become a familiar and loving presence in her life—and unofficially by everyone else in the cohousing community.

Mariposa Grove: An Affordable Slice of Urban Heaven

When I leave my interviews at Temescal Commons, I could have walked to my next interview, with Diane, at Mariposa Grove. It was less than two miles away. Diane, though—knowing no more about me than what I had told her in my email request to talk to her—offered to come get me, and I happily accepted.

Diane parks on the street, and we walk into a vibrant stretch of trees, flowers, vegetables, and herbs tucked in and around an outdoor stage; a chicken coop; a colorful hammock; and tables, benches, and chairs. When it is time for dinner in the common house, the cook walks out into this space and rings a bell.

One of the raps against cohousing is that the homes can be pricey. Mariposa Grove, though, is affordable housing. To qualify to live there, Diane had to demonstrate just the right amount of income—enough to pay her bills but not so much to place out of the low-income criteria. There was a time when Diane made quite a lot of money. It was right after she finished her second degree in computer programming (her first was in nutrition) and was hired by Chevron. But she could not reconcile what she was doing with who she thought she really was. Now she raises money for the public schools in Berkeley and also does some photography.

Diane qualified—both in terms of her financial resources and her fit with the community. She had spent some time visiting, and she and the rest of the community knew they were a good match. That was 2008. She was the last person to join the community, and no one has left since.

Diane's place is a modest two-bedroom on the ground level of a two-story structure. Her twenty-three-year old son was recently laid off and is living in the second bedroom, so Diane's bedroom now includes her desk and computer. Beautiful color photos of her son and some great shots of nature are artistically arranged on one wall, as is an elaborate drawing of a huge gabled house on a corner lot of a small Massachusetts town. That's where she grew up.

On our way to the common house, we stop to chat briefly with one of the other women of the community. Then, in an open spacious room in the common house, one of the Mariposa Grove dads is playing with his little son, so we talk to them too. I ask whether the little one has the run of the place as the only baby—and he does—but that status is only temporary; another community member has a baby on the way.

We continue down a hallway past a magnificent collage, covering nearly the entire wall, telling the story of the cohousing community. Photos show the kids (lots and lots of photos are of the kids), grown-ups, buildings, grounds, food, and events. The shared spaces in the common house include an art studio, office space, workshop, and guest rooms, as well as the playroom. Diane and I head to the living room at the far end of a big, open floor plan that includes an ample kitchen and dining room.

Before we get there, we meet still another Mariposa Grove resident. Diane introduces me and says she adores the woman's two little boys. The mom, in turn, effuses about how much her kids love Diane. "You're like their adopted grandma," she says but quickly adds that Diane is too young to be an actual grandmother. (She is fifty-eight.)

The living room is where the community convenes meetings. We sit on a couch under a big picture window. Lots of other chairs are arranged around a coffee table in the center. The painting above the brick fireplace is more than it appears; pull it toward you, and it opens into a whiteboard with meeting notes. Tacked to the wall is the community's mission statement that reads, in part: *We are creating a permanently affordable home, a physical and social space where we share resources and responsibilities, grow together and support each other to fulfill our personal dreams.* Next to it is the reminder: *Never let a problem to be solved become more important than a person to be loved.*

Diane was partnered in the past and thought she "should have been happy [but] there was something about it that I wasn't feeling quite at peace with." It is different now, and her cohousing community and many circles of friends are a big part of that. She has very close female friends nearby, and usually at least one of them is available whenever she wants to see a movie or go to a local event—she just sends out a text, and a plan materializes. Some evenings, she and the other Mariposa Grove residents build a fire in their fire pit, prepare some barbecue, and stay out laughing and talking until nearly midnight.

Diane is also part of a small women's group that has been meeting once a month since 2006. The women have no agenda except to speak, listen, and be heard. Each time they meet, each woman gets a chunk of uninterrupted time all to herself—to puzzle through an issue, to cry, or just to talk.

Another category of friendships are the ones from within the cohousing community. They are special, Diane thinks, "because we have this extra layer of relying on each other." Once a week for six months, while another single mom went to business networking events, Diane took care of her daughter, feeding her breakfast and taking her to school. Now that mom is married, and after she puts her daughter to bed, she often heads over to Diane's just to chat. Diane has also gotten plenty of help from the others in the community.

Diane talks openly and freely in response to every question I ask. When I get to the last few questions, though, her answers are no longer than two words.

"What would you say has been the happiest time in your life?"

"Right now."

What about the most contented time?

"Right now."

"If you had all the money in the world, what would you change about the way you live?"

"Nothing."

"How long will you stay here?"

"Forever."

Karen Hester: Burning Soul, Devoted Friend, and Solo Sojourner

In her senior year of college, Karen Hester lived with twelve other women in a big house with six bedrooms. In graduate school, she again lived communally with other women. More than a decade later, she was living with a partner and about to buy a house with her, for just the two of them and any children they might raise. They even had opened escrow. That's when Karen and her partner realized that their relationship was not strong enough for that step. The house was off, and so was the relationship.

Karen had just turned forty. She wanted to live in a community again, but this time she also wanted a place of her own. So she convened a meeting of some friends—another single lesbian and three families of straight couples with kids. None of them had ever owned a home. They set their sights on three funky, old Victorian duplexes within walking distance of an Oakland metro stop. After consulting with some professionals who knew more about real estate and cohousing communities than they did, they pooled their financial resources, borrowing from friends and family if they needed to, and bought the properties as tenants-in-common (all of their names were on the mortgage).

Then they set out to turning it into a community, tearing down garages, fences, and carports; adding footpaths; painting and putting in solar panels; and planting gardens and trees. That all started in 1999. The people living near the emerging Temescal Creek community were skeptical at first but were soon wooed by block parties and other fun events that convinced them that their neighborhood had not been invaded by a cult.

By the time I visit in 2012, the central green space shared by the cohousers brims with tomatoes, peas, kale, and strawberries, along with trees bearing figs, loquats, pluots, apples, and Asian pears—plus a huge hundred-year-old oak tree. The residents had bought a few more adjacent properties and added a solar-powered outdoor hot tub and shower, a basketball hoop, a Ping-Pong table (also outdoors—it's California), and some chickens and rabbits (but no dogs). Twenty adults, six children, and four teens live in four duplexes and three single-family homes. The housing units have been converted to condominiums so that each family can own their own place and a share of the common house.

Karen has the top half of one of the duplexes—a sunny, welcoming two-bedroom with a big kitchen, high ceilings, hardwood floors, and huge windows. We don't talk there, though; the Conference of the Cohousing Association of the United States is happening. Karen is in full conference mode, speaking on a panel in the morning, helping with tours in the afternoon, and keeping up with friends and contacts whenever she can create some time. So we meet at a Mexican restaurant.

Looking back on that time thirteen years ago, when Karen first gathered her friends to suggest that they create their own cohousing community, she says it was the best decision she ever made. What's so great about it? "I think it's just the daily rhythms of living there, where I depend on other people and they depend on me in so many ways . . . all those little things that make up a feeling, a network, a web of relationships."

Karen is happy to tell me about her "I'm so glad I live here" moments:

I have that feeling at the end of every day where we call a work party . . . you get all this work done and there's such a feeling of camaraderie. And I always look around at everybody and go, "Oh my God, these are the people that I am so happy I am living with." It's just so pleasant. And then maybe we'll even eat dinner together that night.

I would not have predicted that answer. What she is happy about is work. It is not paid work; it can be dirty—community members work on the grounds and do repairs. Plus, it sometimes takes up an entire day. But I should have predicted it. Because when I go back and review my notes from my other cohousing conversations, I find that others, such as Lynne, have said much the same thing.

As much as Karen cherishes her cohousing friends, they are not the only important friends in her life. She often spends weekend time with close friends in the greater Oakland area. Karen is a nurturer, maintaining relationships with the people she cares about for the long term, even when she no longer lives nearby.

With her extraverted personality, her job as an events planner, and her many connections, Karen could keep adding to her social circles indefinitely.

> Actually, I don't want more friends. I want to increase the time I spend with the friends that I really love and adore . . . a lot of my close friends, I mean [they're] twenty- and thirty-year-old relationships. And those are the people I've been through thick and thin with.

Karen is just fifty-three, but she has just illustrated in her own life what scholar Laura Carstensen has learned from decades of studying aging: older people become less interested in meeting new people and more interested in spending time with those who are already important to them. She calls it "socioemotional selectivity."[13]

One of the things I love about Karen is her open-armed embrace of all of the people who matter to her. She does not limit herself to celebrating only those people our culture conventionally acknowledges, such as romantic couples. At a time when one friend after another was celebrating how long they had been coupled, Karen decided to celebrate something else—her twenty-fifth year of living in California. (She grew up in Lubbock, Texas.) She reserved the historic West Point Inn at the top of Mount Tamalpais, about forty miles north of San Francisco, and invited her sister, her nephew, and about twenty of her closest friends. "We don't really have rituals for celebrating these long-term friendships or . . . just about who I am." As it happens, two of the couples whose anniversary celebrations motivated Karen to celebrate the important people and milestones in her own life have since broken up. Karen's friendships endure.

After hearing about Karen's packed social schedule, I am not surprised when she tells me that during the busiest of times, she is grateful to be able to come back to her home at night and make it her haven. That very evening, in fact, with the cohousing conference still in high gear, Karen says, "I'm so happy I have no plans tonight except to be by myself."

I am stunned, though, when she tells me that she savors her solitude so much that every winter she travels to a different country and spends about six weeks there, mostly on her own. She has gone to places such as South Africa, Peru, Brazil, Bali, and Myanmar. The people she meets along the way are as significant as the places.

> On the other hand, what I love about it and crave about it is I can spend as much time by myself as I want . . . I think if I didn't have that chunk of solitary time every year, I would feel pretty depleted.

How does it feel to come back to her own home in Temescal Creek, cohousing after such remarkable travels? "It's wonderful to come back . . . I'm just like, 'Oh, thank God I live here.'"

Bellingham Cohousing: Big, Open Spaces, Inside and Out

My first cohousing visits were to urban communities, where space is at a premium and communities are fairly small. I went to Bellingham in northern Washington to see a community that was built from the ground up, in a wide-open space. Kristin, who lives in Bellingham (but not in the cohousing community), is my guide to the town and my fellow cohousing explorer. I had been in touch with Kristin online for years, mostly in discussions around my *Living Single* blog posts on PsychologyToday.com. This was the first time we met in person.

We turn into Bellingham cohousing from a country highway and are greeted by a six-acre expanse, its buildings clustered toward the center.

All thirty-three private dwellings are attached, so there are just ten structures, plus the common house. About sixty-five people live there. They have been working on restoring the wetlands that surround the homes.

Marinus, the man who spearheaded Bellingham cohousing in an attempt to recreate the village life he grew up with in the Netherlands, is a designer, draftsman, and carpenter. He co-owns a building and design company that has an office above the cohousing workshop. We meet him there and proceed to the common house.

Outside, the common house is a big, renovated old farmhouse painted a shade close to white. An expansive deck is outfitted with tables and chairs, an umbrella, a sink, and a giant grill. Inside, the styling is Scandinavian. One room is bathed in light from tall windows on two sides; on another side, built-in bookshelves frame a beautiful fireplace. The most magnificent room of the common house is the dining room. A soaring cathedral ceiling and a row of skylights create a wondrous sense of openness. At least a half-dozen oak tables fill the room, each topped with a fresh flower in a clear glass vase. The ample kitchen, with three tall windows in the back, opens to the dining room. This is the fifth common-house kitchen I had seen and the one serving the biggest group, by far. All of the kitchens are open, and none seem institutional; that is by design. As cohousing architect Charles Durrett explained, when cooks work in an open kitchen, they feel like heroes; when they work in a closed kitchen, they feel like servants.[14]

Marinus and his first wife were the inspiration for the Bellingham cohousing community, so it was especially disappointing to Marinus when, after two years, she no longer wanted to live there. They stayed together for nine more years but not in cohousing. Marinus is remarried now and building a home to accommodate another old-fashioned way of living—a multigenerational household. He will live with his daughter, his wife, his wife's daughter, and his mother-in-law.

What did he like best about cohousing when he lived there?

> Just having some friends that you would sit around with, talk about any issues . . . We would just put out the word at dinner time [that we wanted to go dancing, for example], and we'd have, before you know it, five or six or eight people going.

Marinus may have left the grounds of Bellingham cohousing, but he never left the community. He is still on the cohousing email list; and when an announcement goes out about an event or a spontaneous night on the town, he's there.

Cohousing Skeptics

During my time at the cohousing conference, I enjoyed the informality and affability of the attendees. On the tours of the various cohousing neighborhoods, everyone was dressed casually and comfortably in sandals or sneakers, caps, visors, and sunhats. There were men and women from different backgrounds and interests, ranging in age from the thirties well on up. But there seemed to be very few twentysomethings. I didn't know it at the time, but my impression was supported by the available data. Cohousing residents are disproportionately older than the population at large. Rachel (the married-with-children cohouser living in a rural community introduced earlier in this chapter) thought that money was part of the problem. Diane of Mariposa Grove thought life experiences were important. Young adults have certain ideas about how they should live; after they have tried the usual arrangements, some discover that conventional lifespaces are disappointing. By the time they get to their fifties and sixties, they want something more meaningful.

Over the course of my research, I heard from people who were not enamored of cohousing. Some people are turned off by it because they assume it is something that it is not. Rachel said that the question she is asked most often by people just learning about cohousing is, "Is this a commune?" Cohousing communities are not communes. The community members don't all live under the same roof or (as some communes do) share their clothes. Most important, cohousing communities have no shared economies. Individuals have their own jobs (or retirement funds), and households own or rent their own homes.

A friend of Kristin's who had visited the Bellingham cohousing community told me that she was not about to move to a place where she'd have to go to a separate building to do her laundry. Marianne Kilkenny (from chapter 3) wanted nothing to do with the consensus model of decision making. Leanna Wolfe, an anthropologist who has lived in an awe-inspiring array of places around the world (see chapter 8), took a look around a few cohousing communities and thought that people would end up knowing a bit too much about each other.

Some people who had lived in a cohousing community, or still do, also shared their reservations but did not want to be identified. Two were disappointed that they never did develop the close friendships they had so wished for. One found that she just had no interest in all the processing that went on during meetings. Another disliked the very thing that people such as Diane so enjoy—opening the shades and seeing people walking by right outside your window. Two of the same people thought they would prefer to be in the midst of a bustling city.

There is an inward focus to most cohousing communities. The communities are spatially separated from the other neighborhoods, and the homes typically face each other. Many people who love living in cities, though, prefer a more outward momentum. The spatial ecology of some urban neighborhoods invites residents to emerge from their private residences and keep on walking, because the life of the place is on the streets and in the shops, restaurants, and theaters. The intriguing lifespaces— the places and spaces and people—are out there for the city dwellers to discover and make their own.

The Way We Used to Live

Neighborhoods that incorporate the spatial sensitivities of cohousing without any of the other elements, such as a common house, common meals, and consensual decision making, have a long history. They may not achieve the camaraderie and there-for-you qualities of the most successful cohousing communities. Still, they have a better chance at doing so than neighborhoods that are not spatially designed for community building.

The concept of arranging homes around a courtyard or other open space is an architectural tradition that reaches back in time and across continents. In Amsterdam, for example, the Begijnhof is home to more than one hundred single women. They live in tall houses surrounding a courtyard in a lifespace that dates back to the Middle Ages.[15] In Abu Dhabi, the *fareej* is a traditional neighborhood system particularly accommodating to extended-family networks. Private homes arranged around courtyards—also thousands of years old—are connected by narrow paths to shopping, parks, schools, and workplaces so as to create a "complete community."[16]

Los Angeles, California, has a courtyard tradition too. In the opening decades of the twentieth century, L.A. had an image of itself to project to the rest of the nation—it was the "city of homes," meaning the detached, single-family variety we have come to associate with the suburbs.[17] One advertisement proclaimed, "Los Angeles is the home of the bungalow . . . surrounded by palms, lawns, and flowers throughout the year."[18]

People of modest means, along with the poor, were unlikely to achieve that version of home. As more people poured into the area and land became more scarce, the opportunities diminished even more. Los Angeles, though, was not about to go the way of the tenements that marred New York City. An alternative that became popular was the bungalow court, comprising individual cottages, usually rentals, arranged around a shared space. The best-known bungalow courts were upscale versions with houses built in the American Craftsman architectural tradition. Those neighborhoods boasted "individually-designed, well-appointed, and beautifully-crafted houses sharing a spacious, lushly landscaped lot."[19] Residents did not have lots of their own, but they did get to enjoy the privacy of their individual homes in a setting of natural beauty.

Far more numerous than the Craftsman bungalow courts were the collections of smaller, simpler structures that became home to people of more than thirty nationalities.[20] By 1924, more than 7 percent of all dwellings in Los Angeles were located in a house court.[21]

Cohousing's Cousins

The number of communities adopting the entire cohousing package is likely to grow slowly, but already, I see indications that different people are incorporating different elements of cohousing into the lifespaces they are creating. Many have never even heard of cohousing. What seems contagious is the concept of combining the autonomy of a home of your own with the neighborliness of an old-time village.

The New House Courts: Pocket Neighborhoods and Cul-de-Sacs

In Southern California as well as around the nation, about a century after the heyday of the house court in Los Angeles, that lifespace has been reimagined as a pocket neighborhood. Architect Ross Chapin, who wrote a book on the topic, describes a pocket neighborhood as "a cohesive cluster of homes gathered around some kind of common ground within a larger surrounding neighborhood . . . a neighborhood within a neighborhood."[22] These communities often earn high walkability scores for their proximity to shops and restaurants. The homes, which tend to be small and compact, are more manageable for older people than the bigger, more sprawling suburban variety, and more affordable for younger people.

Psychologically, the draw of the pocket neighborhood is the promise of the privacy of an individual home within the community of a neighborhood that feels like a small village. When Sally Abrahms visited pocket neighborhoods for her story in the *AARP Bulletin*, residents told her the same kinds of stories so many cohousers told me—about easy sociability, informal borrowing and sharing, and caring neighbors who show up with homemade meals when someone is ill.[23]

The suburban approximation to the pocket neighborhood is the cul-de-sac. These spaces have been demonized for making neighborhoods harder to navigate and less accessible to emergency vehicles.[24] Interpersonally, though, they work—especially the cuter, bulb-shaped versions. In his studies of bulb cul-de-sacs, dead-end cul-de-sacs, and linear through streets, sociologist Thomas R. Hochschild, Jr. found that people who lived on cul-de-sacs were likely to say that their friendships with their immediate neighbors meant a lot to them. About a quarter of the residents of bulb cul-de-sacs said that "a feeling of friendship runs deep" between them and their nearest neighbors. None of the people living on through streets agreed with that sentiment.[25]

Writing for *Atlantic Cities*, Emily Badger explained why cul-de-sacs are so good for community building: "If you want to throw a block party on a through street, you need a permit. If you want to do the same on a cul-de-sac, the street is already effectively blocked off . . . Cul-de-sacs create a kind of natural panoptican [sic] around children at play." They also pose problems amenable to group solving, such as "fallen trees or unplowed snow blocking every family's exit."[26]

Kristin, Katrina, and Keith's Creative Condo Community

Kristin, who toured the Bellingham cohousing community with me, has created her own version of cohousing in her condo complex, also in Bellingham. She calls it *cohousing lite*. Just one unit separates her condo from the one owned by Katrina and Keith. The humans hardly knew each other until their cats, Kali and Nimby, became friends. Every morning, Kali came calling for Nimby, and at the end of each day, Kristin escorted her back to Katrina and Keith. There were three other cats around who were Kali and Nimby's size, but those two made it happen. The cats created those initial connections that turned into meaningful human friendships.

The humans also bonded over an aggravation they shared. The person who lived in between them was loud, hostile, and sometimes even threatening. His music blared into the wee hours of the night, and he was not receptive to polite suggestions to turn it down. When at last he moved out, Katrina and Keith approached Kristin with a suggestion: What if the three of them rented that unit together?

Keith had been looking for an office to rent downtown, and Kristin and Katrina were avid crafters who quickly became enamored of the idea of having a sunny space to spread out. Keith set up his office in the one bedroom, and the women took over the living room. The three of them gave up the residential internet service they had in the two units they owned and upgraded to business level, with Wi-Fi broadcast into all three units. Because of the rental unit, they all have an extra kitchen and bathroom to share too. It is their own little common house.

They see each other often in that space that they share—no planning needed. They often text each other when they need something; the item can simply be left in the middle unit to be collected and returned when convenient.

Behind their three units is an open grassy space. A wooded area beyond it offers a sense of privacy. Just about every Sunday evening during the summers, Kristin, Katrina, and Keith gather in that space for dinner. Sometimes friends and family join them for the meal and bocce ball. To accommodate my visit, they move their feast to Thursday. In what is clearly a well-practiced routine, Keith prepares perfectly grilled chicken and romaine, thereby bursting my long-held skepticism that lettuce is a grillable vegetable. Kristin brings tasty Asian green beans and big, beautiful strawberries and blueberries. Katrina contributes an array of appetizers. I bring the lemon squares I made just before leaving for the trip, plus some chocolate, because it would be shameful to pretend that dessert is complete without it.

The experience reminds me of a ritual I have enjoyed off and on throughout my adult life. At the end of the week—on a Friday night, or maybe even a Sunday—a group of friends and I would have a standing appointment (for a time, at least) to dine or drink and watch a movie or some bad television. Eons ago, during my first university job, it was *Dallas* (the original show) and drinks. When a couple of colleagues were spending their sabbatical at the university where I taught, we did dinner and a movie in my living room just about every Sunday. Later, a group of friends convened around the same time and in the same place to watch *The Practice* (which at that point had gotten so bad it was only tolerable in a group-ridicule format), sometimes with dinner, other times with just snacks.

As much as I enjoyed all of the various iterations of the end-of-the-week events, I suspect that our events were more fragile than the gatherings of Kristin, Katrina, and Keith. In my versions, everybody except the host had to get in a car and drive. If some little thing came up, the plans could fall apart pretty easily. It seems different when friends live just steps away. Coming together becomes part of the routine of everyday life. No one needs to pack up food—they just carry it from the kitchen to the open space in the back. There isn't even a host, really. The backyard where Kristin and Katrina and Keith set out the food and the chairs is shared space.

Kristin is not growing any fonder of her condo complex, and neither is Katrina or Keith, so I doubt their arrangement will last much longer. In the meantime, though, they have found a felicitous way to enjoy both privacy and community.

The Tiny-House Movement

Dee Williams came up with a different way to create a pint-size community. She built a house tiny enough to fit on a truck trailer and drove it into the backyard of her friends'. They live in two ordinary-size houses, both off the one yard. In one home are Dee's friends Hugh O'Neill and Annie McManus, their two kids, and RooDee, the dog that was once Dee's. In the other, at first, was Hugh's Aunt Rita. After she died, others moved in who are happy to be part of a unique space where they can have the autonomy of a place of their own, and the sociability of people nearby who want to be part of a real community.[27]

Dee's house is just eighty-four square feet—that's really small, even in the context of the hip, new tiny-home movement, which is itself tiny but generating plenty of interest. She arrived in her little abode by way of personal crisis. She was diagnosed with congestive heart failure when she was forty-one years old, and suddenly, she had a better idea than the rest of us of when her life would end: sometime in the not-too-distant future. She was proud of her spacious, lovingly restored home in Portland, Oregon, but she did not want to spend the remainder of her days maintaining it, worrying about paying for it, and dealing with all her stuff. She intuited what science has demonstrated—that it is our meaningful experiences and our positive relationships with other people that make us happy, much more so than our possessions. So she got rid of the stuff, built the miniature house, and set it up in the midst of her friends in Olympia, Washington.

Now, she and the kids and RooDee and the friends in both houses all share the backyard. It is their group living room and playground. They call it the Compound. Hugh McManus, speaking to the *New York Times* for a story called "Square Feet: 84. Possessions: 305." said, "I can walk outside and Dee is on her porch, and I can look up and say, 'You want to go for a walk?'"[28] Those sorts of warm, spontaneous encounters, repeated over long periods of time, are what intimacy is made of.

The graciousness about practicalities is of great significance to Dee as well. She has been able to squeeze a mattress, laptop, sink, toilet, and one burner in the place she calls home, but to take a shower or bake a pie, she relies on the kindness of her friends next door.

The tiny house enthusiasts have books (Dee wrote one of them[29]), a conference, and a raft of creative projects in the works. They aim to enhance the experiences of those who choose to live large in small spaces. They also want to help the generations adapt to economic challenges, as when a young adult just getting started or a grandparent in need of some help set down their miniature places in the yard of the generation in between.[30]

Hope Meadows: Prepare to Have Your Heart Melted

If you drive about two hours south of Chicago toward the heart of the Corn Belt and visit a five-block stretch that used to be part of Chanute Air Force Base in Rantoul, you might not think you were anyplace special. The streets are lined with late 1950s-style split-level brick duplexes with lawns and driveways. Standard middle class, maybe blue collar.

If you try to pigeonhole further, though, you might become flummoxed. There are lots of older people, but it is clearly not a retirement community. Kids are everywhere. Young and middle-aged adults are around too. Many of the kids are black, yet no one raises an eyebrow when they rush to greet one of the older white people in the community with a big hug and a "Hi, Grandma!"—well, at least no one within that neighborhood known as Hope Meadows.[31]

The place was designed to seem ordinary. In fact, though, it is perhaps one of the most magnificent innovations in living and caring ever imagined.

The children you may see running around, happy and smiling and playful, were once among the most wounded in the nation. Earlier in their young lives, before their Hope Meadows days, more than a quarter were sexually abused. The same high number were exposed to cocaine in utero, a third have medical problems (including, for example, cerebral palsy and fetal alcohol syndrome), and nearly two-thirds have behavioral and emotional problems.[32]

Among the Hope Meadows children are those who had been locked in a room by themselves for days, burned with cigarettes, and neglected by parents who may have been abused themselves. All had been referred into the child welfare system, and some had been in four or five foster homes before they arrived at Hope Meadows. They were considered the "unadoptables." (Apparently, people really use that word.) Their problems were often severe; many were not the little babies who can be so appealing to foster and adoptive parents, but were children or even teenagers; and some had a set of siblings, meaning that a potential parent would be asked to take all of them. At Hope Meadows, all of the parents take in at least three children with the goal of adopting them and giving them a permanent home; some have biological children as well.

The older people in the community do not all come from places of great emotional fulfillment either. For some, their lives before they moved to Hope Meadows seemed dreary. They had reached retirement, and were feeling bored and lonely. Irene Bohn used to leave her tiny apartment to walk the mall—back and forth, back and forth; she did not want to believe that was all that was left of her life.[33] David Netterfield looked ahead to his remaining years and figured he'd just sit in front of the television until he died.[34]

Brenda Krause Eheart had seen quite a lot of the usual foster care system, and she was appalled. A scholar with a PhD in child development, Eheart knew that all children need stable, safe, predictable, and nurturing environments—loving adults who are responsive to their needs and a consistent presence in their lives. Yet, too many children who enter the system get shuffled from one placement to another, where they are sometimes neglected and abused all over again. Sure, there are plenty of foster parents who are conscientious, dedicated, and loving, but even they are often overwhelmed. Left to care for wary and traumatized children with little support, too many just can't do it.

Eheart knew these children needed something much better, but what? Her imaginings were guided by one crucial question: What would I want for these kids if they were my children?

First, she wanted to give them families and a neighborhood. She envisioned about a dozen families, all of whom would adopt kids from foster care and live next to each other. That way, all the children would have parents and siblings under the same roof; and up and down the block, they would have playmates and grown-ups who cared about them. The adoptive parents would have other parents living right next to them—a real support system of people who truly understood their challenges and joys.

While Eheart was still imagining the ideal community for healing children who had been abandoned and hurt, she went to a talk by Maggie Kuhn, the founder of the Gray Panthers. Kuhn described an innovative solution for keeping seniors out of nursing homes: they could invite young adults, perhaps college students, to live in their homes in return for providing the help the seniors needed. Eheart's flash of brilliance was the realization that Kuhn's script could be flipped—the seniors could be invited into the community to *provide* help rather than receive it. They could be surrogate grandparents to the children, and sources of support and guidance to the parents.[35]

What she had not fully anticipated until Hope Meadows became a reality is that by providing help, the seniors are themselves healed. Irene Bohn, the once-bored mall walker, told the *New York Times* years later that her time at Hope Meadows has been the happiest and most meaningful of her life.[36] Before moving to Hope Meadows, George King had a collapsed lung and heart disease, and so little interest in helping himself that he had a home health nurse visiting him regularly. A few months into his Hope Meadows experience, he loved waking up every day and going out to spend time with the kids. He volunteered as a crossing guard and a playground supervisor. He also relished the time he got to spend with the other seniors. He didn't need his nurse anymore.[37]

Hope Meadows is part of the foster care and adoption system of the state of Illinois, but it is the least institutional iteration imaginable. There are staff members such as social workers, therapists, and community facilitators, but they are members of the community, not outsiders who just show up for appointments. There are all sorts of programs designed to help the foster and adoptive children, but they are open to the families' biological children as well. The emphasis is on what *all* of the members of the community share, not what sets them apart.

Eheart and her colleagues were explicit about the philosophical principles upon which Hope Meadows would be founded: it is fundamental to the spirit of the community and to the model of helping that the children are viewed "not as problems to be managed but as ordinary people requiring the same embeddedness in family and community that we would want for ourselves." They aren't "cases;" they are "family members, friends, and neighbors."[38]

The founders of Hope Meadows share with the cohousing innovators a sensitivity to the power of spatial design in creating community. The Rantoul neighborhood includes an accessible intergenerational center (similar to the common houses of cohousing communities), houses that are close together, open green spaces, footpaths, and bicycle paths. Shared spaces include play areas for the little kids and hanging-out places for the teens. Every design decision was guided by the goals of increasing "the odds of residents encountering one another" and making relationships "easy to form and maintain."[39]

When Hope Meadows opened in 1994, fifteen of the duplexes had been converted into six-bedroom homes for the families. The adults who raise the children do not get paid according to the number of children in their care, as is typical of foster care arrangements. Instead, one person, the family manager, spends a lot of time at home with the kids and gets a stipend plus health insurance for the family. Rent is free.

The number of parents and seniors has varied over the years, but a ratio of about 3.5 senior households to each family household is considered ideal.[40] Seniors live in the duplexes at a greatly reduced rent and are expected to devote about six hours a week to the children. Most end up giving more than that, as they read to the children, tutor them, coach them, play with them, and give them rides. Much of the time is unscheduled. The kids show up at their "grandparents'" doorsteps, and the seniors let them into their homes and their lives.

The children who come to Hope Meadows as part of the foster care or adoption system range in age from a few days old to young teens. About 90 percent of the children who came to Hope Meadows "achieve permanency"—they are eventually adopted or returned to their biological parents. That does mean, though, that for about 10 percent of the children, even all that Hope Meadows has to offer is not enough; and they go back into the foster-care system.[41]

To Eheart and her Hope Meadows colleagues, who are so invested in their mission, success is not just measured in the number of children who achieve permanency. It is also about the magic ingredient—the interpersonal relationships, made all the more powerful by their embedding in supportive neighborhoods and communities. Hope Meadows "has facilitated the emergence of thousands of supportive neighbor-to-neighbor relationships and over a hundred enduring grandparent relationships, and significantly, these relationships often cross the barriers of race, age, class, and religion."[42]

The year before Hope Meadows was founded, Eheart created the nonprofit corporation Generations of Hope. Over the years, the corporation has attracted funding from organizations such as the Kellogg Foundation and the Heinz Foundation. Other financial support comes from government programs, private donations, and rent paid by seniors.

Hope Meadows has inspired similar communities, such as Bridge Meadows in Portland, Oregon, and in Massachusetts, the Treehouse at Easthampton Meadow. Other possibilities that have generated some interest include a community designed to help children who have been in the juvenile justice system and one focused on adults with developmental disabilities. In another version, veterans of Iraq and Afghanistan would be part of a community in which the seniors are Vietnam vets.

Meanwhile, back at the Hope Meadows community center, kids are staring intently at one of the walls. Every month, Cheryl and Patty, two sisters who are among the seniors of the community, create a new mural and embed in it the names of each of the children. Squeals of delight fill the air as one child after another finds that very special name, and so much more.[43]

5

NOT-SO-SINGLE PARENTS
Finding New Kinds of Community

Carmel Sullivan[1] did not understand what was happening to her. First she had the chills. Her feet were cold, and her throat was tight. She had trouble swallowing. Then it got even worse. She felt powerless, out of control, and nearly paralyzed with fear.

She thought she might die.

She called a hotline and learned that there was a name for what she was experiencing: it was a full-blown panic attack.

She did not need an explanation for the panic. For seventeen years Carmel had enjoyed a financially secure and often happy marriage. But that had recently ended. After the divorce, she and her son, Cooper, moved from Aspen to Boulder, where she knew no one. It didn't help that she stayed home to "unschool" Cooper. She loved following her son's lead in pursuing what interested him most; that was more satisfying to her than a more structured home-schooling curriculum. But she was home alone with a seven-year-old.

Carmel is not a person who had spent a lot of time on her own. She grew up on a farm in Ireland, where she and seven other kids were looked after by her mom and her great aunt. Carmel's mother was married, but her husband's job involved so much travel that the youngest of the children never saw her dad until she was two years old. For all practical purposes, two single moms were raising the houseful of kids.

Carmel's parents divorced when she was ten. Her mother moved to San Francisco and raised eight teens through what Carmel calls "the hippie time." So for the first sixteen years of her life, Carmel lived in one house or another with about nine other people. Then she spent a few years in Australia living with an older sister, who had moved there.

Had Census Bureau officials come knocking during the seventeen years when Carmel was married, they would have recorded her living arrangement as conventional—a married couple; and once Cooper was born, a nuclear family living in a place of their own. Carmel, though, is a person who always seems to be standing at her front door with open arms and an open heart. Close friends and family would come and stay— some for three or four months, others for eight.

With nothing to ground her in Boulder, and with loneliness pushing her away, she moved to Los Angeles, where she had friends and family. But even living within driving distance of people she knew and loved was not enough. At night, after Cooper fell asleep, she'd curl up in bed in the room she was renting and just cry.

Meditation had long been part of Carmel's life. It used to be a source of joy; now, it was an escape that she craved. It was during her meditation time, at this very low point in her life, that she came up with the idea that would change her life—save it, really. Suddenly, she knew with certainty what she needed to do: find another single mother and child, and share a home with them.

First, she found a house big enough for herself, Cooper, another mother, and another child or two—a three-bedroom, two-bath home in west L.A. Then, she placed a notice with a local rental service: *Single mom seeks same to pool resources and share a house with a garden. Let's work together to create a safe environment for our children.*

In short order, eighteen single moms responded, and she met many in person. One particular mother and her two sons seemed just right for Cooper and her. After another month of getting to know them, Carmel was sure she had found the perfect match. Her personal quest was successful.

But she could not get the other seventeen mothers out of her mind; they wanted to share a home too. Some, she thought, would be great matches with each other. For example, one had a four-year-old and another had a five-year-old, and they lived very close to each other.

She started calling the mothers and telling them about the others. Every one of them appreciated the tip. That got Carmel thinking: "If eighteen single moms were looking to share with another single mom in my small neighborhood, how many hundreds must there be in the greater Los Angeles area? How many thousands in California? How many millions in the United States?"

She was just wondering. She had no idea that within a year—in 2000—she would launch CoAbode, an online matching service for single mothers looking to share a home with other single mothers. She would have been shocked, if anyone could have told her then, that by the year 2013, seventy thousand single moms from every state in the nation (and from Canada too), would have profiles on the site; and that big-time media, from NPR to *Time* magazine and *USA Today*, would all want to do stories on CoAbode. It would have been inconceivable to her that up to six million people would visit the site each year.[2]

At that moment, she did not even have a computer.

Carmel and Cooper were heading into the park where they were to meet Donna and her two boys for the first time. Cooper ran ahead and began playing with a little boy he met along the way. Carmel watched them for a moment and was totally smitten with the new kid. She did not yet know that he was Danny, the younger of the two brothers they had come to the park to meet.

It was an easy connection for Carmel and Donna too. They were both artists. Donna was from Australia, and Carmel had spent a few years there. They also had similar approaches to raising children.

About four weeks later, Donna and her boys, Doug and Danny, moved in with Carmel and Cooper. Carmel and Donna each had a room of her own, and the three boys took over the third bedroom. All of the rest of the space was shared.

It must have seemed like a big step to begin to share a home with a mother and two boys who, just a month before, were total strangers, so I ask Carmel to share her early concerns and worries. She had none. Those early days were so exciting. Her son had a buddy. Everything was new and fun.

Her favorite thing about the living arrangement, Carmel says, was the camaraderie: "the sitting down and having a cup of tea with somebody, and talking." She also appreciated that "you [could] run out and do a quick yoga class . . . There was always someone there to watch the kids if you need[ed] to dart out for a half hour. And that never became sided one way or the other."

There was lots of companionship for the boys too. Carmel continued to pursue alternative education for Cooper, and Donna's sons joined in. Soon, there was a tribe of nine boys romping through the house, learning, playing, and taking field trips together. That continued for years, with some girls making appearances, too, as the boys became teens.

Five of the tribe mothers also bonded, forming a version of a mastermind group that meets every two weeks for dinner, often at Carmel's place. In business settings, members of mastermind groups challenge one another to set goals and stick to them. Carmel's group is more spiritual. In the meetings, each woman has twenty minutes to discuss her intentions for the next two weeks and the progress she made in the past two. The group is still meeting.

Deep into our conversation, I finally ask a question that is met with a long pause: "Was there anything you didn't like about sharing?" There is something Donna's son Doug does not like—his younger brother is closer to Cooper than he is. Doug gets his feelings hurt sometimes and takes it out on Danny. As for what Carmel doesn't like, she notes, with little sense of grievance, that sometimes the food she buys mysteriously disappears.

CoAbode: Two Single-Mother Families Equals One Big, Happy Household

Once Carmel had found Donna and had put some of the other seventeen single mothers in touch with each other, it was time to buy her first computer. Cooper, who was then eight, showed her how to use it. Carmel shared her fantasy for CoAbode with a friend who had a whole lot more money than she did, and he became a believer. He provided start-up funding for a tiny staff, a website, and a marketing campaign.

Carmel thought her first press release would bring mostly local responses; instead, her vision reverberated nationally. Calls came in from reporters looking to interview single mothers sharing homes with other single mothers, when the project was still so new that Carmel had no such list of names. She found a few single mothers matched by CoAbode who were willing to be interviewed, the stories got written, and CoAbode was already on a roll.

Today, single mothers interested in CoAbode follow a straightforward process: they register on the site by signing up with the name they want others to see; then they create personal profiles, which include brief descriptions of themselves and their parenting philosophies, along with some key information, such as where they want to live, the approximate amount of money they can put toward housing, their ages and the ages of their children. At that point, they can search the other profiles, and other single mothers can reach out to them by using a private email system.

The CoAbode philosophy goes beyond the notion of mere room-mates. Single-parent families flock to CoAbode not just to share dwellings but also to share lives. To make that work takes more than an exchange of brief personal profiles. Carmel urges potential matches to take the time to get to know each other well by spending plenty of time with each other and with the children, as she and Donna did.

In addition, the website offers registered single mothers an extended questionnaire they can use, if they'd like, to share even more about themselves and their children. They indicate whether they like to have overnight visitors and whether another parent is involved in their children's lives. They are asked to fess up about any bad habits, their use of alcohol, and their preferences for neatness and for sharing. There are also questions about their religious and political views. Lots of items pertain to child-rearing: How do they discipline their children? What is their perspective on allowing their children to watch television, use computers and electronic devices, eat junk food, and stay up late?[3]

Carmel estimates that about 20 to 25 percent of the mothers who sign up for CoAbode have homes of their own that they want to share. Most are low income, but others live in mansions. As Carmel explained, the motivation to live together is not just about money—it is also about loneliness.

In the early days of CoAbode, Carmel worried about the single mothers living in places where few other mothers were registered. Her heart sank when she saw that a woman with seven children in Texas was on the site. In just two weeks, though, that mom found another nearby mother with five kids.

The two Texas moms reached out to other single mothers in the area for friendship and support. More than a dozen of them socialize; carpool;

and share childcare, information, and resources. The CoAbode website now includes opportunities for other single mothers to form their own Circle of Friends who do not necessarily live together but are there for each other, emotionally and practically.

Toward the end of our conversation, I push Carmel once more to tell me something bad about CoAbode. There must be problem areas and things that don't work. She thought a while and came up with a few examples in which the children were not a good match. She has learned, over time, that it works better if the kids are all boys or all girls.

The children's ages matter too. Two mothers sharing a Brooklyn brownstone had two girls the same age and another much younger. The younger one felt excluded and hurt so often that her mother eventually moved out.

Wait—that's not the end of the story. The mom who moved found another single mother with whom to share another brownstone in the same neighborhood. Just a few more blocks away was a third CoAbode brownstone. The six moms have their own village in which they raise their children. Like true villagers, they socialize, help with each other's kids, and exchange resources and favors and tips. Two of the mothers— the original two, with the kids of mismatched ages—started a business together.

One of the reasons that so many people have good experiences with CoAbode is surely self-selection. If you are the kind of person who would not want to live with anyone other than your own kids, you are not going to register with CoAbode.

I think the wisdom Carmel has developed over the years and shares with the CoAbode community helps. Some of her advice is practical:

Take enough time to get to know the other family. Be sure everyone gets along—the adults and the kids. Visit the other family in their home; that can tell you a lot about them and how they live.

Other insights are more psychological. Carmel thinks that CoAbode experiences are more likely to be positive when the two mothers search for a home together than when one moves into another's place. There is more equality that way. Evenness is also important in splitting up the tasks and covering for each other when one of the mothers has an errand to run or a class to attend; the mothers who don't let those kinds of things get too one-sided tend to do best.

To a lot of single mothers living together, Carmel thinks, pitching in and helping each other seems to come naturally. When one person is overburdened, "the other one just jumps in and starts doing whatever needs to be done." If you are a single mother living alone:

> You're the chauffeur, and doing the laundry and the homework; and there's shopping; and then all of that and the house clean-ing. That all gets cut in half when you have another single mother there. That does not happen when you have a husband.

I think Carmel is saying that the single mothers for whom CoAbode works best are following a particular relationship model, and that model is friendship. They enjoy each other's company without becoming enmeshed. They pitch in to help when help is needed in a way that tends to even out over time. They see each other as equals. Even in the hetero-sexual relationships that are most committed to fairness, the overlearned dynamics of men's roles and women's roles make it difficult for men and women to truly share equally in all of the tasks of raising kids and main-taining a home.

Carmel has accomplished quite a lot since those days of such intense anxiety, panic, and loneliness just after her divorce. But she is still not finished dreaming. She wants CoAbode to transcend the bonds of virtual reality and establish a footprint on the earth:

> My vision for the future is to make CoAbode part of the infrastructure . . . economic, political, and commercial that provides actual brick-and-mortar communities for single mothers where hotel housing, apartment buildings, and even whole condominium complexes cater to their families. I dream of actual villages with play structures and picnic areas, and cooperative childcare facilities, and anything else that would enhance the life of these single moms and their kids.[4]

Carmel knows CoAbode is beneficial for the single moms and their kids who want to share their lifespaces. But she also thinks "it will serve society as a whole long into the future."[5]

The Way We Used to Live

When I was in Dunmore High School in the early '70s, one of the "good" girls a grade or two ahead of me got pregnant. She continued to come to school. At mass every Sunday, there she was. Her boyfriend, though, mysteriously disappeared. We were told that he moved away to take care of an ailing grandparent.

Her shame, we imagined, grew in tandem with her belly, as her condition could not be concealed by even the most ample jumpers and winter coats. She was not about to search for another single mom with whom she could share a home and a life.

If her family had wanted to hide her pregnancy and escape the stigma it brought upon them, they could have made up a story about how she was visiting an aunt and sent her to a maternity home. Many white families *did* send their young pregnant daughters to those homes for unwed mothers, an option available since the late 1800s in countries such as the United States, Canada, and those in the British Isles. (In the early years in the United States, African Americans were not welcome, though separate homes were opened for them eventually.)[6]

Most maternity homes were run by religious organizations such as the Salvation Army, and they were on a mission. To the religious matrons in charge, "the pregnancy was more than a mistake, it was a demonstration of the state of a woman's soul." In the Misericordia Home in Montreal in the first half of the twentieth century, the women were forbidden from using their real names and were called "penitents."[7]

The women had usually traveled a distance, so their residency at the home would not be discovered by anyone they knew. In theory, these women—who were coping with the meanings, stresses, and symptoms of their pregnancy; were separated from family and friends; and were seen as ruined and disgraced—could have drawn comfort from bonding with the other women in the home. Instead, in the Misericordia Home, they were all discouraged from sharing anything about their past lives, or even talking at all to one another.[8]

The women were typically pressured to give their babies for adoption if they had not already decided to do so. Some had to commit to never trying to find their children in the future.

In the thinking at the time, the women could walk out of the homes, having excised that whole slice of their lives, and pick up where they left off before they became pregnant.

Once the pill was approved in 1960 and abortion was legalized in 1973, women in America had more control over their reproductive experiences. Attitudes were changing, too, and more women were opting to raise their children as single parents. The number of maternity homes dropped precipitously from about two hundred in 1965 to ninety-nine in 1980. There was a jump in that number for a while, when antiabortion forces looked for ways to persuade women that there were resources available to them if they were to have their children.[9]

A few such homes still remain. Although most are still administered by religious organizations, they are quite different from the nineteenth- and early-twentieth-century varieties in other ways. The homes are run more like social service agencies that offer counseling about nutrition, pregnancy, and sometimes careers; and provide food, clothes, shelter, healthcare, and recreational opportunities. Many support the women who do not want to place their babies for adoption; and they encourage the residents to get to know, trust, and help one another.[10]

For the single women who leave the maternity homes with their children in tow—and for all of the other single parents in America, for that matter—there has been very little envisioning (much less implementation) of entire lifespaces. There are piecemeal efforts, such as housing subsidies and food stamps for the poor, but few carefully articulated options for single parents from every segment of society to find the place, the space, and the people that make up a home and a life.

CoAbode is a contemporary vision of a lifespace for single mothers. Cohousing is another rather recent innovation that many single parents find appealing. Significant numbers of today's single parents choose to do what others have done for generations, which is to live with their own parents or grandparents in a multigenerational household, or with other relatives in an extended-family household. Other single parents have lived in shared households that may or may not include other single-parent families.

But what about the single parents today who are not sharing a home with mothers or others, or living in cohousing? How are they finding their place, their space, and their people—and their children's? Later in this chapter, I share the experiences of two single women who succeeded in very different ways.

Single-parent households have long been part of the social landscape of the United States, but they typically came about in a different way than is customary today. When lifespans were far shorter, women most often became single parents when their husbands died.[11] People born in 1900 could expect to live an average of only forty-seven years. The percentage of single-parent households decreased steadily from 1880 (one of the earliest years for which reliable data are available) to 1960, as lifespans increased to nearly seventy.[12]

By the time the pregnancy scandal hit Dunmore High in the early '70s, the tectonic plates of American culture and opinion were already shifting, and the experience of single parenting would never again be quite so deeply mired in stigma and shame. The sexual revolution had begun, second-wave feminism was gaining steam, the counterculture was in ascendance, and cohabitation was growing. Divorce was increasing, too, and far more women would become single parents though divorce than through widowhood.

Even more significantly, the percentage of births to unmarried women was at the cusp of a spectacular rise. In 1970, only 11 percent of all births were to single women.[13] By the turn of the twenty-first century, it was 33 percent; and by 2008, it surpassed 40 percent and has not dipped below that 40 percent marker since.[14] The question of how single parents create a lifespace for themselves and their children has never been more timely.

Pryor Hale: Adopting Lucy and Creating a Village for Her

Pryor Hale was forty-nine years old in 1992. She knew she was "just way too old and too single" for what she wanted to do, but she was determined. She really wanted to adopt a child. It was a struggle to make it happen, but on a momentous day, she got that magical phone call letting her know that her daughter Lucy had just been born in Paraguay.

The adoption agency faxed Pryor a picture of baby Lucy, but she was not allowed to go to Paraguay to get her for four months. It was excruciating to have to wait, but during that time, Pryor would execute the plan she had been pondering for quite some time: she would build Lucy's village.

She thought about what Lucy would need in her life. She wanted to find people who had strengths that she—Pryor—did not have. Pryor had never raised a child before, so she wanted people in Lucy's village who had. She also wanted Lucy to have male role models, so her brother and several more of her dearest friends would be among the chosen ones. People who had been there for her during some of the most painful times in her life and friends she had cherished since childhood were included, and all would be named godparents. When she asked the last two people, a couple who really knew and cared about Pryor, the woman cried. She told Pryor that she had been afraid that they would not be asked.

A month after Pryor brought Lucy home from Paraguay, there they all were—all twelve godparents and Pryor—gathered around Lucy for her christening in St. Paul's Church. There they would stay, at Lucy's side—and Pryor's—for birthdays, holidays, and the personal milestones of a young life. One of the godmothers realized that the children of single moms need special help buying presents for mom; so every Christmas season, she took Lucy shopping and then sat on the floor with her, the wrapping paper, and the ribbons. Some of the godparents were better at the baby years, and others were more attuned to the childhood or teenage years, but all of them loved her. One even talked about setting up a college fund for her but died before writing a will.

I first met Pryor and Lucy when Lucy was around six years old and I was still living in Virginia, just two miles from them. Back in the day, I was a willing conscript into the imaginative games she would devise for us to play upstairs while her mom made us dinner. On my return visit in 2012, Lucy is a nineteen-year-old college student at the same community college where her recently retired mother taught.

The weekend of my visit includes Mother's Day; and on Sunday, Pryor's ninety-year-old mother, her brother (six years younger), two grown nieces, Lucy, and I gather around the festively set dining room table. Beautifully plated food is arranged tastefully among the fresh flowers. (Luckily for me, I am seated next to the prosciutto-wrapped asparagus.) The conversation is easy and affable, with none of those awkward silences or passive-aggressive digs that sometimes punctuate the family gatherings of less-compatible households. Lucy is especially attentive to her grandmother, but that isn't just a Mother's Day thing. Just about every day, at the end of her school day, Lucy calls her grandmother (who lives nearby) to talk and to ask if she needs anything. If she does, Lucy is right there for her.

Pryor and Lucy have such an easy rapport. Maybe they save their eye rolls and exasperated sighs for times when guests are not around, but the fundamental there-for-you quality that they have—I don't think that can be faked.

What I hadn't realized, until I sat to talk privately with nineteen-year-old Lucy, is how challenging things had sometimes been for her. Lucy has always known she is adopted, but when she was around eight, she struggled with that.

Being the child of a single mother was also difficult for her when she was younger. Throughout her entire childhood, storybooks narrated the tales of just one kind of family—the kind that had a mom, a dad, and kids. In the fourth grade, the students in the Family Life class included Lucy as well as the daughter of lesbian parents, yet even there, the message seemed to be that there was just one proper family—and Lucy's wasn't it.

Lucy is very introspective and psychologically minded. She has come to terms with being adopted, and tells me repeatedly how much she loves her mom and appreciates her unwavering support during the most trying times of her life. Lucy no longer feels self-conscious about being the child of a single mother:

Now that I'm older, I realize that having a single parent really doesn't mean much in the world. It doesn't separate you from anybody else. It's part of who you are; and I'm grateful with the experiences, both positive and negative, that I've been through in my life.

Have there been times, I asked Lucy, when she is particularly grateful to be living the way she is? Oh yes, she answers—when she goes to other people's houses. She has sat around dinner tables with families who never say a word to each other the entire time. She has been with other families who are at each other's throats. Pryor is the consummate entertainer. She has hosted graceful dinner parties all her life, and even though most of the guests have been grown-ups, Lucy has always been included in the conversations.

Lucy will probably stay with her mom until she finishes college. After that, she would like to live with lots of people she cares about, all under one roof. "I want to be married to a man," she tells me. It makes me smile that she feels the need to specify that last part. Lucy has grown up with friends who have lesbian parents; to her, it is not a given that if she wants to marry, it would be to a man. Lucy wants three to five kids who grow up in a spacious and kid-friendly home.

There is something Lucy has kept secret from her mother. It happened right after Pryor retired. Lucy was quietly telephoning and emailing people from all parts of her mother's life, all around the country, to tell them about it. Not one of them betrayed Lucy's confidence. When Pryor came home one day, she found her home festooned with decorations and rooms full of people who loved her, all gathered to celebrate the end of her long and distinguished teaching career. She was stunned and cried like a baby. Along with the day she first held Lucy in her arms, it was one of the happiest days of her life.

Feminist scholars and authors such as bell hooks and Patricia Hill Collins have pointed out that in African American communities, children have often been cared for and mentored by a network of people, in addition to their mothers. Grandmothers, aunts, and other relatives (sometimes including men) and even some people who are not relatives but who come to be treated as family, have all been part of the care network. For mothers who work but cannot afford daycare, these "other mothers" are essential. But even mothers who stay at home appreciate the extra sets of eyes looking over their children as the kids head to the store or the playground.[15]

When bell hooks described the tradition of multiple parents and people who do not have children sharing child-rearing, she called it "revolutionary parenting."[16] Perhaps it is revolutionary when considered alongside the popular Western, white ideology that only parents—mothers in particular—should be raising their children. Yet what evolutionary scholars call "alloparenting"—the caring for children by people in addition to their mothers—may date back as far as the hunter-gatherer era.[17] Anthropologist Sarah Blaffer Hrdy believes that such "cooperative breeding" has been vital to human evolution. Human children remain dependent for years, but their mothers have almost always worked. They "gathered, gardened, farmed, fished, built huts, made clothing and other necessities, even hunted in some cultures"—in addition to raising kids and doing other domestic chores. They needed help, and they almost certainly got it.[18]

In the big picture, then, what Pryor did when she named twelve people to be Lucy's godparents was not unique. It did, though, have its own special and contemporary inflection. By asking the godparents in advance and then arranging events when they would all come together to be with Lucy, Pryor acted with marked intentionality and deliberateness. Her approach may also have fostered more continuity and commitment in Lucy's village than in many of its historical precedents.

April McCaffery: Mother, Blogger, and Visionary

The person who first told me about CoAbode was April McCaffery, a single parent I first got to know online as a blogger who wrote movingly and insightfully about single parenting and single life.[19] For several years, she was a contributor to the *LA Moms* blog and has been recognized by the Circle of Moms online community as a top blogger. If something intriguing was happening among single moms, especially around Los Angeles, April would probably know about it.

I already knew that she was not sharing a home with another single mom but never asked her about it until we met in person.

"Oh," she says, "there is no way I could ever live with somebody else's kids."

Since I don't want to live with any other humans of any age, I can relate.

I had taken the train from Carpinteria, California (the little town just south of the even littler town of Summerland, where I live) to Burbank, where April agreed to meet me over her lunch hour at a restaurant I could walk to from the train station.

April is a slim forty-year-old with long dark hair and a warm, open, and engaging manner. We settle in, and I know within moments that by the time she has to head back to work, I will be wishing we could keep talking for the rest of the afternoon.

April's story, like Carmel's, began at a time when she had tremendous responsibilities and frighteningly few resources. She was living in Rochester, New York, in 2003 when her marriage ended. She had custody of her two daughters: Sylvia, who was five, and Riley, who was just two. She had only enough money to fly with the girls to her parents' home in Los Angeles. When she arrived, she had no car, no job prospects, and no college degree. She was thirty years old, and living with her parents and her kids.

135

With their three-bedroom house, April's mother and father were able to provide a room for April and another for the girls to share. They respected April as the authority figure for her children, and were welcoming and gracious. April's father even built a special space outside for Bobbie, the cat. But April wanted a place of her own.

She set her sights on a full-time job, but she started with a temporary position as a paralegal. She must have done excellent work because the temporary job became permanent; and she was promoted within five years. As her job standing improved, so did her living situation. When she first left her parents' place, she rented a one-bedroom apartment. The girls slept in the bedroom, and she took the living room. Later, when she upgraded to a two-bedroom, she gave the master bedroom to the girls.

Early in the mornings, sometimes even before the night is ready to relinquish its darkness, April is up tossing ingredients into the slow cooker. It could be many hours before she is home again, and by then, neither she nor the girls want to wait even the twenty minutes it might take to prepare a quick meal. April's job is only moments away—that's not the issue. But she wanted more for her daughters than the nearby public schools could offer. She researched alternatives and found the perfect charter middle school for Riley. Sylvia is now enrolled in a high school focusing on the arts, just as April had been when she was that age. To get the girls to their schools, though, adds an hour and a half of driving before April's own workday even begins.

After school, Sylvia sometimes has dance class, so April is back on the road, dropping her off and picking her up again. Oh, and April is taking classes. She has already completed her college degree—both girls were there at her graduation to cheer her on—but she is not finished pursuing her education.

The CoAbode website shimmers with testimonials from grateful single mothers whose lives became so much more joyful after they discovered CoAbode. Many of them had "before" stories that sounded a lot like April's—their schedules and obligations were exhausting. To them (and to single mothers such as Diane Dew and Lynn Elizabeth, who found comfort and community in cohousing), and perhaps to people such as Lauren, who felt that her father changed her life when he welcomed her and her sons into his home, April's determination to go it alone is baffling. She could have stayed with her parents. She could have signed up for CoAbode. There is even a cohousing community in L.A. *Any* of those options might have slashed her bills, multiplied her sources of help with the kids, and offered adult conversations for her and perhaps some friends for Riley and Sylvia.

Yet to April—and to me—what is unimaginable is not having a home of your own, and a full measure of privacy and autonomy.

Most of the people I interviewed for this project have a zone of privacy that they value and guard. For Marianne Kilkenny, it is her own space within the home that she shared. As much as she loves living under the same roof with other people, she also wants to be able to close the door of her suite and be by herself, undisturbed.

For April, her zone of privacy extends beyond her individual apartment to the apartment complex. In one of the buildings where April lived, the girls befriended the kids who lived upstairs. "At first it was nice; but other times, it just felt like every time we got home, they were knocking on the door. And it stopped having that sort of safe-haven feeling to it." In her current place, one of the things she likes best is that everyone pretty much keeps to themselves.

Sometimes, behind closed doors, April and the girls will "turn on the music, and dance and be silly." Or they just talk. April believes that in a house full of females, there are topics that come up more naturally and organically. Other times, they retreat to their own private spaces—Riley in April's room, Sylvia in the girls' room, and April in the living room. Each evening, April craves an hour during which absolutely no one speaks to her.

In many ways, though, April is an intensely social person. It's just that her social life is outside of the space where she lives.

Those first few years in L.A.—when she knew hardly anyone other than her parents—were hard. She opened up to some of her coworkers, and they became close and lasting friends. She set goals for herself such as going back to school; that widened her circle of friends a bit more. She got involved in her daughters' schools and joined the PTA. The principal at one of Sylvia's schools was impressed with the talented young girl; he started coming to her performances and became a close family friend.

April has loved the theater since she was six years old. She performed as a child; trained in vocal music as a teen; and managed, performed, directed, and produced plays as an adult. When she first started her life as a single parent in Los Angeles, she wondered whether she would ever again find the time for the theater. Eventually, though, she did. The summer before I interviewed her, theater had become a family affair. All three of them were in the cast of *The Music Man* at the local community-theater troupe, Stepping Stone Players. The rehearsals and performances became another wonderful source of friendship and fun. Sometimes, they all go out afterward.

Even after April moved out of her parents' home, her family connections stayed strong. Her parents adore the girls. Sometimes her father will call and say, "You know, it's been six days since we've seen them." April also talks often to her sister, who lives farther south, in San Diego.

Still, April yearned to connect with other single parents. Back when she was a stay-at-home mom, a few years before her divorce, she thought about blogging but just did not have the confidence. But that changed. With some of the other single-mom bloggers, her online conversations deepened. Then the moms jumped the bounds of cyberspace and met in person. One moved to Arizona; that wasn't too far for April to visit. Disneyland with all the kids was a nice excuse for the Arizona mom to return to California for more time with April.

April is drawn to "people who inspire me and people who are smarter than me." In those early days in L.A., she wondered whether she might serve on a board of directors someday, but that seemed daunting. Joining the PTA had been one small step in that direction. For another organization, she volunteered to write a grant, so she could learn how. She started a single parents' group at work, but the members—herself included—were just too busy to come to the meetings with any regularity.

Fast-forward to the present and April is now on the board of directors of Leadership Burbank and the Stepping Stone Players. She also chairs a section of the Los Angeles Paralegal Association. She has found even more inspiring people to be part of her life.

On Valentine's Day of 2013, April wrote a blog post called "Celebrating Friend-Love." "In my pre-kid days," she said, "there were always a few people that I considered my pillars. These days, we have our tribe." She went on to describe the special place in her life and in her daughters' of so many of her friends. "We love you, we thank you, and we are honored to celebrate our love for you. Not just today, of course, but every day."[20]

It must be quite a balancing act, I think, as I contemplate everything that April is juggling, such as working, raising the kids, maintaining the home and the car, pursuing her education, working on boards, performing, blogging, and nurturing her relationships with friends and family—almost all of them full-time activities by themselves. Aptly, the name of her blog is *It's All About Balance*. Her children are part of the team, and they help make it all work out. Riley does all the laundry. Sylvia does the dishes and helps in other ways around the house. Both girls know how to snake a toilet. (Can I adopt them?)

Somewhere near the end of my interviews, I get to one of my favorite questions. I ask people how they would live if money were no object and they had all of the resources they wanted. It is a question about pure fantasy. Less than halfway through the interview, though, with no prompting from me, April volunteers her dream. She would like to create a community of single-parent families in Los Angeles. Moms who like taking care of kids would do that; others would work outside of the community. Training classes would be available for the mothers who had stayed at home and now wanted to venture out. There would be children's clothing swaps and other creative activities likely to be welcomed by the mothers and the children.

Of course, April doesn't have the money for such a venture at this time, but the main reason she learned grant writing was so that she could attract funding for the community she is designing in her mind. She knows the odds are long; just finding available real estate in L.A. is daunting.

Two weeks after I interviewed April, a local paper published a story about her theater group beneath a huge photo of the set, the stage, and the entire cast of *Oliver!* In the very front, beaming, were the associate producer and the producer—April. The company that had hired April as a temp all those years ago now recognized the hundreds of hours of service she contributed to the community, and nominated her for the President's Volunteer Service Award. She won. The award came with one thousand dollars to be given to the charity of her choice (she chose the Stepping Stone Players) and a note of thanks from President Obama.[21]

Maybe she really will make that single-mothers community happen.

Lifespaces for Not-So-Single Parents: Visions from Around the World

More than a half century before April shared her dream for a community of single parents, visionaries of their time had their own fantasies for what a great place for parents and their children might look like; and they, too, had Los Angeles in mind. They wanted sun-filled, affordable townhouses and apartments built around lots of attractively landscaped spaces suitable for ambling and playing. They wanted childcare centers, community kitchens, and a shopping center. They tilted at windmills, though, and never did get the variety of layouts they wanted—or the daycare centers, community kitchens, or shopping center. But in 1942, Baldwin Hills Village did open in Los Angeles. With its parks and play-grounds, common laundries, a community center with a pool, and private outdoor spaces for each family, the village offered residents a measure of both privacy and community in an urban oasis unspoiled by L.A. traffic. By the 1980s, however, another group took over the village. Ironically, they reinvented it as a child-free condo complex.[22]

Even before Baldwin Hills Village was conceptualized, activists were already pursuing major changes in lifespaces. In the opening decades of the twentieth century, feminists aspired to improve the status of women left behind in the home. They wanted housework and childcare to be recognized and compensated. It seemed nonsensical to many of them that untold numbers of women were toiling away at the same chores, one by one, all alone in their homes. One solution was for the women to come together in neighborhood cooperatives where they would work on tasks such as sewing, baking, cooking, laundering, and caring for chil-dren, and charge for their goods and services. For a few decades, many such experiments were tried and some even prospered for a while, in places such as Massachusetts, Ohio, and Illinois.[23]

Other proposed solutions in the early 1900s were even more radical. Proponents of the industrial strategy wanted to remove kitchens from apartments entirely. Meals prepared on an assembly line would be served to masses of people in huge dining halls. Daycare and other services would be institutionalized, and women would then be free to dedicate themselves to paid work.[24] It was a strategy that aimed to maximize efficiency while neglecting people's cravings for meaningful human connections. The Soviet Union flirted with those ideas under Lenin, but Americans preferred to continue viewing their homes as warm and nurturing havens. Even today, when plenty of Americans have shed their sentimentality about home-cooked food, they still want their kitchens and their connections. In my experiences of eliciting people's fantasies of their ideal living situations, both in interviews and online, no one suggested anything even remotely resembling an industrial model of living.

In London in the 1960s, a broke, twice-divorced mother wondered how she was going to find housing and daycare, not to mention a job to pay for it all. She knew she wasn't the only one facing these kinds of challenges, so she borrowed money to start a nursery school. By 1972, her unstinting efforts had resulted in the opening of what would be the first of the Nina West Homes (named for its founder) for single-parent families. One of them, Fiona House, includes a nursery school on the ground floor, where some of the mothers can work for pay and others can drop off their children and go to their workplaces—just what April has in mind for her Los Angeles community. On the second floor, two sections of the building face an interior corridor where children can play and their mothers can watch them from their apartment windows.[25] West was as focused on the children as earlier activists were on the mothers. Describing what she especially liked about Fiona House, she said, "A child looks out of the window and can see the nursery. From the nursery, she or he can see the apartment and home. This is reassuring to the child."[26]

For Joan Forrester Sprague, the American architect and planner who began designing housing for poor women and their children in the late 1970s, the title of one of her books captured her mission: *More Than Housing: Lifeboats for Women and Children.*[27] She said that people who work on housing for the poor "have to deal with people's whole lives. They can't just give them a place to live and forget about them."[28] Ultimately, she wanted the women who would live in those dwellings to not just be sheltered but also to be empowered. The housing, she thought, should be located close to workplaces that offered more than just a subsistence wage. In a project in Providence, Rhode Island, in which run-down buildings were rehabilitated into residential housing, some of the women who would live in the new housing broke gender barriers and got jobs as builders and developers.

Sprague wanted her projects to incorporate many of the basics that others had already recognized as important, such as childcare, access to transportation and shopping (as well as jobs), and spaces for counseling and other services. She also thought about the psychological needs of the people who would call these buildings home. She wanted people to have spaces for their activities—for example, places where kids could play, places where the mothers could get together informally, and more formal spaces where events could be scheduled and where people from the broader community could be welcomed. The designs could be practical as well as emotionally satisfying. Kitchens, for instance, could open to living rooms so mothers could watch their kids play while they cooked dinner.

It is commonplace for people of means to think about the design of their homes as reflective of their individual personalities and preferences. Public housing for the poor, though, is often generic and cold. Sprague upended that expectation too. The entryways of several of the projects she described in her *Lifeboats* book "incorporate a small peaked roof that recalls the generic child's drawing of a house."[29] Others have porches or sheltering roofs.

In her advice to fellow professionals about the design of permanent housing, Sprague reminded them that it's important to keep the entire life course in mind, and to plan for the ways in which families expand and contract over time. Among the possibilities she suggested were the inclusion of smaller accessory units (mother-in-law apartments), rooms that could be closed off to provide greater privacy, and suites of bedrooms and bathrooms that could open up to a shared living room and kitchen.

In the Netherlands, near the center of Amsterdam, is a "mothers' house" for single-mother families so structurally innovative as to be impressive to architects, and so colorful that laypersons are taken with it too. The lodging features separate spaces for the children and the parents, a shared dining room, offices, a roof terrace, and a courtyard. It is not a place for families to settle for the long term, though; it is just transitional housing.[30]

In the book *Going Solo*, sociologist Eric Klinenberg delighted readers with his description of innovative lifespaces for single mothers and single women in Stockholm, Sweden. One of the collective houses he described, which opened in 1938, "contained a restaurant (with a small elevator system that could deliver meals into every unit), a communal kitchen, a laundry (with chutes for sending down dirty clothing and a paid staff of launderers), and a nursery."[31] A contractor who built other nearby collective houses included childcare and shared dining rooms in each building, but he decided against the delivery of prepared food. As Dolores Hayden explained, his goal was not just convenience but connection; he believed that "a large dining room with private family tables was more conducive to social contacts."[32] Not all of the collective houses have maintained their restaurants and other services. Nonetheless, many parents want to stay in those places long after their children have grown and left.

A site of continuing innovation in lifespaces is Vienna, Austria. I am taken with the commitment of their architects and planners to study patterns of behavior first, and then design the appropriate dwellings and spaces. A project designed by and for women aspired to simplify the lives of mothers by including a kindergarten, a nursery, and a doctor's office in the development and by building it near public transportation. That way, mothers have a convenient way to get to work and school, and the other places they need to go. Called Women-Work-City I, the 360-unit complex includes courtyards, footpaths, playgrounds, and apartments with lots of light and good views. The 1993 project was so successful that two more iterations followed.[33]

"Asking for a Child" and Creating a Brave, New Community

What Americans call the Vietnam War is called something else in Vietnam—the American War. So many men perished that by the time of reunification in 1979, for every one hundred women between twenty and forty-four, there were only eighty-eight men.[34] Some married men who survived the war abandoned their wives, and many single soldiers preferred younger women, leaving many unmarried Vietnamese women who wanted to marry—including some who had themselves served in the war—but felt that their only option was "a bad, older man."[35]

One of those women was Nguyen Thi Luu. She decided that she could forgo marriage, but she was not about to give up on motherhood. So she did something that shocked her family and left her marginalized, stigmatized, and poor: She asked a man to help her conceive and then walked away. She would raise the baby herself.

Luu moved to the edge of a sparsely populated town in Northern Vietnam where the land was inexpensive and the distance offered some protection from harsh judgments. Already, there were a few other women there who had done the same thing. Eventually, seventeen single mothers settled in the village of Lang Loi (now called Do Cung). "It was comforting to be in a group with other women in a similar situation," Luu said.

Across the country, other single women were also engaging in the practice that was recognized by the name *xin con*: "asking for a child." In Vietnam, the desire for a child is about more than motherly love; it is also about security in later life. There are few special housing facilities for the elderly. Instead, old people count on their children to continue the long tradition of caring for their parents. The fear of dying alone takes on a special urgency among women with no children, and fuels their commitment to have those children any way they can—even if it means flouting conventions and risking stigma, poverty, and shame.

Over time, attitudes toward the single mothers softened. Nearby villagers sometimes offered food to the women of Lang Loi. Activists recognized that these women who had given—and given up—so much during the war were now being treated badly, and organized to change that. Credit programs that assisted the women economically were instituted, and laws were passed that recognized their children as officially legitimate. The mothers also helped one another, sometimes in big ways. For example, when the son of one of the mothers died, the community built her a new house.[36]

Today, in the United States and other Western nations, single women approaching the age at which they no longer want to delay having children have opted for their own innovative approach. It is as radical in its context as "asking for a child" was decades ago in Vietnam. Men have embraced it too—in fact, several of them spearheaded it.

Parenting Partnerships: How to Raise Children with a Partner When You Are Single

Darren Spedale was in his midthirties when a realization became more acute than it had ever been before: he was not leading the life he had envisioned. He wanted a partner but didn't have one, and he also really wanted kids.[37]

He knew there were options for single people such as himself who loved children. He had nieces and nephews—he could be the fun uncle. Theoretically, single parenting was also a possibility. Neither, though, felt right. He wanted to be more than an uncle—he wanted to be a parent. But he did not want to raise a child on his own.

There was something else Darren did not want to do: settle. It was a temptation, he knew, for plenty of single men and single women who so passionately wanted to be parents (and not single parents), yet were inching their way toward forty and still had not met a person they truly loved.

His friends knew how he felt; and two of them, independently, told him about single women they knew who also wanted to be parents but not single parents. Darren made plans to meet each of them for drinks.

Here's the part that's revolutionary: he was not looking for that romantic spark that would light up a life of coupledom and kids. He was willing to skip past the quest for conjugal love and focus on a different kind of love—the love of parenting—with another person for the long haul. He wanted what he would come to call a parenting partnership. (He prefers that term to coparenting, which others sometimes favor, because *coparenting* is sometimes used to describe other arrangements, such as the practices of divorced parents.)

The two women understood what Darren wanted. In fact, they wanted the same thing. If Darren and one of these women—or a different woman—decided to pursue the parenting partnership, they would be committing to being there for the child for the rest of the child's life. They would also be there for each other—as parents—but each would also be free to pursue romantic interests.

Darren realized that what he was seeking was unconventional. He even knew that, to many, it was unfathomable. But he has faith that what seems kooky now could seem ordinary in just a generation or two.

His faith is grounded in a lifetime of scholarship. When he was just an undergraduate at Duke, Darren wrote an honors thesis on domestic partnerships. Then, in the late '90s, he went to Northern Europe on a Fulbright Fellowship to study contemporary family structures. By 2006, he had published, with William Eskridge, *Gay Marriage: For Better or For Worse? What We've Learned from the Evidence.* He has a law degree and a business degree from Stanford.

Darren has witnessed the decades-long process by which the gay pride and gay rights movements awakened and enlightened a once-clueless nation. When Americans saw so many gays and lesbians not just settling into long-term relationships but also raising children together, something fundamental shifted. The bond between romance and reproduction, which seemed unseverable (even if it wasn't), was now broken.

If gay and lesbian couples could welcome another person into their lives, not just as a surrogate or an anonymous sperm donor but as another involved parent, then why couldn't straight people create parenting partnerships too?

Neither of the two women seemed to be the perfect person with whom to partner and raise children. But the experience, he said, "really got me thinking: I have to read the book on how you do this whole parenting partnership thing. And then I realized there wasn't a book!"[38]

Darren wanted to write that book. First, though, he did what Carmel Sullivan had done—he created a website. His would serve as an online meeting place and resource for people from just about anywhere looking to find a person with whom they could have and raise children.[39]

The website, Family by Design, launched in the fall of 2012. By February 2013, the *New York Times* was writing about it, as well as other sites with similar missions, such as Co-parents.net, Coparents.com, Co-ParentMatch.com, PollenTree.com, MyAlternativeFamily.com, and Modamily.com.[40]

Among the people interviewed by the *Times* were two who had met through Co-parents.net in 2011. At the time, Dawn Pieke was a forty-one-year-old in Omaha, Nebraska, who had just ended a decade-long relationship. She wanted a baby, and she wanted that baby to have a father who would be involved in the baby's life. Fabian Blue was a gay man living in Melbourne, Australia, who had wanted to be a father for years. He had met some women from parenting websites, but none seemed right.

With Dawn, it was different.[41] They communicated intensively, on Facebook and then on Skype. They probably discussed a greater variety of matters, both trivial and profound, than most dating couples ever do. Parenting philosophies, family backgrounds, religious beliefs, and much more were all on the table. They even did background checks on each other and went through medical screenings.

After about five months, Fabian left Melbourne and moved into a separate room in Dawn's Omaha home. A month later, Dawn said, "He handed me a semen sample, we hugged, and I went into my bedroom and inseminated myself."[42] Their daughter, Indigo, was born in October of 2012. Dawn now introduces Fabian to others as her coparent.

By the summer of 2013, when the Family by Design site had been live for less than a year and little marketing had been done, several thousand members had already created profiles. Modamily had launched a few months before Family by Design, and by the middle of 2013, boasted four thousand members.[43] (The origin story for Modamily is strikingly similar to Family by Design. A single, thirty-six-year-old man was feeling haunted by his biological clock when he decided to create the site.)[44]

The United Kingdom is years ahead. Co-Parent Match launched in 2007. By 2013, it had attracted thirty thousand members from around the world. The site, though, is not exclusively for people who want to find parenting partners. Those who want to be sperm donors or who are looking for sperm donors also have a place there.[45]

Having a child together (naturally, or by IVF) is not the only option for parenting partnerships, however. Some partners adopt together. In other instances, one parent already has children and the other agrees to be a coparent.

Long before there were any online parenting matching services, creative and open-minded souls found their own way to the same solution. In 1991, Rachel Hope had baby Jesse with her close friend and coworker, who was eighteen years older than her. He did most of the childcare; she provided most of the income. They both pursued their own romantic interests.[46]

Rachel was delighted with her parenting partnership experience. "I get all the benefits of being married, but I didn't have all the weather patterns of sexual-romantic destabilization."[47] In 2009, she had another child, Grace, with another man. As of 2013, she and Grace's dad were sharing "separate wings of a rented house, with Grace shuttling happily between them."[48]

Rachel has Carmel Sullivan's arms-wide-open approach to living with other people. For a while, her best friend also moved in, and Rachel is looking for more people to join them. Her ideal living arrangement would be what she calls "tribal parenting," in which many adults live close to one another and raise a number of children together.[49]

Parenting partners do not always live together. Apryll, who lives in Los Angeles, wanted to have a baby by the time she was thirty, so she had Cheyenne with her best friend, Charlie. Later, she met her husband, Damian, and she now lives with him and Cheyenne. Charlie lives twelve miles away. Apryll and Charlie still talk nearly every day, and the four of them often socialize together.[50]

Friends with Kids: The Hollywood Version of Parenting Partnerships

When Americans begin to experiment with something as intriguing as parenting partnerships, Hollywood notices. The big screen gave big play to the idea with the release, in 2011, of *Friends with Kids*. Julie and Jason (the kinds of long-time platonic friends who are so close that they call each other late at night just to ask silly quiz questions) watch with yearning as two of their married-couple friends have kids, and then with horror as the kids wreak havoc on their households and their relationships.

Neither has a serious marriage prospect in the wings. They are not so young anymore. Why not make a baby together and share totally in the parenting, while continuing to pursue their love lives independently?

Their friends are confused and threatened. Their parents cast icy daggers of disapproval. But they carry on, creating beautiful baby Joe by having awkward, passionless sex just that one time. Their married friends settle into a pattern of acting outwardly supportive and sharing their skeptical remarks only with each other—until, that is, the friends meet in a cabin at a ski resort to celebrate the New Year. As the whole gang gathers around a festive dinner table, one of the married men rises and delivers a drunken, scathingly hostile attack, culminating with the (accurate) accusation that Julie and Jason never even discussed what they would tell Joe about the circumstances of his birth and upbringing.

In the real lives of real people who sign up on a site such as Family by Design and follow the recommended process, what happened to Julie and Jason would never happen to them. These sites offer more than just a world of possible partners and a treasure trove of resources, information, and forums for discussions; they promote a strong perspective on how parenting partnerships should be pursued.

Darren believes that prospective partners should spend six months, if not longer, getting to know each other. They should, he thinks, meet each other's friends and family. They should see how the other person interacts with kids. Maybe they should take trips together. By the time they are feeling sufficiently confident to commit to the parenting part- nership, they should know a great deal about each other, and especially about their perspectives on parenting.[51]

The deep knowing begins with the first step of creating a profile. Prospective partners describe their approaches to discipline, education, food, religion, and many other parenting issues. They reveal the financial contributions they are willing to make and their vision of how parenting responsibilities would be shared. They indicate their preferred living arrangements, and other lifestyle preferences and habits. An algorithm compares each person's profile with others and generates compatibility scores. Help from the site's moderators and users is always available.

It is not Darren's first choice to raise a child with a partner who is not also the romantic love of his life. For others, it will not be either. Critics of the arrangement point out that it is a form of settling. Yet, as Darren notes, there are "adults who never envisioned themselves in a traditional romantic relationship," and for them, "parenting partnerships actually are a 'Plan A.'"[52]

The Plan B criticism is among the tamest. Every time a serious alternative emerges to the sentimentally favorite family form of two married heterosexual parents and their children, angst and outrage erupt. The very foundations of civilization are always said to be imperiled. Pained expressions of concern for the children rule the day.

When I first started reading the original research reports on single parenting, I was shocked to discover that the actual findings of the studies rarely matched the ominous reports in the media. Ways in which the children of single parents were purportedly disadvantaged were often exaggerated or misrepresented. Studies documenting advantages enjoyed by children of single parents rarely made it into the headlines or our cultural conversations.[53]

So far, there is no substantial body of research on the actual experiences of the children of parenting partnerships. I'm optimistic, though, about what future studies are likely to show. These children have at least two parents who were so committed to parenting that they were willing to endure the possible skepticism and stigmatizing from others. If the partners followed the advice of the parenting partnership websites, they probably had deeper—more thorough, extensive, and thoughtful—discussions of parenting and of life before conceiving than most conventional dating couples ever do. These are not the fortysomething adults who panicked at their advancing age and lunged into a marriage they knew would be risky just so they could have children in the socially approved fashion. Those children born of panic are probably most at risk of ending up in a hostile or tumultuous household.

Rachel's observation that her children were spared "all the weather patterns of sexual-romantic destabilization" is telling. Her bold suggestion is that the children of parents who are friends rather than lovers may actually experience a calmer and more stable family life. Is that so? We just don't know.

I am less interested in other people's romantic relationships than anyone I know, but I have to admit that when I first learned about parenting partnerships, I wondered what would happen if one or both partners became romantically involved with someone else. It seemed dicey.

Later, though, I was embarrassed by the realization that I had committed the same error for which I had so often criticized others: I was comparing the parenting partnerships not to real married-with-children families but to idealized ones. Real married couples, like parenting partners, have also been known to get romantically involved with people outside their partnership—they just do it sneakily rather than openly.

Any disapproval or outrage vented at parenting partnerships is likely to subside over time. Younger generations have tended to be more open-minded than their predecessors about all manner of social change. The attitudes of the millennials are already in line with the values of those who pursue parenting partnerships. A Pew Report found that 52 percent of them said that being a good parent was one of the most important things in their life, but only 30 percent said the same about having a successful marriage.[54]

Meanwhile, the law is making room for nontraditional family forms. In October 2013, California Governor Jerry Brown signed legislation allowing children to have more than two legal parents, as, for example, when same-sex couples have a child with a different-sex biological parent. In this regard, California lagged behind Pennsylvania, Florida, Maine, Delaware, and the District of Columbia, where it had already been legally recognized as sometimes in the best interests of the child to have more than two parents.[55]

Before I got deep into the research for this project, I tried to imagine the kinds of creative lifespaces I would discover, and I never, ever imagined anything like what Carmel Sullivan created with CoAbode or Darren Spedale achieved with Family by Design. All of the parents or prospective parents whose stories I told in this chapter—Carmel, Pryor, Apryll, Darren, and the many others mentioned along the way—asked themselves what every caring parent does: *How can I create the best possible life for my child?* Then they went about doing so, often sharing their wisdom with others along the way. What makes them special is that they were not deterred by trepidations about what others might think. They lived their dreams rather than their fears.

6

THE NEW COUPLES
So Happy Not Together

A ndrew, who is fifty-nine, did not come out as gay until he was in his forties. When he told his eighty-two-year-old mother, she locked eyes with him and asked, "Aren't you kind of old to be figuring this out?"

Andrew was open to getting some help in figuring things out. Before he came out, he had never had a relationship with a man. So he signed up for a men's therapy group. One of the assignments was to spend some time in a place where he might meet other men. Andrew is shy, and he put off the assignment until the last possible evening, when he stopped at a bar on his way home from work. A man next to him struck up a conversation. Then, at the same moment, they both stopped talking. It was karaoke night, and the guy who was singing was so amazing that they both just had to listen.

When he finished the song, Brian did something the reticent Andrew would never do: he gleefully bounded right up to Andrew and announced, "Hi, I'm Brian. I was great, wasn't I?"

That was nearly a decade ago, and except for two brief breakups, they have been a committed couple ever since.

They are not, however, living together and never have been. They do not face any insurmountable obstacles to sharing a home. Neither has a job in a far-flung location. Neither is pursuing an education in a faraway place. Brian does help care for his aging parents; he shares a duplex with them, where he lives in the three upstairs rooms. But he does not need to live with them in order to provide the assistance they need. There is room for him in Andrew's place, and there would be no financial costs to either of the men if they shared Andrew's space. They are also not trying to figure out whether they are truly committed to each other; they decided that long ago. They are not using their separate residents as secret sanctuaries from which to launch clandestine affairs. They are not avoiding each other. They love spending time together, and do so for a few hours most evenings; they live just ten miles apart.

Andrew and Brian are staying together as a couple but staying apart in their own separate places, because that is how they want to live. They are a serious, long-term, committed couple, so they could have what so many people covet about traditional coupled living—the day-to-day intimacy of living under the same roof, sharing a home and a life. Instead, by staying together but living in homes of their own, they chose to have a measure of both intimacy and independence.

Andrew lives outside of a big Midwestern city. It is a suburb but without the characteristics so often disdained by contemporary planners, and with some of the features that new urbanists like to recommend. The houses on his block are not huge, not set too far back from the street, and not too far apart. There are sidewalks alongside stretches of grass. Andrew can walk to shops and a grocery store (and before it went out of business, a bookstore). There's a bike path too.

Andrew suggests that we sit in the sunroom for the interview. He tells me that he sees himself as "semi-nerdy." He's wearing blue jeans and a quarter-zip, black-and-gray-striped pullover that somehow seems coordinated with his short, graying hair. We're both wearing clear-framed glasses. I think he's "semi-nerdy" only in the endearing sense that the term has come to assume. From pictures he has shown me, I can see that the sandy-haired and handsome Brian is the taller of the two.

When social scientists first started studying the rules of attraction, they produced stacks of studies on competing clichés. In the end, the weight of the evidence favored the cliché about similarity ("birds of a feather flock together") over the one about complementarity ("opposites attract").[1] In research with humans, though, hardly any rule is unbreakable; and with Andrew and Brian, there are some significant complementarities.

Brian, for example, has been out since he was fifteen, and he looks to Andrew to be his primary support system. Brian is important to Andrew, but so is a whole circle of friends he has developed. It is "hugely important" to Andrew to stay connected to them. Andrew has a home in Florida, and Brian would happily move there permanently; for Andrew, though, not even the harsh Midwestern winters are incentive enough to leave his friends.

Andrew has a serious work ethic and has always planned his life with financial stability in mind. Brian has some significant injuries that limit the kinds of work he can do. To make some money, he cuts hair (including for Andrew's mother, who adores him). His real passion is music.

Andrew does higher-education consulting work for three universities. He started out as a community organizer, then worked for nonprofits for eighteen years, and still contributes significant time and resources to the social justice causes that are closest to his heart. His paid work requires significant travel. All of that adds up to some hectic and sometimes stressful days. Coming home, he says, "gives me a sense of calm that I don't get anywhere else." Heading toward the front door, he thinks, *Ah, I really like this place.* His home is his "safe sanctuary." He loves walking in the door and finding everything just as he left it. He loves being able to watch junk television, or sit and read, or do anything else he wants. In the mornings, he basks in the deep contentment that comes from lying in bed and reading or just looking out the window at the wooded wonderland.

Home is the place we are sitting in now, and it is also his place in Florida. Being with friends feels like home. So does being alone. Home, to Andrew, is any place that "feeds [him] in some positive way."

He and Brian have a favorite place they like to go. It is a little mom-and-pop motel on the water with a view of islands and a ferry. Andrew has also gone there on his own and has felt totally happy spending four days alone. (By then, though, he is ready to come home and re-engage socially.)

Andrew has craved his own space for about as far back as he can remember. Growing up, home was his married parents' suburban ranch house, where he lived with a sister and a brother. He shared a room with his brother but did not want to wait until that sibling headed to college in order to claim the room as his own. He had designs on the downstairs, even though it was unfinished.

In college, Andrew had to share a dorm room—he hated it. He has never lived with anyone ever again.

Although Brian and Andrew spend most evenings together—almost always at Andrew's suburban place—Brian only stays over once every week or two. The two of them do spend time traveling together, and when they are in the Florida home (often for a week at a time), Andrew has no separate space to himself. They used to get on each other's nerves, but they have figured out how to let the small stuff go and use humor to dispense with the rest. Sometimes Andrew hops on his bike and takes off. "I need my alone time, no question."

I ask Andrew if he would mind offering some advice to younger people about how to live. He thinks they should ask themselves, *What are my values? How do I want to live my life? What do I care about?* And then, *Does my living situation feed that or does it take away from that?*

Oh, and one more thing: Don't look to someone else to save you—they are not going to live forever anyway. "We come into this world alone and we go out alone, so we better be able to be okay with that."

Andrew is so eloquent about the appeal of living alone, and I greatly appreciate and even identify with it; but I push him on the matter of whether he ever wishes he were living with Brian. So many people think that's one of the true joys of committed coupledom—you get to live with the person you love.

He thinks about it a moment. Sometimes, he says, when something important has happened, it might be nice to come home and tell Brian about it. But then again, he can call or email. Occasionally, he thinks he might like to have Brian living in one part of the house, but "I can't say it's a superstrong feeling." There's also "that holiday myth of family." Around Christmas time, he might get sucked into that.

Finally, he comes up with one more thing: when he gets snowed in, that can be isolating.

"But then, sometimes I love that too."

Living Apart Together (LAT)

When I told a friend that I was writing about committed couples who choose to live separately, he said, "Oh, that's just what Hollywood celebrities do." Woody Allen and Mia Farrow are probably the most famous couple in that category, with Helena Bonham Carter and Tim Burton coming in second. (Though neither relationship is ongoing, there's no evidence that living in separate residences caused the splits.) Attorney and scholar Anita Hill, who testified against Clarence Thomas in the infamous Senate hearings on his nomination to the Supreme Court, has had a committed relationship for more than a decade with a man she sees every day—but they each have their own homes. British novelist Margaret Drabble, the American National Book Award–winner Jaimy Gordon, and the Indian Booker Prize–winner Arundhati Roy all have living-apart committed relationships with their partners. Artists Frida Kahlo and Diego Rivera lived apart from each other, as did the intellectuals Jean Paul Sartre and Simone de Beauvoir.

Today, if you wanted to count on your fingers all of the ordinary Americans in committed relationships but living apart from their partners, you would need several million fingers. The practice—called "living apart together" (LAT), or more felicitously, dual-dwelling duos—is no longer a quirk of the rich or famous, if it ever was.[2] Studies from the 1990s found that between 6 and 9 percent of all adults in the United States, France, Germany, and Australia were in LAT relationships.[3] In California in 2004 and 2005, about 12 percent of heterosexuals were in LAT relationships. Among gay men and lesbians, so often ahead of the curve in reimagining marriage and family and friendship, about 16 percent were part of a dual-dwelling duo.[4]

The Way We Used to Live

Committed couples have often lived apart from each other for extended periods of time. For centuries, military deployments have kept couples separated. So has imprisonment. Jobs in construction, entertainment, sports, and politics have often entailed extended absences. Seasonal workers sometimes leave behind partners and families for months at a time, as do women from developing countries who seek work as live-in help in wealthy nations. All of these people, though, are separated by constraint and necessity. They are living apart because they have to.

In the 1970s, as career opportunities for women multiplied and growing numbers of women were eager to seize them, a new style of marriage grabbed headlines and changed lives. The cutting-edge couples of the time wanted greater equality of roles for husbands and wives. In traditional marriages, husbands' jobs were paramount; and if that meant moving to pursue better opportunities, then wives typically went along with that. The second wave of feminism washed that away. Many women who wanted to be married wanted to pursue their careers too. Some found husbands who shared their egalitarian values, but what these couples—usually professionals—often could not find were desirable jobs in the same place. So they pioneered commuter marriages, in which they each had separate residences near their jobs. They maintained their marriages long-distance, traveling to be together on weekends or in the summers, or whenever their work schedules permitted.[5]

Although couples in commuter marriages chose their distance relationships over the alternative of asking one member of the couple (typically the wife) to abandon her professional aspirations, they were not embracing separation in the way that Andrew does. They were not challenging one of the most fundamental assumptions about coupling, as *New York Times* columnist Frank Bruni (who was forty-nine at the time) did in 2013:

> Moving in with each other: that's supposed to be the ultimate prize, the real consummation. You co-sign a lease, put both names on the mailbox, settle on a toothpaste, and the angels weep.
>
> But why not seize the intimacy without forfeiting the privacy? . . . Isn't *that* the definition of having it all?[6]

Frank and his partner, Tom, have lived separately for more than four years—Frank in Manhattan and Tom in Brooklyn. "We'd made our own homes before meeting each other. We'd tailored our budgets accordingly. We relish a measure of independence, can vanquish loneliness with a subway ride, and don't feel much loneliness in the first place." With the continuous availability of emailing, texting, sexting, and Skyping, even the subway ride can be forsaken now and then.

Bold New Couples or Cautious and Fearful Ones?

To some scholars—I'm one of them—couples such as Andrew and Brian and Frank and Tom are twenty-first-century lifespace pioneers. They are redefining what it means to be in a committed long-term relationship. They value their partners but not to the exclusion of every other important person in their lives. They embrace bigger, broader meanings of love.[7] Andrew was speaking the new language of inclusion when he said that it was "hugely important" to him to stay connected to his friends.

Others, though, are more dismissive. To talk back to fellow therapists who considered living apart together "a condition to be cured rather than a legitimate lifestyle option," Judye Hess and Padma Catell, who coined the term *dual-dwelling duos*, published an article in the *Journal of Couples Therapy*. The authors batted away the presumption that couples who want to live apart are suffering from a "fear of intimacy," and that those who live together have achieved a higher developmental stage.[8]

A related contrarian view maintains that LAT couples are just overly cautious about taking the next step in the evolution of a serious relationship. They are not on the leading edge of contemporary relationships; they are lagging behind. Still others discount the LAT phenomenon as little more than today's version of going steady—only without the admonition against having sex. From that perspective, it is mostly just the youngest adults who are living apart from their partners. Let's take a look at a few more dual-dwelling duos to see how these critiques hold up.[9]

Dorothy Hackett and the Table of Seniors at Heritage Harbour

Dorothy Hackett won't tell me her age. After we've been talking for a while, she tells me all sorts of things, including her complaint about Simon, the man she's been with for more than eight years (his "damn body is changing"), but she never will tell me her age.

When I say that Dorothy is "with" Simon, I don't mean that she is living with him. She has her own place—the townhouse where I am interviewing her—and he has his own home nearby.

I ask Dorothy if I can take her picture, and she stands up straight, with the poise that perhaps came from her two years at Julliard a long time ago. She has red hair that she has probably had done every week for decades. She is wearing a short-sleeve V-neck floral tee, turquoise slacks, and clip-on earrings. She has one simple gold bangle bracelet on one arm and a watch on the other. I think she must be in her eighties.

Dorothy does not like to spend too much time by herself; it is too hard to keep loneliness at bay. But there's plenty to do at the Heritage Harbour fifty-five-plus adult community in Annapolis, Maryland, and lots of people to see. (More about those senior communities is in chapter 7.) "I could be out every day," she says. She is in the drama club and the chorus, and took a creative writing class for a while. She uses the indoor and outdoor pools and the exercise room, and she's a regular at the Friday dances. When she *is* at home, she sits on the porch. Sometimes her friends pull up in their cars and stop to talk. She loves all the company, but she doesn't want Simon living in her house.

I want to know why. We settle into the sitting room just inside the front door. Except for the glass-top table in the center, everything about the room suggests, at least to me, an era from the past: the ornate lamps; the many traditional end tables and side tables; the shiny, velvety wallpaper; the paintings on the walls illuminated by their own lights; the artificial flowers perfectly color coordinated with the apricot floral couch; and the turquoise upholstered chairs and soft carpeting.

Later, she will show me the rest of the downstairs—the dining room, kitchen, den, and small patio out back. Photos are everywhere—on the glass table, the end tables, the mantle, the refrigerator door, and the table in the hallway (that one has a wedding picture on the wall just above it).

The dining room reminds me of my late grandmother's, with its lace tablecloth, candles, and cut-glass candy dish; the chairs with ornately carved backs and upholstered seats; the sidebar with lace doilies beneath silver serving pieces; the elaborate hutch; and the statue of Jesus in the corner.

Dorothy and her one and only husband moved here in 1989 to retire. Ed would only live here for six years. He had a stroke and then another stroke, and then died in a nursing home. The couple had two children, a son and a daughter, but neither ever lived with Dorothy as adults. "My kids didn't stay around, and they're not coming back either. Oh, no. We didn't spend all that money educating them to come back and live with us."

Ed and Dorothy's courtship, which began more than sixty years ago, lasted just a few months. Ed was a firefighter recently back from serving in World War II. He had vacation time coming in December, and a friend could get him a good deal on an Atlantic City vacation if he and Dorothy wanted to get married and then honeymoon there. It was an easy call for the twenty-year-old Dorothy: "He had a job. Came from a nice family. Had a future. He was my kind of guy. That was it!"

It was in her role as the treasurer of the Friday Night Dance, nearly a decade after Ed died, that Dorothy met Simon. She was taking tickets at the door when a friend said she wanted to introduce Dorothy to a man with a swagger. The twosome exchanged some friendly banter, and not long after, they were on their way. "He had a Buick, and he had a convertible Chrysler. It was springtime, and I love a convertible; so we put the roof down, and like two kids with caps on their head[s], we take off."

In the first year or so of their relationship, Dorothy and Simon tried living together in Dorothy's home. Dorothy "tolerated it," but a number of things bothered her. She didn't feel that she had the same level of privacy she did when she had her house to herself. "Some men get to be nosy . . . He has the freedom of my house, and I leave papers around upstairs; how do I know?"

He wasn't much help with chores, such as making the king-size bed. He tried once but screwed it up, "so I said forget it."

What seemed to annoy Dorothy the most was Simon's obliviousness to her high standards of cleanliness:

> He'll always say, "I never use the front door." I said, "Do you wipe your feet?" He said, "Oh, I didn't walk on the grass." I said, "But you walked on the concrete, and it has dirt on it." He said, "Oh!" I said, "Listen up. You stay where you are. I'll stay where I am."

Simon did go back to living in his own place. It is close to Dorothy's, but she hasn't been there in seven years: "The less I know, the better my heart beats."

When Dorothy and Simon go to Heritage Harbour dinner events, they sometimes sit with three other couples. One couple is hugging sixty. The others are in their seventies and eighties. All four couples are committed to each other—they have been together as couples between eight and eleven years—but not one of them is married. Three of the couples live apart from each other. The fourth lived apart for more than eight years and just recently moved into a place together at Heritage Harbour.

I'm a social scientist, so I know better than to draw conclusions from anecdotes; but still, I have to wonder about the table of unconventional couples. Is it possible that at the vanguard of the living-apart-together phenomenon are our seniors?

I reviewed the research, and it's clear that, statistically, dual-dwelling duos are not most likely to be found among the oldest demographic. In fact, every relevant study has shown that the proportion of couples living apart from each other decreases steadily from around age thirty on. In other significant ways, though, it is the seniors who are most resolutely committed, both to their relationship and to having places of their own.[10]

Ask young adults (between twenty-five and thirty-four years old) who are living apart whether they plan to move in together within the next three years and nearly 80 percent will say yes. Ask seniors, and only about three in ten will say the same.[11] They know of what they speak. Young couples are actually likely to move in together within a few years. Seniors, in contrast, have remarkably enduring living-apart relationships. In one study of couples between fifty-five and seventy-nine, nearly half of them had been living apart together for more than nine years.[12] Seniors don't want to marry their dual-dwelling partner, either, and they are less likely to do so than younger couples.[13]

Seniors are also least likely to hedge when it comes to explaining why they prefer to live apart. They are most likely to declare that they have made a positive decision to live apart—that they did not just settle into their separate places out of indecision.[14] There are lots of reasons people give for their dual-dwelling arrangements, from lack of confidence (couples who just aren't sure they are ready to live together) to an array of constraints, such as having kids—including grown ones—who may be attached to the family home; concerns about leases or mortgages, or selling one place and moving into another; and more. The one reason seniors give most often is simple: they want their independence. Across all ages, 17 percent give that answer. Among seniors, it is 40 percent.[15]

I'm not the first to be intrigued by the living-apart lifestyles of the oldest couples. In Sweden, a pair of researchers surveyed more than one hundred such couples, ages sixty through ninety, and then talked in depth with a few of them. Those people treasured their independence. One woman told the authors, "Now, I am free." Freedom, to living-apart-together seniors, means the option of carving out time to themselves if they wish.[16] For the women especially, it meant easier resistance to traditional female roles of doing dishes, cleaning up after men trekking dirt into the house, and playing nurse to the ailing and injured.[17]

Most important, it also means maintaining relationships with the other significant people in their lives on their own terms. The Swedish women were adamant about wanting to have guilt-free time to spend with children, grandchildren, and friends. Although close to 90 percent of them included their partner in at least some of their get-togethers with their children, nearly three in ten kept their time with their friends for themselves.[18]

Homes and the objects that fill them may also take on special symbolic significance among the oldest adults.[19] Every surface of every room of Dorothy's home was filled with photos, mementos, and cherished possessions. Packing up and moving in with Simon—or anyone else—would not just be a matter of disassembling a house; it would mean closing down a home and a lifetime of memories. Even the less dramatic option of welcoming Simon into her home would mean making room for his stuff and his style, and letting go of some of her own.

At different times and in different places, that's just what a dutiful woman would do. She would do all that and more, and be married too. Not now. Not even among the oldest among us. Stereotypes tell us that the elderly are old-fashioned and set in their ways, protective of customs and traditions, and wary of radical innovations in living. Yet there they are, in Heritage Harbour in the United States, and in communities in Sweden, other Scandinavian countries, and many other Western nations, living life their way. I'd like to think that with age comes a strong sense of self: an understanding of who you are and what works for you, and a noble resilience in the face of quizzical or censorious looks from others.

Dorothy has a ready answer to my question of how she would live if she had all the money in the world. It does not include any mention of sharing a place with someone else. "I would happily buy a small, rambling house on the water but up on a cliff," she says. Then she pauses a moment to reconsider. Where she lives now, her friends are nearby and they can get around without driving. If Dorothy lived in that house on a hill, she would have to pick them up. "I don't know if I'd really be happy. I'm so secure here, and I feel safe."

Kerry and Tony: Together, Apart, Then Together Again

Scholars and pundits who dismiss LAT couples as people who just aren't sufficiently committed to their relationships have missed a big part of the dual-dwelling phenomenon. Some of these couples care so much about what they have together that they separate in order to save it. At the point when other couples might be filing for divorce, they are signing separate rental agreements. In fact, when Lise Stryker Stoessel wrote her book on her LAT experience, *Living Happily Ever After Separately*, she subtitled it, *How Separate Spaces Could Save Your Marriage.*[20]

The practice of living apart together continues to grow and to capture the imagination of reporters, bloggers, and essayists. For most couples, though, the customary way of doing things still holds enormous sway, even for those who are the least suited to the traditional married-and-living-together life.

Kerry is a thirty-six-year-old African American woman so strikingly beautiful that I fake-named her after the actress Kerry Washington. Growing up, she used to feign feeling ill when the rest of her family was headed out of the house so she would have the place to herself.

Kerry fell for a "charmingly Midwestern" man, Tony, and moved in with him a few months before they married. She adores his sweetness, his love of animals, his fundamental decency, and his brilliant political mind. Right away, though, small things started to annoy each of them. She loves cooking with garlic; he can't stand the smell of it. She likes listening to music and would turn it on first thing in the morning, if it were up to her; he prefers quiet. He craves solitude even more than she does, and sometimes felt that she was intruding on his space. There were bigger issues too: "It got to the point where when we got home, we would go to our separate corners; and we were not communicating at all." A little over a year after moving in together, when they were in Chicago, Kerry moved to a place of her own a five-minute walk away.

Tony and Kerry's friends viewed their new arrangement as ominous; they were sure it was the first step toward divorce. Kerry said they just didn't know anyone else who had done anything like that. Her attitude was different: "I am living here; he is living down the street. We will work it out or not work it out, but no one died."

For several years, they lived that way—together as a couple but in separate spaces. She played Lady Gaga music and cooked with garlic. He read books about dead presidents in peaceful silence, with no one encroaching on his space. They saw each other about twice a week.

Kerry thinks about her choice to live apart the way I like to think about all of the different ways that people are choosing to live today— in the context of broader historical and cultural trends. She mentions that wealthy Victorian couples often had separate bedrooms and only came together when it was time to have kids. More recently, she adds, moms took their kids to the farm or to the beach while dads stayed in Manhattan to work. She likes that quote from Katherine Hepburn: "Sometimes I wonder if men and women really suit each other. Perhaps they should live next door, and just visit now and then." She is very aware, though, that just getting to even consider having separate places is what she calls *#firstworldproblems*.

Nearly two years after moving into a place of her own, Kerry came to understand two things. She considered this new understanding an epiphany, and from that moment on, she knew her marriage would be fine:

[First], marriage means you have to be comfortable with being uncomfortable sometimes. And [second], don't do anything that can't be undone. Once I knew that moving out, having a separate lease, was not a permanent decision—it can always be undone—I knew everything was going to be fine.

When I last talked to Kerry, she and Tony had just moved to Northern California for Tony's job (Kerry is an attorney who does contract work, sometimes from home and sometimes on the road) and are living together for the first time since they initiated their living-apart arrangement nearly three years ago. In the pricey California market, living separately is no longer financially feasible. They had already decided, though, that they were ready to live together again. Kerry missed Tony and wanted to see him more often. They had made progress on the bigger issues that had separated them far more than physical distance ever had, and they have found work-arounds for the small stuff. For example, Kerry uses garlic powder instead of fresh garlic, or she just saves those dishes for the times when Tony is away: "Who is going to go to divorce court and say, our difference is [whether] I can put garlic in?" She credits the years they spent apart with saving their marriage.

Lindsay and Larry:
They Tried Living Together

Lindsay was born in South Korea and is now living in upstate New York. By email, she tells me that she found her absolute favorite way of living when she was twenty-three and had an apartment of her own for the first time: "Friday nights became my time to sleep and be by myself: reading books, cleaning the apartment, making meals for the next week, whatever I wanted. I loved that time. It was heaven."

When Lindsay first met Larry at a party, she was sure he was not her type. Eventually, though, they made second contact and found that they enjoyed hiking, camping, and going to museums and markets together. Over time, their relationship deepened. Lindsay never cared about marrying or living with someone, but those things were important to Larry, so she went along. They moved in together and got engaged.

Within a year, Lindsay realized she just could not make her living situation work, even though she did think it had its benefits. Larry's personal style was grating. His books, his papers, and the rest of his stuff were strewn everywhere—from his desk to the coffee table in front of his recliner to the living room floor. He was always partway through several different books in several different rooms. Lindsay is not a neat freak, but she contains her chaos to particular places. Larry can't deal with silence. From the moment he awakens until after he falls asleep at night, something or someone is making noise. If the television or the radio is not on, then he's talking. Lindsay grew up in a home in which the television was on only once a week, for family movie night; she still favors that quiet style.

"I couldn't find the me within us when we were living together," she tells me. "I hated this lack of space for me, I hated not having quiet or alone time, I hated the lack of peace. I hated the fact that I could never just be by myself." Yet, she adds, "I was and remain happy in the relationship."

The clashing styles exacerbated other tensions. The two would argue, and then Lindsay would run out to sit in her car "just to get some peace, quiet, and alone time." She also did a lot of shopping. "When I needed time and space, I would say 'I have to go to a store'; then I would buy something and sit in my car in the parking lot."

Lindsay and Larry got engaged, but Lindsay's physical health was suffering. She was also diagnosed with depression. The ring became a symbol of the status of their relationship: every time Lindsay felt particularly discouraged about it, she took the ring off.

She had The Talk with Larry. "Normal people don't go to work . . . come home and cry for two hours, make dinner, then go to bed." She thought they should live apart and work on their separate issues. Once she put that ring back on, she told him, she never wanted to take it off again.

That was about four years ago. At first, Lindsay moved to a different state, though she stayed in touch with Larry. Now she is back, living upstairs in a home in a city; a friend owns it and lives downstairs. Larry is in an apartment a half hour away, in a more suburban area. Lindsay loves her "space, quiet, peace of mind, my own stuff." Things are better with Larry. They spend a lot of time together and have even broached the topic of moving back in together, though they have not made any plans. Lindsay enjoys her friends more now too: "I spend less time running to [them] to bitch and complain about him."

People such as Lindsay and Kerry, who so love having their own places but love their romantic partners, too, have thought a lot about how they might be able to live successfully with other people. Lindsay has already done so—with friends. Then, it helped that they often had opposite schedules or that she worked two jobs when her friend worked one. Looking ahead to a time when she and Larry might live together again, she says that she would "need a place where I can be quiet and on my own. An extra bedroom, an in-law suite, whatever."

As for Kerry, she is leaning on her epiphanies and the compromises she worked out with Tony in order to make her new shared-living situation work. She and Tony have been fantasizing about their ideal living situation since they moved in together the first time. They would love to build two homes connected by a master suite. Each would include its own kitchen, office, bathroom, and dressing room; and they would share a dining room and media room.

As challenging as it can be psychologically for people who love their own space to move into shared space, it can also free them of the defensiveness they sometimes feel. LAT is new enough that, often, friends and family just can't help reading something into it that isn't there. Frank Bruni said, "It wears you down: the murmurs that you must not be fully confident in what you have, the nagging worry that you're being indulgent or adolescent or just perverse."[21] Lindsay tells me that "some people ask me, what's the point of being with someone if you don't want to live with him? For me, it's not that I don't want to be with him—I do (if I didn't I'd have stayed gone!); I just like my space . . . If we lived together in a traditional way, we'd kill each other."

The nattering nabobs of negativity who are the incredulous friends of the LATs often have a conventional view of closeness. They think about that day-to-day sharing of the minutiae of life, add it all up, and get intimacy. What they overlook is the potential for conflict over the small stuff, for pettiness, and for just plain boredom. Couples who have spent time apart, either because they want to (as with many LAT couples) or because they have to (as when distant jobs put time and space between them), often remark on the unexpected perks. They don't bother keeping their small grievances alive when they don't see each other every day. Their communications focus on the positive. When they are together, there is often more passion.[22]

Again, I'm left wondering if it is the older demographic, so often derided as "set in their ways," who are ahead of the curve in truly getting what living apart together is all about. Dorothy's friends don't pelt her with questions about why she doesn't live with her partner. Neither do Joan's.

At that table of unconventional couples at Heritage Harbour, the only couple living together is the warm and gracious Joan Shelley, fifty-nine, and her partner, Pete. (True confessions: Pete is my older brother. I'll tell you more about him and Joan later.) They lived apart for more than eight years. Joan tells me what she loved about the arrangement.

> I like coming home from work and not having to talk to anybody . . .
> Maybe I want to sleep, and get up and watch a favorite TV show—
> I just like not having a schedule, not having to answer to anybody.

If I wanted to get an extra pet, I don't have to ask anybody. I like being able to read in bed at night without worrying that I'm keeping someone else up . . . I like being by myself . . . It wasn't that I didn't love him, but I just didn't think that we needed to live together.

Unlike Frank's or Lindsay's or Kerry's friends, Joan's friends at work totally understood Joan's love of both Pete and her time alone. After she and Pete first moved in together, her colleagues could not wait for her to get into work every day so they could ask *their* question: "Okay, how was it?" She had to convince them that it really was going well.

Will You Be My POSSLQ?

The most fundamental components of marriage and family life used to be all tied up in one neat, tight ball of yarn. In the middle of the twentieth century, getting married, living together and having sex, having kids, and staying married occurred in that order. Sure, people strayed from the script, but when they did, they tried to hide it; and when that failed, they were stigmatized and shamed.[23]

When the Pill was approved by the FDA in 1960, the thread that held sex and procreation together loosened. The sexual revolution pulled on the string that linked sex outside of marriage to shame, and the other trends toward open-mindedness tugged at the knot that tied unwed parenting to a status that was both stigmatized and, for the children, legally unprotected. Cohabitation further unwound the yarn that tied living together with marrying. But who would have ever predicted that the bond between coupling and cohabiting would come undone too?

As scholars and pundits wonder what the living-apart-together phenomenon means and where it's heading, it's worth recalling the early days of unmarried cohabitation. When Americans began to cohabit in sufficient numbers to attract attention, those who disapproved—and there were many[24]—referred to the practice, without irony, as "living in sin." Even as recently as 2002, the president of Northwestern University's Family Institute asked whether the increase in cohabitation was a symptom of the psychological trauma experienced by a generation that came of age between 1960 and 1980, and would therefore subside once divorce rates declined and the whole society calmed down.[25]

Just as we have not yet settled on a way to describe committed couples who do not live together (Are they living apart together? Dual-dwelling duos? Something else?), so, too, were the trend namers stumped in the early days of cohabitation. The Census Bureau had settled on POSSLQ— persons of the opposite sex sharing living quarters.[26] CBS radio-man Charles Osgood even came up with a rhyme that became popular:

> There's nothing that I wouldn't do
> If you would be my POSSLQ
> You live with me and I with you,
> And you will be my POSSLQ.[27]

Cohabiting couples multiplied over time, from a mere fifty thousand practitioners in 1950 to four hundred thousand in 1960, five hundred thousand in 1970 to over one million in 1980, and over two million in 1986.[28] As of 2012, there are more than 7.6 million unmarried cohabiting couples, and that number only includes heterosexuals.[29]

The profile of cohabitors has changed, too, broadening to include people from just about every demographic. The young were the early adopters, but now nearly half are thirty-five or older, and 13 percent are fifty-five and older. Just over half have at least a bachelor's degree and more than 40 percent have kids living with them.[30]

Arlia: Beyond Monogamy

For Arlia, who knew from the time when she was a teen that she craves solitude more than most people do, her need for a place of her own is complicated. She had a husband, Andy, who did not understand the LAT style, and she has kids.

When their first child was just one, she and Andy lived in a trailer with a big screened porch in a wooded area on a lake in Georgia; Arlia thought it was magical. They were hired as part of a program to help teenage boys who had gotten in trouble, and needed guidance and reha- bilitation. Andy commuted into Atlanta for law school, and they stayed for three years.

Andy finished law school, and Arlia thought the experience had changed him. That was the harshest thing she ever said about him. She voiced no complaints about him as a father, a provider (she worked, too), or even as a husband. She was smitten by the craftsman bunga- low they had moved into in an old Georgia neighborhood dotted with bungalows from the '20s and '30s. She knew that, by conventional stan- dards, she had it all. But she was miserable. She did not want a divorce; she just ached for a place of her own and time to herself. That was too painful for Andy.

They got divorced, and Arlia got that place she had coveted; it was a mile or so away. Their two daughters, three and fourteen, lived with Andy (whose parents moved in to provide some extra help) and stayed with Arlia one night a week, every other weekend, and during vacations.

Arlia experienced the predictable guilt that comes with being the parent who does not have custody. She also felt isolated when many friends the couple had made at church rejected her and sided with Andy. But she also felt strong and happy, and she believed that was a better way to be a role model to her daughters than remaining in a despondent place. "I woke up every morning and said, 'if I could go back right now, would I,' and the answer was always no."

One thing she felt totally unambivalent about was having a place of her own: "First time ever. It was wonderful. It was wonderful. I had to rebuild everything, but that was great too . . . I got to redefine who I was in my physical environment."

Up to that point, Arlia's story is a familiar divorce narrative. Then it turns into the most complex and boundary-pushing tale that I have heard. About two years after the divorce, Arlia fell in love with Art and invited him to move into her tiny condo. She had already told him that she "had come to decide that maybe I didn't want to be a monogamous kind of person." That gave them pause about the wedding they were planning, but they decided that they could still define their marriage their own way.

For a while, the marriage remained traditional, despite the understanding that it might not stay that way. Eventually, though, Arlia met Aiden and fell in love with him. She told him about Art right from the beginning. (In the internet age, it is easier to find people who are already on the same page when it comes to the arrangement of our loves and our lives.)

Arlia always wanted to live her nonmonogamous life openly, honestly, and with integrity—no sneaking around. Arrangements such as hers are called "consensual nonmonogamy." The consensual part invites the openness and truthfulness. Although there are no studies of the prevalence of consensual nonmonogamy based on representative national samples, scholars estimate that about 4 percent of all adults in the United States are practitioners.[31]

Art and Arlia had been sharing a bedroom; then Arlia moved to a different bedroom:

> We became housemates. So we shared the house and all the bills, but we still coparented my daughter because she loved him—they had a great relationship. So we were coparents, housemates, lovers, and partners to some degree, but that was still evolving.

After three months, Arlia proposed to both Art and Aiden. They became a V-shaped triad, with the two men involved with Arlia but not with each other. Aiden was still living in a place of his own. At first, he lived about an hour away but then moved to within about twenty-five minutes away.

The triad lasted eighteen months, until Art met someone else and became uncomfortable with his unconventional arrangement. He and Arlia got divorced, but he stayed in the house with her for a while longer. When he moved out, it was to a home about a block away that was nearly identical to Arlia's.

Once again, Arlia is living in a place of her own, and once again, she loves it. Aiden, who has a twelve-year-old son, would love to share a place with her. But, Arlia told me, "when he sees how much I flourish when I get enough time alone, [how] I really need that, how balanced it keeps me . . . he gets it."

Arlia's older daughter has been away since she left for college, but her younger daughter, Art, Aiden, and Aiden's son all have their own postmodern version of family. Of Art, Arlia says:

> [He] is like my brother now. He's a sweetheart. We're family . . . And he can still maintain this great relationship with his stepdaughter, and there's this family sense between he and Aiden and the kids . . . So it is not uncommon on a Tuesday night, when [my younger daughter] is here, or, a weekend night for the five of us to go to dinner together.

The older daughter is the more conservative of the two. Her father is remarried, and she appreciates the structure there. She let her mother know that she thinks her life is weird, to which Arlia replied, "Honey, I am never going to be a normal mom."

The unconventionality is continuing. Just a month before I interviewed her, Arlia became involved with a woman, Amy, that she met in a graduate program in Jungian psychology. Aiden thinks she's great. Arlia considers both Aiden and Amy to be life partners. Unlike Aiden, though, Amy is not pining to live with Arlia. She, too, loves her own space.

Dual-Dwelling Duos: What About the Children?

Logistically, it is undoubtedly easier to live apart from your partner when there are no young children involved. And yet, data from an American study of heterosexuals show that it is only men who seem to shy away from living-apart relationships when they have kids: only 9 percent of LAT men live with kids, compared to 49 percent of married men and 39 percent of cohabiting men. For women, there is no such disparity: 45 percent of LAT, 50 percent of married, and 52 percent of cohabiting women are living with children.[32]

It is not clear, though, how many of those children were the children of both parents. Some, such as Arlia and Aiden, already have children of their own when they decide to live as dual-dwelling duos. In those instances, the emotional case may actually tilt toward staying apart. Vicki Larson, journalist and author of *The New I Do*, has been in a committed, monogamous, unmarried relationship for more than eight years. She and her partner have both been married previously. Unlike so many individuals who lose themselves in their personal stories and the love they feel for their partners, Larson is acutely aware of bigger sociological trends. She knows that divorce is commonplace and even more so for second or third marriages. When her children were younger, it was just too daunting to consider what another possible breakup could do to them. So she did not marry, and she and her partner never did combine households.

It's different now. And yet, it's not. "Now, the kids are gone, so we have no excuse [not to live together]. It's just that we don't want to."[33] Larson's is one of the most powerful lessons about the twenty-first-century lifespace that comprises living-apart-together relationships. There are all sorts of reasons why committed couples feel that they should move in together. Peel back all the practicalities, the externalities, and the pressures, and one last impediment remains: they just don't want to.

The Future of LAT

We don't know whether the current living-apart-together phenomenon will show the same dramatic increase over time that cohabitation has. We do, however, have some hints about who today's LAT couples are and how they differ from their contemporaries.

One of the challenges in studying LAT couples is distinguishing those who really are committed to both the relationship and their separate places from those who are more akin to the going-steady couples of the past. In the most extensive study of the attitudes of LAT couples, based on a representative national sample of British citizens, the authors moved to a separate category those couples who said they were living apart because it was too early to move in together or they were not ready yet. Then they compared the remaining LAT couples to married couples, cohabiting couples, and single people (divorced or always single).[34]

One of the most radical views of people in LAT relationships is that they are rewriting the rules for coupling in a way that knocks the conjugal couple off its throne and elevates the status of other kinds of relationships, such as friendships. And in fact, people in LAT relationships are more likely than the people in any of the other groups to say that they have at least one friend in whom they can confide, and that they have received help with a difficult problem from such a friend. Among the LATs and the singles—but not married people or cohabitors—more than half say that they have more than one close friend who is a confidant. LATs are also more likely than any of the others to agree with the survey item "Relationships are much stronger when both partners have the independence to follow their own careers and friendships."[35]

Is the relationship between a parent and their child stronger than the relationship between any couple? LATs and singles are most likely to agree that it is. Married people have a different hierarchy. They are most likely to reject the statement that "relatives will always be there for you in a way that partners might not be." Pit family against friends, and married people put their faith in family, agreeing with items such as "when things really go wrong in your life, family is more likely to be there than friends."

On hot-button social issues, the group that stood out in the British study was not the LATs but married people, who were the most judgmental about single women having children, lesbians raising children, the superiority of married parents to unmarried parents, and the importance of marrying and not just living together.

To be deeply committed as a couple yet equally committed to living apart, is—I think—a revolutionary act. Many partners who live together look to each other to meet all their needs and make all of their wishes come true. Their social lives become more insular after they merge households; they see their friends less often; they are not there for their parents as much as they were before. These are not just my impressions; they are the findings of research in which couples' social lives were tracked for years.[36]

Dual-dwelling duos may be the couples who challenge the emotionally greedy form of coupling. They are saving a place in their lives for the other people who matter to them while continuing to honor their dedication to each other. Sure, some will say that by insisting on places of their own, they are behaving selfishly. But what if instead, by tending to their own places and their own spaces, they are nurturing their souls? And what if that attentiveness to their own needs is an expansive act rather than an isolating one? What if that very self-care is what makes it possible for them to care deeply about partners and about other people, too, and maybe even save their marriages along the way?

7

LIFESPACES FOR THE NEW OLD AGE
Institutions Begone!

Among those creating some of the most remarkable lifespaces are contemporary seniors. Their places, spaces, and people empower every aspect of themselves—their social selves, their emotional selves, their physical selves, their spiritual selves, and their thinking and learning and growing selves. Most of these seniors are also on a mission of avoidance—they do not want to end up in the dreary institutionalized "homes" that served as the final living places for so many in the generations before theirs.

What they remember of institutionalized senior housing, though, was hardly the worst of it. The forms and philosophies have changed markedly over the years.[1] In the earliest American nursing homes, residents were assigned to beds around the periphery of huge, open rooms, with staff stationed in the center. There were no private bathrooms, and sometimes there were not even curtains between the beds. Even the names of the places were bleak; a Maryland home chartered in 1883, for instance, was called the Keswick Home for the Uncurables. These places were the product of a medical-model mentality. Like hospitals, these nursing homes were clean and antiseptic, and allowed for easy monitoring of the residents from the centralized nursing stations.

The stunning lack of privacy didn't sit well with the residents, and the better off among them began to clamor for more. Eventually, some of the vast wards shrunk to smaller quads, and then to rooms shared by two. When the Social Security Act was passed in 1935, followed by Medicare and Medicaid, nursing-home care attracted more funding and more regulation. But minimum room sizes soon became standard room sizes, and the impersonal, institutionalized feel remained.

In the tiny town of Dunmore, Pennsylvania, where I grew up, my little friends and I walked every day to our neighborhood grade school, William Penn Elementary—all of the Dunmore kids did. There were grade schools within walking distance of every neighborhood. By 1969, though, all of the elementary schools were consolidated into one big elementary center, and my beloved Penn was replaced by a six-story senior high-rise. It was not a local quirk. Across the nation, monotonous towers shot up, reaching much greater heights in cities than in small towns like Dunmore. They did little to add character or personalization to the senior-housing experience.

The nursing-home model of senior living was increasingly at odds with the ever-healthier generations of retired people. For the many older Americans who did not need full-time supervision or medical care, a new model of congregate housing became popular. Residents had bedrooms to themselves and shared kitchens, dining rooms, and sometimes bathrooms with the other residents. The congregate buildings could be multistory or single story. Today, this model is usually called "assisted living" or "independent living."

Initially, the units in congregate housing were studios and one bedrooms. But just as families in the suburbs wanted bigger and bigger houses, so did seniors prefer spaciousness. Over time, many studios were replaced by two-bedroom units.

With their accumulated savings, Social Security checks, and good health, the youngest, fittest, and most affluent retirees saw many more years on the horizon and were not about to spend them marking time in bare-bones senior housing. Active adult communities were built for them. These communities for those fifty-five and older or sixty-two and older—leisure worlds with swimming pools, golf courses, and club-houses—first dotted the sunny landscapes of Florida and Arizona. When the very first one—Sun City, Arizona—was planned, the developers were not sure what to expect. Would seniors really leave their homes and move to a desert in Arizona where they would live only with other people their age? They built six model homes, and on the first day of 1960, invited the public to come take a look. By the end of the weekend, more than one hundred thousand people had toured them. Initially, they had hoped to sell four hundred of the homes by the end of the year; instead, all four hundred were gone within a month.[2]

Senior Cohousing: Communities and Amenities for Later Life

In Stillwater, Oklahoma; Abingdon, Virginia; Boulder, Colorado; and Davis and Grass Valley, California, the people who came together to create a cohousing community knew what they wanted, and it wasn't the same as what every other cohousing community wanted. When they generated their wish list for the kinds of spaces they wanted in their common house, a comfortable meeting room was likely to be included; a playroom was not. For the outdoor areas, a hot tub or a tasteful terrace might get top billing; a kiddie pool would not. In their private homes, wide doorways might be a given; child proofing might not be. In the many discussions that brought them together as they designed their community, they navigated the same practical concerns as every founding cohousing group; in addition, they bonded over matters both personal and profound. These innovators were designing a new variation of cohousing—one in which all of the residents would be in their fifties or older.[3]

They were not avoiding children—grandkids were frequent visitors—but they were focusing on the concerns that become more salient as people age. By the time they moved into their newly built community, they had already discussed their hopes and fears about aging, and maybe even about death and dying. Mostly, though, they planned for the full and rich lives they would share.

The homes in senior cohousing communities are designed with elders in mind. There are grab bars, and wheelchair-accessible bathrooms and hallways. There are open floor plans, few steps (if any), and lots of light. Cabinets and sinks are easy to reach. Foundations are flat, and homes are usually single-story. Often, there is an extra bedroom so there is room for a live-in caregiver, should that need arise. But all of those kinds of accommodations are commonplace in other retirement communities too. What makes senior cohousing special is much more than that.

Psychologist Pat Darlington, who was among the visionaries who created the Oakcreek Cohousing community in Oklahoma, described her motivation to Sally Abrahms of the *AARP Bulletin*:

> I have patients with a ton of money, long-term care insurance, and round-the-clock caregivers, and they sit in their lovely homes bored and lonely . . . When you go to a financial adviser, you're told to have a diversified portfolio. Cohousing is my social portfolio.[4]

Also telling is the vignette that opened a *New York Times* article about the ElderSpirit cohousing community in Virginia:

> When Carol Edwards, eighty-six, returned home after rotator-cuff surgery, her right arm in a sling, she could not bathe, make her bed or fix a meal. She lived alone with no family close by. Still, the thought of a six-week recuperation did not faze her.

If all you know about cohousing is what you have read in an earlier chapter in this book, you already know how Carol's story unfolds. Her friends in the community brought her meals, helped with her chores, and drove her to doctors' appointments. "My every need was taken care of."[5]

In traditional intergenerational cohousing, the caring and sense of community that is at the heart of such endeavors are valued. In senior cohousing, it is vital. It is life-affirming and possibly even life-extending. A popular aspiration of elders is to age in place. Seniors in cohousing want even more than that—they want to age in community. Their hope—often realized—is that by living in a cohousing community, they will put off the institutionalized care of nursing homes or assisted-living facilities for as long as possible—and maybe even forever.

Essential to the senior cohousing compact is that the caring is voluntary and has limits. Ideally, residents of senior cohousing communities decide in advance what they will and will not do for each other. With regard to those who are ill or injured, the will-do list might include, for example, driving them to doctors' appointments when possible and helping them with meals. Giving a bath might be an example of a will-not-do item. When needs become too overwhelming, residents may need to hire outside help or even move into facilities that offer more intensive and professional care.[6]

Some senior cohousing communities have found another way to be cared for that is both personal and professional without imposing too much on the other residents. The seniors who need special care hire someone such as a nurse or a nursing student to live in a guest suite in the common house (at no cost) and become part of the community. Such professionals come to know and care about the people they are helping in a deeper way than those who only see elders as patients in an office or an institution.[7]

Philip Dowds is a sixty-nine-year-old living in an intergenerational cohousing community. He has devoted much of his career to what he calls "eldercare architecture." He's bullish about what the newly retired have to offer to the development of a new community: skills, time, flexibility, and often money. But he is no longer an advocate of communities for elders only.

When a senior community first opens, he says, it attracts

> Go-gos, who are the able and independent elderly [who] bring energy, enthusiasm, optimism about new friends and experiences, and a sense of adventure . . . But time marches on, and energy and capability inevitably decline. The Go-gos morph into the Slow-gos, and finally the No-gos. After a while . . . you have a lot of people hoping for help to get to their doctor appointment but unable to offer much help to each other.[8]

It is the most starkly pessimistic appraisal of any kind of cohousing that I had encountered in all of my interviews and visits and reading. I had to know what the person who wrote the book on senior cohousing, Charles Durrett, had to say about that. I called to find out.

> Ultimately, if you're going to be responsive to seniors, you have to listen to what they have to say on the matter. Seniors certainly don't age anywhere near consistently. We have a ninety-five-year-old in our cohousing community who's just as [energetic] as some fifty-year-old. People don't age in parallel. We have twenty seniors who live in our intergenerational cohousing community in Nevada City. Some seniors like intergenerational cohousing, some like senior cohousing—I respect both of them.

Dowds's opinions of senior communities have changed over time. Had Durrett's?

I am more encouraged than ever . . . I am just astounded by what a great time these people are having. I don't see that anywhere else. I don't see seniors just living at the top of their game like they are in that setting [senior cohousing]. The biggest surprise to me is how phenomenally gratifying it is to see these folks. I mean, it was beyond my wildest imagination. I suggest that Mr. Dowds visit a couple dozen senior cohousing communities before he draws any conclusions. People die; new people move in; some stay longer than others. It is complicated, and slogans do not adequately sum it up.

Tricia and Anja: A Duplex Friendship

Anja Woltman, sixty-five, is a Zen Buddhist. She is on her way back from the Tassajara Zen Mountain Center, inland from Big Sur, the same day I am leaving the cohousing conference in Oakland and heading to check out the living arrangement she and Tricia Hoffmann, also sixty-five, worked out. She offered to pick me up. That is the first time we meet.

In a drive that becomes ever more glorious as we approach the Golden Gate Bridge, she tells me about growing up with her brother on a street in The Hague in Holland, where everyone knew one another and the kids played outside. Her American experiences began in New York, when she won a scholarship that allowed her to teach at the private Bridgehampton Day School, where parents were open to alternative ways of thinking and teaching. Later, she shared a 150-year-old farmhouse in Vermont with three other friends. They gardened and raised turkeys, geese, and chickens.

Once Anja had a husband and kids, they moved into a place of their own nearby—a wood-and-beam structure that they built. "The boys lived like Huckleberry Finn: barefoot, out in nature, fishing. They loved their childhood." In many ways, though, those were hardscrabble and sometimes isolating years. "There was one winter, I remember, when we were particularly poor and I was reading the Little House series to them, and it was like [we were] living it."

Anja and her husband eventually divorced. He moved to California, and then she did too. She was drawn to the spiritual climate as well as the weather.

I am so absorbed in Anja's stories that I almost don't notice that we are in Sebastopol and nearing the street where she and Tricia live. "This is High Street. We have Sharon living here. We have Tammy living there. We have Christine living there. A little post office down there. This is our park."

Tricia's front yard and front porch are what I see first when we get to the duplex. Welcoming tables and chairs and lots of greenery grace each. There is even a small, white picket fence. Anja's house is in the back, separated from Tricia's by two garages. Both houses include ample kitchens and enough room for a dining-room table. Tricia favors lighter woods; Anja, darker ones. Tricia's walls are taupe with white accents; Anja has accent walls in persimmon and golden yellow. Tricia uses her second bedroom as an office. (Luckily for people like me, her third bedroom is for guests.) The materials of a dedicated painter fill Anja's second bedroom. She also has a small, colorful meditation room.

Once I step into Anja's backyard and settle on one of her comfortable chairs to continue our conversation, I know what answer I will get when I ask Anja which space she likes the best. With gardens, trees, flowers, a bird bath, a hammock, and a hot tub—all artistically arranged—the place is a sanctuary.

On days when she is not hosting visitors, Tricia enjoys a tremendously active and sociable life. Her current passion is pickleball (a combination of tennis, badminton, and ping-pong), but she also plays ping-pong and goes hiking, biking, and dancing. Dinner out with friends is on the docket several times a week, sometimes followed by one of the free concerts in a nearby town square.

Tricia's sister, her two grown sons, and her grandkids all live hours away, but she still manages to see each of them at least a few times a year. The grandkids, she sees every month. Still, on a day-to-day basis, Tricia thinks of her friends as her extended family. She has about a half-dozen friends she sees individually and many more in the contexts of her group activities. "I've had more friends and more diversity of friends than I've ever had in my life. It's great!"

I am touched by how warmly Tricia and Anja speak of each other. About Anja, Tricia says, "She's so even tempered and so smart . . . We laugh a lot, which is an important part of any relationship." Of Tricia, Anja says, "She is one of these incredibly nice people . . . Anytime I need a bubbly person in my life, she'll never not be happy to see me." They both tell me they confide in each other and totally trust each other.

To me, their friendship looks effortless. It isn't, though. When they first moved into the duplex, they had to figure out how to live together. Tricia expected to see Anja a bit more often. Anja needed to figure out how to get all the privacy and solitude that she savored without sacrificing the closeness with Tricia that she so cherished.

Anja believes that for an arrangement like hers and Tricia's to succeed, it takes "people who are willing to live consciously...to be honest, respectful, willing to hear what's hard—perhaps invite that. You can't do it and assume it's going to work great."

It has worked great for the two of them. "We've been friends for ten years and we've never had a fight," Tricia tells me. Anja offers, "I love the fact that I have one of my best friends living right next door. I can be there for her, she is there for me. Growing older that way is a wonderful feeling of security."

The two of them occasionally go out to dinner or a movie together. They might take a walk into town or go for a hike. They've gone to Giants games and done stair walks in San Francisco. They also have a really nice tradition of taking several day trips a year. They've visited many of the little towns that dot the coast, each with its own personality.

Mostly, when they see each other, it is casually and spontaneously around the property. If Tricia sees Anja sitting outside, she might join her. Anja describes the boundary between their places as a "gentle" one. I think that describes their interpersonal boundaries too. They do not walk into each other's homes without knocking. They have even developed a special knock, so they know it is the other person at the door. Anja doesn't always answer if she is meditating or just not in the mood. Tricia understands that. With her many activities, Tricia is not always around when Anja is looking for her either.

When I ask how Anja's life would be different if she had all the money and resources in the world, she says it would make the finances of her travels easier; but otherwise, nothing much would change. "Right now, I think my life is better than it has ever been." She'd probably give the money away.

When I ask Tricia the same question, she says that she used to play the lottery. Then one day, she thought, *What if I won the lottery?* And she realized that she loved her life just the way it was.

Tricia doesn't play the lottery anymore. She already won it.

Lucy Whitworth: Seven Community Members and Forty-Nine Angels

Lucy Whitworth, seventy-one, has not been in a romantic relationship for twenty-five years. Her parents died more than forty years ago. She has no children. Her nearest relatives live eight hundred miles away. Two dogs and three cats, but no humans, share the house where she lives.[9]

When she was diagnosed with breast cancer a few years ago (as mentioned in chapter 1), Lucy discovered she had a people problem. She needed a lot of help over the course of her surgery, recovery from surgery, and treatment, but there just wasn't enough need to go around. When word went out about her diagnosis, forty-nine friends near her home in Sebastopol, California, all wanted to help. They were called Lucy's Angels. There were some hard feelings because there were not enough tasks to keep all of the angels as involved as they wanted to be. Mostly, though, the caring deepened their bonds with Lucy and with one another.

During our conversation, I ask Lucy to tell me about the most stressful time of her life. I almost skip that question, because I am so sure she will say it was when she was dealing with cancer. "Oh, no," she corrects me. That wasn't the most stressful time at all. "I was surrounded by so much love." (Her actual answer: It was when she was working with severely emotionally troubled children, and she had too many children in her care and too little help.)

The night before Lucy's surgery, more than a dozen of her friends sat with her out in the sunroom in the back of her home and sang healing songs. Then they asked Lucy if she would lie on the floor and let them each place a hand on her body. She agreed, and the singing began anew. "In that moment, when I said yes, that changed my life."

Lucy lives in a house on 2.5 acres of lush vegetable gardens and flower gardens, fruit trees and beds of berries, bordered by tall oak trees. She believes that the verdant setting, with its spiritual feel, also contributed to her healing.

Six other women also live in the dwellings nestled in the flora. There's a single-family house, a duplex, and a trailer. A charming artists' studio also graces the property, as does a lap pool and pool house.

Lucy was not yet fifty when she took a look at the overgrown piece of land and the damaged buildings that had been neglected by an absentee landlord. She recognized the potential and bought the place. It wasn't the first time she had done such a thing. Many years previously and more than five hundred miles south, in San Diego, she also established the first of her safe communities for lesbians. She did it again when she moved further north. Her Sebastopol community is the grandest of them all (it has more people, more structures, and more inspiring grounds than the others); and it is where she wants to stay.

One of the seven women has been living in the community for twenty years. Another, the most recent arrival, has been a friend of Lucy's for three decades. When Lucy learns about people who are interested in renting, she doesn't try to discern whether they will be enthusiastic participants in the life of the community—she isn't even sure she can say what "community" is—but she has found over the years that the women who are most likely to cherish their experiences there are those who enjoy seeing the other women as they go about their routines and who do not mind being known by the others. The least contented person who ever lived there wanted more privacy.

What Lucy likes least about her community is her own position in it. She would like everyone to feel like equals, but she owns the place, and they all pay her rent; that adds a dynamic that she finds discomfiting. She has never raised the rent and, she never will. To keep the place in good shape, everyone does what she can. To maintain the pool, for example, the women who can afford to pay do so; the others help by cleaning it.

Lucy was familiar with cohousing when she designed the community in Sebastopol and wanted to add a common house, but the building codes were too daunting. The seven women do not have regular meals together, but they do have occasional potlucks; and they often stop to chat as they tend their gardens (each has her own), enjoy the pool, or just sit serenely on the glider alongside the pool, as Lucy and I do when we talk. They also celebrate birthdays, several at a time, and host an annual Fourth of July celebration (actually on the third), to which friends and neighbors are invited. There are kids who have grown up with that tradition and lovingly embrace it.

Lucy's grandsons love to visit. Given a choice between the special treat of Legoland or their grandmother's place, they choose Lucy's, where they know they will have the doting attention of the seven women they call their aunties.

Ever since she retired, Lucy has enjoyed spending many hours of her days in solitude, reading, gardening, taking walks, and keeping up with personal connections and volunteer work on email. As dinnertime approaches, she becomes much more sociable. One of her favorite rituals is Chop and Chat. A few women get in touch, bring whatever is in her refrigerator to one of their homes, and make a meal of it. They get to catch up over the chopping and the eating, and no one is obliged to stay any longer than that.

I'm a hugger and Lucy is, too, but I have never gathered twenty-eight hugs, several nights a week, for months or even years. Okay, I've never accomplished that even once. Maybe I should learn to square dance, as Lucy does. Lucy explained that during a ninety-minute session, there are four "tips," and at the end of each, the eight people cross their arms and offer a thank you. In straight clubs, they shake hands, but in gay ones, they hug. With four tips and seven other people, that's twenty-eight hugs. Sometimes Lucy stays for three hours instead and gathers fifty-six hugs. It's a life-enhancing experience, physically, mentally, and emotionally.

As she grew older, Lucy wasn't always certain about the changes in her life or in her own body, and she wasn't one to keep her misgivings to herself. In her forties, she organized a group of lesbians to discuss their experiences; it was called the Hot Flashes. When she retired, she put together a group of similarly situated women to mull over what this new stage of life meant for them. Currently, she is the inspiration for a group of single lesbians over fifty. At the most recent gathering she hosted, fifty women showed up.

As I heard all of these stories, it became more evident to me how she ended up with forty-nine people who wanted to be involved in her care during her illness. Maybe, though, the most important thing she had done was to be there when others had needed her.

About seven times before her own diagnosis (and at least three since), Lucy organized a team of angels for people she knew who were facing a crisis. There was a system to it, improvised at first, but then systematized in templates such as *Share the Care* (a book by Sheila Warnock) and more recently, in online formats such as LotsaHelpingHands.com and Caring Bridge.org.

When Lucy was figuring it out (mostly on her own), she would sit down with the person who, say, was about to have surgery, and ask her to think about every single thing she does in her everyday life. Then Lucy would be the point person for the friends and relatives who wanted to help with the various tasks, asking them to sign up for different things on different days. The power of the system is that helpers get to contribute in ways that best suit their talents and preferences and schedules, and no one person or set of persons feels overburdened. The person in need of help can specify what she does and does not want, when she wants it, and then focus on healing—without always worrying about asking for help.

Even though Lucy was only in her late forties when she bought the land that would become the site of her community, she was already thinking about the future. She liked the location, just a block or so away from shops and restaurants and a supermarket; that would be a boon to the women in their later years if they could no longer drive. Looking ahead, she hopes that she and the other women who are interested can stay in the community for the rest of their lives. She thinks some of the living space can be adapted to accommodate a caregiver, who could be invited to stay there for free.

If she needs more help than her own community can offer, Lucy knows where she might go—to the Redwoods Retirement Community in nearby Mill Valley. The residents, Lucy says, "are a bunch of old hippies who are politically active and have been all their lives . . . It's not like going into a sterile environment, especially as a queer." Lucy is willing to go back to many of the places she has been in her life, but the closet isn't one of them.

Santa Barbara Village: Helping Seniors Stay in Their Own Homes

On a clear, sunny January day, I show up at an open meeting at a Santa Barbara community center. I want to hear about a brilliant way of helping seniors live exactly how so many of them want to: in their own homes, for as long as possible.[10]

The thirteen people who are already there when I arrive have come to learn about Santa Barbara's Village—the nonprofit organization, its people, and its services. The Village helps seniors with those sometimes small but crucial chores, tasks, services, and outings that can make the difference between staying in their own familiar, comforting homes and landing in a more institutional setting.

The Santa Barbara version of the Village—as of 2014, one of more than one hundred around the country—was just two years old at the time. The Village that started it all, Beacon Hill, has only been around since 2001. That's when a dozen people from that storied and historic Boston neighborhood were about to start a movement, though that's not what they had in mind at the time. They were just thinking about their own advancing age, and what they could do to stay in the neighborhood they cherished and the homes they loved.[11]

Would it be possible to access many of the services that would be a given if they moved to assisted living or some other retirement community? Could they find a way to stay that would honor their sense of responsibility and independence without burdening family members who may not even live nearby? That's what they hoped for.

If you are young and feeling invincible (or if you are sixty-one years old like me and in denial about the help you might need in the years to come), you might not realize all of the kinds of things that you may no longer be able to do on your own or might not *want* to do on your own. You may not want to think about what it would take to find someone to help you each time. If you share another one of my flaws, you might not like asking for help. There are services you can pay for, of course—which also need to be tracked down—but then there's another issue: do you have enough money to pay for all that you need?

Inside the community center, a woman with long, curly, black hair steps to the front of the room to tell newcomers what the Santa Barbara Village is all about. She is Naomi Kovacs, who brought to her position as executive director an impressive resumé of relevant experiences, from her Peace Corps days in Cameroon, Africa, to her work on affordable housing and neighborhood participation programs in Los Angeles, to her contributions to the Livable Communities Project in Southern California.

Anyone fifty or older from the county of Santa Barbara, she tells us, can join the Village for a monthly fee. Then, with one call or one email to the Village, members can usually get what they need—often for free—from someone in the Village; or they can get referred to someone or some service from the outside, often at a discount. Membership fees are on the high side because Santa Barbara is such an expensive place to live (though scholarships and more affordable rates are available). In other places, Village fees are lower. A few don't charge at all.

The youngest of the forty-five Santa Barbara members is in her late fifties; the average age is about seventy-five. Nationwide, about a third of Village members are between sixty-five and seventy-four, and 40 percent are between seventy-five and eighty-four.[12]

Across the many Villages, what members ask for most is a ride.[13] In Santa Barbara, too, members have gotten transportation to places such as grocery stores, friends' homes, hair salons, doctors' offices, and Village social events. Usually one of the trained and vetted volunteers helps with that. Local members have also gotten help with errands, light housekeeping, filing and organizing, techie troubleshooting, replacing lightbulbs and smoke-alarm batteries, and finding information (for example, about the banks that have easy parking). Some want friendly visits or daily phone check-ins. Other members are the caregivers for parents, partners, or other loved ones who need constant attention, and what they most want from the Village is a break. When someone from the Village comes by for a while, the caregivers can finally get some time to themselves.

Sometimes the help that Village members need is beyond the expertise of the volunteers or staff or fellow members. In those instances, the Village functions as a concierge service, putting members in touch with the roofers, accountants, computer experts, professional drivers, and others, all of whom have been screened and typically provide their services at a discount to Village members. Then Village staff follow up to make sure that members were satisfied with their experiences.

"We think of you as our Village family," Naomi says in wrapping up her presentation. "We want to get to know you."

True to the tradition of the twelve seniors who started it all in Beacon Hill, the Santa Barbara Village is a self-governing, grassroots, bottom-up organization. There is a national Village-to-Village Network, which provides resources, tools, webinars, and other support to the registered Villages. It also organizes an annual conference. The national organization does not call the shots, though—each individual Village does.[14] It seems fitting, then, that the last three speakers are not directors or other staff members but two Village members and one volunteer.

Adele, who has been a member of the Santa Barbara Village for two years, pushes her walker to the front of the room. She leans over it as she recounts one thing after another that Village volunteers and staff have helped her with, from setting up her answering machine to assembling a living-room table to getting her watch fixed. She admits that she used to be one of those people who loathed asking for help; now, it's easy. Adele lives in a senior community where many of the other residents rarely leave their homes. That's not an issue for Adele. The Village events keep her active and involved. Blanche, another two-year member, tells us that she already had a network of friends before she joined the Village but likes knowing people from the Village too.

The formal part of the meeting, before we head to the back where we can gather pamphlets and flyers while enjoying refreshments, ends with a presentation by the man Naomi introduces as the Village's star volunteer. Joe, who lives alone, has been helping for a year, calling members just to say hi, going on walks with them, watering their plants, and driving them wherever they need to go. That saying about how it takes a village—Joe thinks that applies to seniors too. He also has a more personal motivation. When his mother was in need of a great deal of care, Joe lived hundreds of miles away, and his sister, who lived nearby, did nearly all of the work. Joe still feels bad that he was not able to help his mother more and share the care with his sister. Now he can give to others the help he could not give to his own relatives.

I'm not a sappy person, but I am totally taken by the caring and love that I hear in the voices of the people who spoke that day. I guess I am not the only one. Naomi tells us about an email she received from one of the members that said, simply, *Thank you for caring.*

Appreciation seems to be commonplace among the Village people. In 2012, the eighty Villages registered with the Village-to-Village Network were invited to participate in an extensive survey of their experiences. Sixty-nine agreed. More than 50 percent of the participants said that the quality of their life had improved; 80 percent said that overall, they were very satisfied or extremely satisfied with their experiences as Village members; even more than that said that they would refer a friend. One of the core missions of the Villages seems to be highly successful: 81 percent said that they are more likely to know how to get help when they need it. Members were also more socially engaged. For example, 77 percent said they know more people since joining the Village. Most important, 79 percent said that they are more likely to stay in their own homes now that they have joined a Village.[15]

Villages are, most fundamentally, ways for people to stay in their own homes as they age. In Santa Barbara, though, one woman who had moved into an assisted-living facility joined the Village too. If she hadn't, she says, she would be around old people too much of the time.

I do wonder, though, whether Villages are primarily for people who already have plenty of resources. After all, Beacon Hill is a place known for affluence and education, and so is Santa Barbara. Ray Suarez had the same question, and in an interview on PBS, he put it to Susan McWhinney-Morse, one of the founding members of the Beacon Hill Village. She had a quick and confident response: "I really think that this model is a terrific answer, particularly for people who are low to moderate income and middle class, who simply have no other options. Who can't move to retirement communities. Who don't have the resources to go to Sun City."[16]

On the average, membership fees account for just under half of the operating budgets for Villages, so other sources of funding are necessary.[17] Private foundations, corporations, individual gifts, and fundraising often make up much of the balance. Sometimes organizers and directors go without pay.[18] Not all Villages survive, and even Beacon Hill saw drops in membership during the recession.[19]

Though the federal government funds long-term care programs for the elderly, they are overwhelmingly focused on nursing-home care. Activists such as Henry Cisneros, former secretary of Housing and Urban Development, have been urging a shift in resources toward more community-based solutions (such as Villages), with some success. Seniors who can stay in their own homes longer seem to be happier, healthier, and more socially and civically engaged. The tab for the services they use is a lot less too.[20]

When I was researching the Village concept, I brought it up in conversations with all sorts of people who I thought would be interested, or who were close to someone else who could benefit tremendously from what a Village has to offer. But none of them joined. A member of the Beacon Hill Village Board of Directors described some of the same frustrations. Plenty of seniors had told her they loved the idea of the Village, but they just weren't ready yet. Some of them were in their nineties.[21]

I'd like to think that the issue is largely one of familiarity; people just don't know enough about the Village concept yet. Once it catches on, and there are more media reports, and more friends telling friends about their good experiences, and more adult children sharing their stories of how much their own parents were helped, Villages will become one of the cool ways to age.

Pismodise: A Mobile-Home Community on the Cusp of the Pacific Ocean

For a while, my father co-owned a mobile-home park with a relative. It sat in front of a rocky ledge in mountainous northeastern Pennsylvania. As a kid, I loved climbing the rocks and exploring, but even those fun-filled experiences did nothing to undermine the standard prejudices against those kinds of homes. I shared them.

That is, until I moved to the California coast. Here, the parks come with names like Summerland by the Sea and Silver Sands, and many really do have unobstructed ocean views. People talk about their friends and relatives who live in mobile-home communities and their own plans to move there, with no self-consciousness.

When Lisa Margonelli came to Pismodise to interview the residents about their community, her interviewees were not about to stand for it. Instead, they walked. Starting at 7:00 AM, seven women met her and they all set off at a good clip, covering the various roads in the community and, along the way, greeting people sitting on their porches. Sometimes, the residents—and not just the women—walk to the grocery store in town or to the beach. Both are close enough to reach without a car, even for people in this community, all of whom are at least fifty-five.[22]

Pismodise is the name the residents gave to the central California mobile-home community of Pismo Dunes Senior Park. It is a paradise to them. For rents of less than five hundred dollars a month, they can live close enough to the ocean to eat their lunch there every day. Perhaps even more important, they have turned their park into a real community. They have what they call their therapy sessions, where they meet regularly and shoot the breeze. There's a clubhouse where they play cards and have lunch twice a week. They look out for each other, too, especially when someone is ailing or caring for someone who is ill.

Margaret Julkowski had been hospitalized with a condition that left her weakened and left her daughter ruminating over whether it was such a great idea for her mother to return to the mobile-home park. "But when she saw the parade of visitors, some carrying food, she realized Margaret was probably in the best hands here."

Ernie Link, ninety-three, also has a daughter who lives nearby. He doesn't need to stay in the park. But he wants to live alone, in a community where there's always someone else around.

Even beyond any lingering stigma, mobile homes still have disadvantages. They don't appreciate the way other homes do. Although residents in parks might own their trailers, at Pismo Dunes and many other parks, they do not own the land beneath them.

Still, as Margonelli learned from her research, even the very small trailers at Pismo Dunes (usually under eight hundred square feet) have a lot to recommend them. Owners can modify them as they wish, adding porches and carports and sunrooms. They have patches of land where they can garden. Their dogs are welcome, as long as they are not too big. The boundaries around the parks can provide some safety; most residents don't bother locking their doors.

Seniors in mobile-home parks typically spend less of their income on their housing than people who rent or own homes, even though their overall income is smaller. Yet residents can be surprisingly diverse economically. At Pismo Dunes, they have assets ranging from under twenty-five thousand dollars to more than a half million.

The members of Pismodise also have a lot of what we all want: control. That balance between time alone and time together is easy to tip in just the right direction.

Bienvenida Torres: Public Housing, Private Parties

It is 2012 and Bienvenida Torres, seventy-eight, is living alone in an apartment on the fifth floor of a public-housing building in New York City. No other relatives live there. She and her husband split about two decades before. The previous year, her daughter was stabbed to death by the man who was living with her in the Bronx.[23]

Back in the Dominican Republic, her mother's life had been very different. She lived with her five kids, and with other families all around her. As Bienvenida told the *New York Times*, "They were more united. When they killed a pig, everyone would eat from the pig, and she'd fill burlap bags with food for all the children and grandchildren."

Bienvenida, though, is not pining for a life like that. She likes living on her own. She cherishes her family but does not want to live with them.

In a way, Bienvenida has all the warmth and closeness and love and support any family could offer—all around her in the other apartments on her floor. There's Brunilda De Leon, eighty-nine, her next-door neighbor, who has been bringing Bienvenida coffee every day for years. Bruna also calls Bienvenida at the end of each evening to be sure she's okay. Mercedes Morel is on the same floor too—she likes to treat her neighbors to their favorite foods. Rene Cavallo, eighty-six, does the same. Frank Ramos and Ana Lopez's sons are the handymen—when Bienvenida has something that needs fixing, they are there.

The caring goes both ways. Bienvenida has a nurturing way about her. Neighbors know they are welcome to stop by and share their troubles or just drink coffee and chat. They don't even knock anymore—no need. Bienvenida tells Bruna that if she ever feels sick, all she has to do is knock on the wall, and she will hear her. The two women let each other know when they are headed out. If it has been a while since one has seen the other, she'll call, just to be sure.

Bienvenida has been a huge help to Rene too. When his wife had Alzheimer's and needed the help of an aide, Rene would sometimes have to leave long before the aide arrived. No problem—Bienvenida would be there at 5:00 AM and stay until 9:00.

More than a dozen of the residents on Bienvenida's floor had already been getting formal help with living alone through the Visiting Nurse Service of New York. The camaraderie was contagious, and the nurses became friends as well as helpers. Even their own family members were drawn into the embrace.

The building where all of these residents live has a senior center on a lower floor, but none of the fifth-floor residents use it. They have their own senior centers—in each of their living rooms.

And none of the other floors in the building have that same neighborly spirit. Many of the residents throughout the building are Dominican, so anything special about that culture is unlikely to be the answer.

Are the other floors missing that special person who gets the whole community vibe started by knocking on a door and offering the first cup of coffee? Do they comprise groups of people who just don't click? Or are those people living exactly the way they want to, on their own, with autonomy and privacy, in places of their own?

In 2012, there were more than forty-three million Americans who were sixty-five or older, just under 14 percent of the total population.[24] That number will continue to climb. AARP pointed out that the first of the baby boomers reached retirement age in 2011 and projected that "for the next 18 years, boomers will be turning 65 at a rate of about 8,000 a day."[25] Many of them will be innovators like Tricia and Anja; or visionaries such as Marianne (from chapter 3), sharing a home with other seniors; or talented community builders such as the residents of Pismodise or of the fifth floor of that New York City apartment building. Complementing these lifespaces are others more specifically designed to accommodate the changing needs and wishes of today's seniors.

Return to Heritage Harbour: Choose Your Neighborhood, Follow Your Interests

Active adult communities, so new in the early '60s, now stretch across the nation. I get my first glimpse of one when I interview Dorothy Hackett, who lives apart from her partner in the Heritage Harbour fifty-five plus community in Annapolis, Maryland. (See chapter 6.) The person who introduced me to Dorothy is Joan Shelly, fifty-nine, the long-time partner of my older brother, Pete. Now she is volunteering to show me around the rest of the community.

I knew she would do so with gusto. She and Pete discovered the community after taking in a craft beer festival in Annapolis, and they became instant enthusiasts. I still have the email from my brother when they had just moved in. He and Joan had already met some of the other residents and the people who were visiting them. Then, when they left the garage door open, someone called to let them know. Pete already had a good feeling about the community on two counts: it was going to be friendly, and it was going to be safe.

When news got out that there was a new young (sixty-one) man on the street, widows began stopping by, just to say hi. Joan tells me, though, that some of the other women have a whole different attitude.

> I've talked to women here who have said, "I wouldn't get married.
> I don't want any man in my life. I had a great marriage, but now I'm

all about me and my friends and what I want to do, and I don't want
to answer to anybody, and I'm having the time of my life."

To see all of Heritage Harbour, you need to get in a car and drive.
The neighborhood of townhouses where Dorothy lives is just one of the
sections, each with its own character and type of dwelling. Turn one way,
and you are in a genteel neighborhood of single-family homes. Drive a
bit more, turn again, and you are in the high-rise section, with an entirely
different sensibility. There are also neighborhoods of duplexes and patio
condos. Joan and Pete live in one of the villas—sections of single-story
homes attached in sets of four.

The social center is the community lodge, an immaculate, spacious,
sunny place. A bulletin board near the entry announces the week's upcoming events (a jazz pianist) and daily activities (ping-pong on Tuesday,
bocce ball and billiards on Wednesday, horseshoes on Thursday, and the
dance on Friday night). A big sitting room with a wood-beamed cathedral
ceiling, a fireplace, lots of comfortable seating, and a puzzle station off to
the side is the centerpiece of the lodge. Probably just as important is the
auditorium, the venue for the Friday night dances, monthly movies, and
occasional plays starring the community members. (Joan tried out for
comedy and landed one of the leads.)

In a fitness center—one of Pete's haunts—a few men are working
out vigorously on the equipment. In another room, others stay seated
for their exercises. There are many other amenities in the lodge, such as
the pool room, arts-and-crafts room, woodwork shop, plant-care room,
Jacuzzi, and saunas; I am happy to see that there is also a library.

Joan and Pete moved into the community as a couple. Would a single
person feel lonely, I wonder? "There's no excuse for being lonely here,"
Joan tells me. You can always go to the lodge: "There will be people sitting around doing puzzles . . . You could go to the pool, and someone
would talk to you." When Bonnie, a single person, moved in recently,
Joan and Pete invited her to join them at an event where they introduced

her to some of the others. She—like everyone else who first moves into the community—was visited by a member of the orientation committee, who brought a welcome package with a directory of all of the residents and a list of groups to join, both within the community and in the greater Annapolis area. Bonnie is already active in a number of groups.

Heritage Harbour is an active adult community, not assisted living, so nursing care is not part of the package. There are, though, great hospitals nearby. Within the community, volunteers in the caring network take their fellow community members to doctors' appointments and help in many of the same ways that Villages do. Lots of the caring is informal, as when one neighbor learns that another is ill or in the hospital and might like a visitor, or when the blind person next door would really like some hard-boiled eggs but is wary of turning on a burner.

Joan is so enthusiastic about her fifty-five-plus community, I wonder what she will say when I ask if there is anything she does not like about it. She admits that she hadn't realized, until after they had moved in, that the fifty-five-plus community is really more like an eighty-plus community. Joan is not one to whine, so she recast even that in a positive way:

> Really, that hasn't been a negative because it gives me hope for what kind of a life I could have when I got to be that age, because they're all really active, and a lot of them have had very interesting and high-powered jobs.

But still.

From Active Adult Communities to Continuing Care

What Joan described about the overwhelmingly older ages of the residents in the fifty-five-plus community has become true of many other active adult communities. Some, at first, really did include many of the very-young-old. As Philip Dowds cautioned when describing the likely

fate of senior cohousing communities, Go-go seniors can become Slow-gos and then No-gos. It was just that dynamic that provided one of the motivations for the next innovation in senior living, the Continuing Care Retirement Community (CCRC). For an entry fee and a monthly fee—both of which are often quite steep—residents can move from the most autonomous living situations (independent living), to an arrangement that offers more help (assisted living), to skilled nursing facilities—all on the same grounds.[26]

The CCRC generation often wants more than the tennis, golf, and shuffleboard of the GI generation. In response, the most upscale of CCRC settings have become like amenity-rich resorts, catering to residents' interests in fitness, spiritual and emotional wellness, intellectual enrichment, and social engagement. Pools, fitness centers, libraries, cafés, and art studios are among the offerings residents can access—all without ever leaving the neighborhood.

Also in keeping with changing preferences and expectations of well-off seniors, the private living spaces have become bigger and homier. There are grab bars, wide doorways, and all of the other features of senior-friendly living integrated into attractive designs. Contemporary seniors do not often share the preference for formality of the generations before them, and so elegant dining halls have been replaced with more informal spaces with plenty of food choices.

When I lived in Virginia, an esteemed colleague retired to an upscale CCRC. I remember walking down the long corridors to her beautifully appointed apartment; I felt like I was in a fancy hotel. This place was where only the most affluent seniors could afford to stay. And yet, it never appealed to me. Hotels—even the nice, welcoming ones—just don't feel like home.

Green Houses: Nursing-Home Abolitionism

That feeling of home is what Dr. William Thomas set out to create in a lifespace for elders that took everything that was wrong with the earlier

versions of senior housing and made them right. He calls his innovation Green Houses: intentional communities "dedicated to fostering the
most positive elderhood possible."[27] He calls himself a "nursing home
abolitionist."[28]

Step into a Green House and, instead of finding long corridors, mas-
sive dining rooms, and rigid schedules, you will find a hearth. That's
the common area—an open space with a kitchen, a table big enough to
seat the elders and the staff, and a living room. Private rooms—usually
between six and twelve of them—are arranged around the hearth; that's
how many elders live in a Green House. Thomas insists on places that are
"family sized" rather than "factory sized."[29]

Traditional nursing homes might boast of their efficiency, the long
list of activities available to their residents, and the skilled nurses, or designated care managers, available around the clock; Green Houses offer
meaningfulness. Rather than set mealtimes, Green Houses encourage
elders to eat what they want, when they want it, and where they want it.[30]
When NPR visited the Baltimore Green House around lunchtime, some
of the elders were gathered around the table. Charles Taylor, though,
wanted to relax in the recliner in the living room a while longer. He
wasn't worried. "Anytime I get ready, just press the button, and they'll
bring me a raisin-bread sandwich. That's my favorite."[31]

Elders. That's Thomas's term of choice. To him, an elder is "a person
who, by virtue of age or life experience, has transcended or has the potential to transcend the limitations and shortcomings of adulthood."[32] It is a
definition so startlingly defiant of ageism and declinism that after I first
read it, I had to read it again just to be sure of what Thomas was saying: it
is the adults and not the elders who have "limitations and shortcomings"
that need to be transcended.

Thomas is not putting down adulthood—it has its place—but elderhood has its own developmental potential. Adulthood, Thomas believes,
is all about doing; elderhood is more about being. Adults like their
achievements; elders value emotional rewards. Adults compare them-

selves to others; elders value intrinsic satisfactions. Adults are shaping their identities and meeting more people; elders want to deepen their intimacy with the people they already care about. Adults like to get stuff done; elders like to savor their experiences.[33] That's why there are no meaningless activities foisted upon the elders in Green Houses. Telling your stories and understanding everyone else's stories, for example, are valued ways of being in Green Houses.

A growing stack of studies shows that older people are more focused on the positive than are younger adults. For example, they remember positive events better than negative ones, and they are more influenced by the positive experiences than the negative ones.[34] Green Houses, though, don't try to sweep the bad stuff under the pretty rugs. Of course, illness, loss, and grief are part of elderhood; those experiences are "reframed [as] elements of an ancient way of living that gradually brings emotions and relationships to the center of an elder's experience."[35] In so many places—and not just places for elders—people work hard to suppress conflict or pretend it's not happening. Not in Green Houses. "We say, oh, we've got conflict? Let's talk about it. We're human beings. We're going to have conflict."[36]

The first of the Green Houses were built in Tupelo, Mississippi, in 2004.[37] Before they were constructed, an environmental gerontologist (yes, the concept was new to me too) was sent to visit dozens of homes in the area and take more than a thousand pictures. Green Houses are designed to have layouts that feel familiar and exteriors that look architecturally consistent with their surroundings. Elders who move in are encouraged to fill their spaces with their own furnishings and decorations. You won't find nurse stations, chart racks, or medication charts in Green Houses. In fact, you won't find much of anything in a Green House that you would not find in any other house that you would call your home.[38]

Green Houses are "green" in the broader environmental sense, but more important, they are garden-green. There are plants on the inside and easy access to the outside, where elders can enjoy nature, sunshine, fresh air, and the changing of the seasons.[39]

William Thomas's "aha" moment came many years ago, when he was called to take a look at a rash on the arm of a woman in a conventional nursing home. He examined the rash, asked the woman what he needed to know about it, and tried to leave. She grabbed his arm, pulled him back, and said, "I'm so lonely."[40]

Thomas now believes that the greatest part of the suffering that older people often endure comes from loneliness, boredom, and helplessness.[41] Companionship is Thomas's answer to loneliness. It comes from sharing the rhythms of daily life with other people—knowing them, being with them, and trading stories. Companionship is not just for the elders; it is also central to the role of the Green House staff members. "Without companionship," Thomas noted, "long-term care can only offer the cruel comfort of strangers feeding, bathing, dressing, and entertaining strangers."[42] It has become fashionable to invite visiting animals into some nursing homes; Green Housers look down on that practice. They want their pets to be full-time residents, too. There's nothing like a friendly dog to create the spontaneity, unpredictability, and variety that are the kryptonite of boredom. Kids are welcome for the same reasons, among others.

In institutionalized nursing homes, staff members give plenty of help—too much help, Thomas believes. By doing for elders what they could do for themselves, these well-intentioned professionals create helplessness. In Green Houses, elders do as much as they can for themselves and for others too. They can, if they like, help with gardening, meal planning and preparation, laundry, cleaning, and caring for pets.

Elders also make their own decisions. If they are truly incapable of doing so, then the people who know them best are consulted. That, too, is part of the philosophy of Green Houses that values elders' autonomy, dignity, and individuality. When the staff members listen closely to the elders, focus on enhancing their skills rather than just remedying their deficits, and share meals and other everyday life experiences with them, then their dignity is honored too.

As of 2014, there were more than 150 Green Houses in thirty-two states either open or in development.[43] Some are licensed as assisted-living centers, others as skilled nursing homes.[44] Some senior facilities are incorporating selected aspects of Green Houses, but they don't count as Green Houses.[45] Although Green Houses can be expensive to build, once they are up and running, they are generally no more costly than other nursing homes.[46] The Baltimore Green House featured in the NPR story, for instance, serves mostly low-income elders on Medicaid.

The results of the first long-term studies of Green Houses are becoming available, and they are promising. Compared to residents of other nursing homes in nearby areas, Green House elders report physical health that is just as good, in addition to emotional health, spiritual well-being, privacy, dignity, autonomy, and meaningfulness that are all much better.[47]

Back in Tupelo, in the early days of the project, an adult son brought his mother, Mildred, to one of the first Green Houses. She had been in a traditional nursing home, where she would not walk or talk or feed herself. Mother and son sat around the common table with the eleven other elders, and the son picked up a spoon to start feeding his mom. That's when Mildred said her first words in years: "Give me that spoon!" Years later, she was still feeding herself—and walking, singing gospel songs, and telling stories of her life.[48]

Think again about all the different lifespaces I've described in this chapter. Every one of them is distinctive, and every one is a source of great joy and meaningfulness for the people who choose to live that way. What strikes me as most remarkable, though, is what is missing from each and every example: not one of them is based on the assumption that people come in couples or in nuclear families. Sure, there are couples and relatives in many of these lifespaces, but no one is required to be married or a parent to qualify. These twenty-first-century seniors are finding companionship, caring, and help in their friends, their neighbors, and in the families and communities they have created. They are lifespace pioneers, ushering in the new old age—and inspiring those who will follow them to create the next set of innovations.

8

THERE'S NOTHING SWEETER THAN SOLITUDE
Living Alone

This book is biased. I wasn't looking for a representative sample of people, taking the happy with the unhappy. I set out to find people who were (mostly) proud of their lifespaces. As I listened to one after another, I was so delighted and impressed by them—they had found their places, their spaces, and their people.

I was intrigued by many of the arrangements I knew little about before starting this project—probably cohousing most of all. If there were a cohousing community not too far from my little town of Summerland, I would have checked it out. But I know I would not have joined, even if they would have me. My work on this project has made me even more certain (if that's even possible) that there is only one way I ever want to live: by myself, and not in any sort of intentional community.

I grew up with a sister and two brothers in a ranch house on the corner of Sherwood and Ward in the small town of Dunmore, Pennsylvania (near Scranton). My parents were married and stayed that way. Ours was an intensely social home. My father's one sibling and my mother's six all lived nearby. For us kids, birthdays and christenings and First Holy

Communions and Christmases and Easters were all marked by a gaggle of cousins running, playing, and pouring the multihued sodas into one big stream until it all turned a disgusting shade of brown. (We did the same with the Easter egg colorings.)

When we got to high school, all the relatives kept gathering in the Dunmore dining room, but then, so did our friends. Over the holidays, my mother would add the leaf to the table and put out a spread of coffee and cookies for the family (cutouts, chocolate with chocolate icing, peanut blossoms, butterballs, rum balls, and crispelli dipped in honey); then the relatives would leave and she'd do the same for the first round of friends, then again for the next.

My father started each event at his seat at the head of the table, but then at some point, he quietly disappeared. When I went to fetch more cookies from the kitchen downstairs (did you think we only had one kitchen? We're Italians!), I'd see him in the den, reading or watching television by himself. At first, I didn't understand that. I loved the excitement of a house full of company. I shared a bedroom with my sister until my parents built an addition to the house, and I thought that was fine too.

By my high school years, however, I started to feel a connection with the dad who went downstairs. There was usually only one time when the house was totally empty—no parents, no sibs, no visiting aunties or uncles or cousins. That was Sunday evening. I couldn't wait for it. All I did was kick back in the recliner, maybe read or perhaps just close my eyes and take in the utter quiet. I considered it my first taste of real luxury.

That savoring of solitude has continued for the rest of my life. In response to one of my survey questions, a woman said:

> Another person in the house, even if they're not talking to me or interacting directly with me at the moment, seems to take up a lot of my emotional energy. I can only really relax and be creative when I'm on my own.

I, too, can only think with my whole mind and feel with my whole heart when I am totally and completely alone.

I sometimes invite friends and family to visit for days at a time. They are the world's best houseguests—otherwise, they would not have been invited. But no matter what I'm doing and what they're doing—even during those down times when they're reading and I'm at my computer—there's a piece of my mind that's attending to them. As much as I enjoy their visits (I'm the one who invites them again and again!), I'm happy when they are gone. I get to have my whole house back, and my whole mind.

The research for all of the other chapters in this book felt like an anthropological exploration into ways of living that only other people experience. This chapter is like coming home for me. I already knew how much I cherish living on my own, and now I can explore more deeply how other people experience it. I'll start with someone whose big-city lifespace is about as different from my tiny little Summerland as I can imagine.

Going Solo in the City

In the East Village of Manhattan, in a neighborhood with a Middle Eastern restaurant, a vegetarian place, a pub, several hair salons, and actor Jennifer Esposito's gluten-free, sugar-free, vegan bakery, is a brick townhouse, five stories high. In 2001, it was in bad shape. The façade was crumbling, the beams were poorly constructed, and the windows looked more industrial than residential. Dan Scheffey, who was forty-five at the time, looked at the wreck and saw a home. He, four friends, and two investors bought the building, gutted it, and put it back together. In the rehabbed version, each floor is a generous twenty-five-feet wide, with two bedrooms and two baths spread out across about twelve hundred square feet. Dan moved into the third floor within a year and has lived there ever since. And he didn't have to look too hard to find others eager to take up residence on the other floors.

Michael, one of Dan's friends and fellow owners, moved into the first floor; Mel and Chris, two other owner-friends, shared the fourth. Michael's mother owned the second floor and rented it to Beth, a single mom with a teenage daughter. Two more friends of Dan's owned the fifth floor, which they also rented. It was "a building made porous by friendship."[1]

"I've had dinner on every floor," Beth said, "and my daughter saw a real sense of community. How many buildings do you know where each floor simultaneously throws a party?" Every year, the residents hosted a Christmas party. Once, three hundred of their closest friends showed up.

When I read stories like that, I always wonder how the lifespaces evolve over time. Do the residents stay there? Do they remain friends?

Fortunately, my sister Lisa DePaulo knows Dan, and invites him to visit her Bridgehampton cottage (on Long Island) on a weekend when I am there with my friends Bobbie and Susan. Bobbie, a psychology and law professor in Virginia, spent decades living alone but is now married. Susan, a clinical and forensic psychologist in North Carolina, was married briefly and is now going solo in a home of her own. Lisa, a talented and accomplished magazine writer (she didn't make me say that) has always been single and lives in her beachy, artsy, comfy cottage with her Havanese, Joey Obama (or Joey O for short).

I claim the seat next to Dan for dinner on the deck. Dan's story of his current lifespace also began with a step outside. As someone living in the heart of a thriving city, Dan does what so many other urbanites do—he walks out the front door of his building and into the streets that are his living room. No advance planning, no reservations necessary. His slice of the city is just as he likes it, with shops and restaurants but not a lot of noisy bars.

Perhaps befitting a person whose expertise is in communications and public relations, Dan has an abundance of friends. He's kept in touch with some for decades. A core group of about seven of them are from his University of Pennsylvania days and live in the city; they and other close friends have a lively social life.

Dan is also at the center of a nexus of friends from his days working at Disney. Recently, one of them, Caroline, with whom he's had a complicated relationship, visited the city and ran into Fran and Deena and Susie, each of whom then asked Dan what had happened with Caroline. "And I said, 'nothing happened,' but I realized that if anything was going to break the logjam, it was me." So he emailed Caroline, saying how nice it was to hear about her and suggesting that they get together next time she was in the city. They did. They had a long talk in which Dan told her, "my most important family is the family that I've selected and brought together," and he wanted her to be a part of it.

When Dan turned fifty, he threw himself a party in his East Village apartment. For the first time in his life, he brought together what he calls "the family I have" and "the family I chose." About one hundred people were there. They included his mother, father, stepmother; his brothers and a sister-in-law; and his friends from different times and different parts of his life. "Speech! Speech!" they implored him. He spoke from the heart, telling them how much they all meant to him, and how touched he was to have both of his families there with him and with each other.

As Dan's story has progressed, so has our dinner. By now we are back inside my sister's place, dipping big, fat, freshly picked strawberries into a decadent warmed chocolate sauce. It was also time to go back inside that five-story townhouse. What happened to those people?

It's a fairly small building, so the people who live there run into each other spontaneously about once or twice a week. They share a rooftop and see each other there too. The housing is structured as a condominium, so they also meet twice a year to discuss repairs and such. They do neighborly things such as picking up packages and taking in the mail when someone is away. None of the current residents, though, are the same people who moved into the building when Dan did. Dan's friendships with those people have endured, but now they live elsewhere. The current townhouse residents have not hosted a Christmas party in years, and they only have dinner together a few times a year.

The 2005 version of Dan's lifespace was a better fit to chapter 4—about people who live in private residences but within self-conscious communities. The way Dan lives now is closer to the topic of this chapter—living truly alone, residentially. In that lifespace, there may or may not be other people nearby, down the hall, on different floors, or across the street; if there are, it is not because they all made a deliberate decision to nurture real interpersonal connections while living in a place of their own. When I say that the people in this chapter are truly living alone residentially, the *residentially* qualifier is essential. Whether people who live alone residentially really *are* alone is a whole different question. Clearly, Dan is not.

Demographers have long kept careful records of the popularity of living alone, though none, so far as I know, have distinguished those who live truly alone, residentially, from those who live in self-conscious communities. In *Living Alone*, Lynn Jamieson and Roona Simpson compiled data from around the globe on the percentage of all households that are one-person households. They focused on the years 1950, 1980, 1990, 2000, and 2010 and found forty-two countries for which data were reported for at least two of those years.[2]

In the earliest year, 1950, solo living was rare. In eleven countries (of the nineteen for which data were available), no more than 12 percent of all households were one-person households, and in only one nation did the number top 20 percent (Sweden had 21 percent).

By 2010, living alone had become commonplace. Data were available from twenty-nine nations, and in only three of them—China, Mexico, and India—did one-person households make up 12 percent or fewer of all households. (Brazil, Argentina, and Chile reported data from the previous decade, and those numbers were similarly low.) Sweden led the world in solo living again; 49 percent of its households were one-person. Solo living was next most popular in Finland at 41 percent, and Norway at 40 percent.

In forty-one of the forty-two nations, solo living increased over time. The most dramatic increase happened in Japan, where only 5 percent of all households were one-person households in 1950, but 31 percent were by 2010. Only in India did the rate of solo-dwelling remain flat, at 4 percent.

The Way We Used To Live

The architect Witold Rybczynski, in a book called *Home*, pointed out that in the sixteenth century, it was unusual for anyone to have a room of his or her own, much less an entire apartment or house. "Houses were full of people, much more so than today, and privacy was unknown. Moreover, rooms did not have specialized functions." Typically, houses had just one or two rooms for as many as two dozen people, including workers as well as family. "It was more than a hundred years later," Rybczynski added, "that rooms to which the individual could retreat from public view came into being—they were called 'privacies.'"[3]

Rybczynski was talking about Europe, but in Colonial America, the story was much the same. As James Averill and Louise Sundararajan noted in their review of experiences of solitude, "Within a household, privacy was rarely possible, even in bed; and since households served multiple functions (educational, commercial, etc.), they were, in turn, under constant guidance and surveillance by the community."[4]

Eventually, rooms designated specifically as bedrooms, with doors that shut, became popular, but the rise of private dwellings was much slower. Many decades passed, and still, by 1950, less than 10 percent of all American households had just one person. A faint stirring of social forces pushed that number to nearly 13 percent by 1960. Then all demographic hell broke loose. By 1970, more than 17 percent of all households were one-person households; by 1980, it was more than 22 percent. Afterward, the climb slowed, but it never stopped. In 2013, 27 percent of all households were maintained by solo dwellers—that's thirty-four million people just in the United States.[5]

Something else broke loose in the second half of the twentieth century: the tight grip that marriage and family held on the youngest adults. The twenty-year-old first-time brides and twenty-two-and-a-half-year-old first-time grooms of 1956 were the youngest on record. From that year forward, the age at which adults first married—of those who did marry—would inch ever upward. By 2013, half of all women reached the age of 26.6 without ever having married, and half of all men made it to twenty-nine. That's a lot of time to be finished with high school (and even college) without ever starting married life.[6]

Those who had already married were doing something different too—in bigger numbers than ever before: they were divorcing.[7] That added another sizable chunk of the population ready to live some way other than in a married-couple household. Meanwhile, at the other end of the age spectrum, women continued to outlive men. In large numbers, women who had once been married became widowed, joining their divorced and ever-single sisters in their opportunities to live in a new way.[8]

In theory, the widowed could move in with their grown children, and young adults could have just continued to live with their parents until they married. The most celebrated family form in the second half of the twentieth century, though, was the nuclear family, not the multigenerational or extended family. It was no longer assumed that aging parents would live with their grown children, and increasingly, the seniors who were living on their own preferred to stay that way for as long as possible.[9]

As for the young adults, as more and more of them sought work or pursued their education outside of their hometowns, they got a taste of independence that was hard to give up. As the age at which people first married stretched further into the distance, marrying lost its status as a marker of adulthood. Other achievements, such as landing a place of your own, took that esteemed place.[10]

The life options available to young women increased even more dramatically than those available to young men. In the later decades of the twentieth century, more and more women went to college, got jobs, and supported themselves. Effective forms of contraception became available, abortion was legalized, and the stigma against premarital sex subsided. Women no longer needed to live with a husband in order to lead full, exciting lives.[11]

Many young adults who came from middle-class or wealthy families got to experience autonomy and privacy long before they left home for jobs or college. Unlike the kids in the generations that preceded them, late-twentieth-century children often had rooms of their own. Those who grew up in single-parent households or in married households in which both parents had jobs outside the home developed useful skills. They made their own decisions and took care of themselves while their parents were at work. They got their own snacks, did their homework, and entertained themselves.[12]

Going Solo in Twenty-First-Century America

For twenty-first-century kids, choices have proliferated beyond anything imaginable to children or adults who came of age before the revolution in communication technologies. No more gathering in front of the television with the whole family on Sunday nights to watch *Lassie* or *The Ed*

Sullivan Show. Now, all the kids and all the adults can choose their own television shows, their own movies, and their own music and call them up on their own devices. No more family phone attached to the kitchen wall either. Now there are cell phone family-plan contracts, so everyone can have a pocket-sized phone of his or her own. By the time kids are old enough to leave the family home, they have developed their own tastes and sensibilities, and they are already accustomed to arranging their lives in ways that express their individuality. The leap to a place of their own has never seemed so short.

People who live alone in the modern world do not get to avail themselves of the contributions that a spouse used to bring to old-fashioned married-couple households. Cooking, cleaning, and doing laundry, for example, used to be women's work. Now, even women living alone might not have time to do those things, even if they want to—they are too busy working. That's okay, though—they don't have to, and neither do men. With the growing availability of takeout, fast food, and prepared foods at grocery stores, meals are covered. Laundromats and dry cleaners are everywhere, as are house-cleaning services. In some cities, online opportunities offer new ways of finding people to cover all sorts of random errands for you.

All of these services are available—but at a price. Not everyone can afford them. Nor can everyone afford to live solo, with sole responsibility for the rent or mortgage and every utility bill. With no obvious backup source of financial support during a time of crisis or even during a month in which income trickles in too slowly, solo dwellers can be economically vulnerable.

The financial factor is perhaps the most important driver of the rise of solo living. Individuals who have benefitted from their nation's economic development have the option of using their resources to pay for a place of their own. The advent of Social Security was a boon to seniors who wanted to live on their own. Countries with far more generous social-welfare programs, sometimes including social housing, make solo living even more possible. They tend to have the highest percentages of people living alone.[13]

And yet, not everyone who can afford to live alone chooses to do so.

Leanna Wolfe: There Is Only One Way She Cannot Live

Leanna Wolfe, fifty-nine, is a free-thinking anthropologist living in the San Fernando Valley region of Southern California. In the home that she owns, she has space for three other people. Two people live there as long-term roommates; the other space is typically filled by guests who often find her through Airbnb. That fluidity is by choice. Leanna is a self-professed "variety junkie": "I need the energy of new people," she tells me.

When I ask Leanna about other ways she has lived in the past, she gives the longest answer of anyone I ever interviewed. Apart from the twenty-five years she has lived in a "marriage like" relationship with boyfriends, she has shared different houses with different people—once with a couple, another time with five housemates, and still another with her sister and her fiancé. She did the typical dorm-room sharing in college and once rented a room in the home of the mother of a friend. A cousin had a houseboat, and she stayed there for a while; when the cousin had a girlfriend over, Leanna had to leave for the night and typically ended up on someone's couch. One summer during her college years, she and about twenty other students took a month-long backpacking trip through the Sierras, carrying with them a manuscript version of a not-yet-published Carlos Castaneda book. Leanna has also lived in Mexico, Africa, New Guinea, Borneo, and India. When she was younger, she traveled through France, Spain, Italy, Germany, and Scandinavia, backpacking, staying in youth hostels, and sleeping on trains.

I try to maintain my quietly encouraging facial expression as I listen to Leanna's stories of her adventures in living arrangements, but inside,

I am just blown away. As she describes one experience after another that strikes me as uncomfortable, unfamiliar, and sometimes just plain scary, I kept thinking, *I could never do that!* Then Leanna reaches the part of her life story when she was thirty-seven and got a place of her own for the first time. She had friends in the building and a boyfriend nearby, but this was the situation that the intrepid Leanna just couldn't handle. "I would come home and cry. I was just so lonely."

Finding Community: Solo-Social Networks

People who live alone do not have that built-in plus-one that is often part of the job description of a spouse. Those who truly live alone—not alone within a deliberate community—also do not have the other built-in option of finding companionship next door. Yet one by one, they each find ways to foster just the amount of human connection that they desire—or they are working on it.

The revolution in communication technologies has redefined what it means to be in touch with other humans. We are all potentially connected. Distance is no obstacle, and neither is living on your own, even in a place that is not part of a deliberate community. Anyone can go to a computer or hold some other device, and email or text or phone or Skype or tweet or post to Facebook, anytime, anywhere. Contrary to the scare stories, our devices do not typically take the place of real social interactions—they add to them.[14]

But what about those face-to-face interactions? How do people who truly live alone, residentially, make them happen?

Maartje Duin: Attracted to Bustling City Life

Maartje Duin, a thirty-seven-year-old Dutch journalist and radio producer, is one of just a few people from other countries I talked to for this book. She lives in a suburb east of Amsterdam that is filled with families.

226

She finds it "a bit boring." True, "there's a nice pizza place nearby and there's one bar . . . but to me, as a single person, I really miss just going out and being in the middle of things." Maartje feeds on the energy of other people, and she makes sure to have enough time with other people to feel interpersonally fulfilled. "But I had to organize it myself . . . and that was a bit tiring." Eventually, she may move. In the meantime, she has found a creative solution—she got an office in the center of Amsterdam, with a café next door. Now, she says, "I go out; I have my own bookstore, and I have my own restaurant and bar; and I feel much more connected . . . There, I still feel part of a bustling city life."

Tom Giesler: Still Close to His Best Friend from Fourth Grade

Tom Giesler, forty-one, who is a case manager for patients awaiting transplants, lives in the suburbs, and he likes it there. He is still close to his best friend from fourth grade, and often gets together for dinner with him and his wife. The couple lives about fifteen miles away, but with Chicago's great public transportation, it seems closer. Distance just doesn't keep Tom from the people he cares about. His sister and her family live out in the country in the neighboring state of Indiana, about an hour and a half away. Tom sees them just about every month. His widowed dad is just ten minutes away; the two of them spend time together almost every weekend. Sometimes they read the paper and watch television; other times they go out to lunch.

Tom and his sister grew up in what Tom describes as a traditional family, in which social life was grounded in the family, church, and school. "Most socializing was just the four of us, or the church, or the people at work." Of trying to find more friends from outside of work, Tom says, "That's something I'm trying to work on." He's open to finding friendships in church groups and tried joining one of them. The members were friendly to him, but they all were already so close to one another that he never felt like he fully belonged. He'll probably try again with another church in the future.

Jane: Grandmother, Activist, Teacher, and Friend

It was the birth of her ten-year-old grandson that brought Jane, a sixty-nine-year-old retired professor of speech and language pathology, to the small North Carolina town where she now lives. The child is a steady part of her life, calling when he needs help with homework, sleeping over on the weekends (and sometimes one night during the week) in the attic-style loft that is just for him. For adult company, Jane has created what I think is one of the best solutions for people living alone who want to spend time with friends but don't want to have to figure things out from scratch all the time: she and a friend have a semiregular time marked on their calendars. That evening is saved for Netflix, popcorn, and wine. Book club meets regularly, too, though less often. There were as many as seventeen people in the group at one point, and Jane has become close to a half-dozen of them. The book club really is about the books; Jane's dinners out with friends are separate events.

Jane hates the phone, but she's fine with Skype. About once a month, she Skypes with a couple from Buffalo who have been her friends for decades. Many of Jane's other activities are also social ones. She takes pottery classes, does Medicare counseling, and teaches English as a second language. She's active politically. She seems to have traveled to just about every corner of the globe.

Sarah Stokes: Planning for the Best Possible Solo Life

Sarah Stokes, fifty-seven, didn't know anyone when she first moved to Santa Barbara, California. She had quit her corporate job in Northern California and was doing event marketing and management from home. Leaving her job was the most gratifying thing she had ever done in her life. But she missed the easy sociability of it—how grabbing dinner or a drink after work just happened naturally. She had anticipated the challenge of living on her own in a whole new place and had plans for dealing with it. She purposefully chose to live close enough to the downtown area to be able to walk there. She signed up for a gym. She joined two nonprofits and eventually ended up on the board of one and the steering committee of the other. She did the kinds of things she always wanted to do but had never gotten around to, like taking voice lessons.

Sarah soon had Santa Barbara friends. When new neighbors moved next door to her two-bedroom bungalow a year or so ago, she got to know them fairly well too. Sarah's sister and her family live in Los Angeles, about one hundred miles away; they visit each other fairly regularly and sometimes travel together. A few years after Sarah moved to Santa Barbara, one of her friends did too. That friend shares a place with another friend. When the two of them mention that they spontaneously decided to go to a movie or for a long bike ride, Sarah thinks that sounds pretty good and wouldn't mind being included the next time.

Sarah loves to cook and entertain, but she has had less time for those things since moving her recently widowed mother a few months ago into a place in Santa Barbara where she can receive the care that she needs. Sarah visits her often. She and her siblings did most of the research and decision making about the new living situation once their mother could no longer manage in the big, two-story dream house in the mountains near Yosemite—the house that she and her husband had built when they were in their fifties. Sarah will get back to having more time with her friends once her mother is more settled. For all of us, she notes, "priorities kick in differently" at different times.

In planning for how she will live in later life, Sarah will be as deliberate and as forward thinking as she was about moving to a place where she knew no one. She knows she wants to maintain her connections to other people who are important to her, and she wants to be the one who makes the decisions.

Lisa Cook: The Three Levels of Human Connection

After living in Ohio, Colorado, California, Maryland, Virginia, and Washington, DC, Lisa Cook, forty-nine, just wanted to find "home." She hadn't lived very long in Minneapolis, the place where she was born—she mostly grew up in DC—but she felt drawn to the Midwest. "My toy of choice [as a child] was never dolls, it was my farm-animal sets."

She had a fantasy of living on one of those ten thousand lakes that define the area and was delighted to land an apartment on the top floor of a building with a great lake view. The lake did not disappoint, but the social life did. Lisa's town was an out-of-the-way place, and her neighbors were mostly transient and not very friendly.

She thought she would feel more connected if she became a homeowner living among other homeowners. She took the big step of buying a place on her own in a townhouse complex about fifteen minutes from downtown Minneapolis, then she set out to build her circle of friends. She went to Meetups and organized social events for other transplants to the area. She joined the Single Volunteers of the Twin Cities and two Unitarian Church conversation circles. She invited professional colleagues and other women in her social network to her place once a month for coffee and conversation.

But those early efforts proved disappointing. Lisa wasn't looking for one-time meet-and-greets and acquaintances; she wanted substantial and reciprocal friendships. The women in her Coffee Talk group did show up every month, but the conversation never deepened; and none of the women ever initiated activities beyond the monthly gatherings or offered to host the event. "Being invited to someone's home," Lisa says, "I think there's just something magical about that."

Lisa believes that we all need three levels of human connection: an emergency contact (someone to call if you fall or need a ride home from the hospital), activity pals (people to do fun things with), and meaningful connections. Activity pals are the easiest to find; but if all you ever do is work out at the gym together, then you are probably not going to develop a close friendship. Meaningful connections are the most important—and also the most difficult to develop.

Lisa had made friends easily in the other places she lived, but this was different. She thought about returning to one of those places where she still had close friends. Instead, she doubled her efforts to create the connections she so craved. Lisa understood something that many other lonely people do not fully appreciate: many other people feel the same way. They, too, are looking for relationships with depth.

Her personal quest for meaningful connections became a mission. Lisa didn't just want that third level for herself; she wanted to learn as much as she could and then share those understandings with others.

One of the things she learned is that language and framing matter. She led a few conversations at a local library on social isolation, but who wants to admit they are isolated and lonely? She set out to create a website called Plan B Connections with the tagline, "Living Alone, Living Connected." She envisioned a site with resources and strategies for connecting, a blog, and a list of upcoming events. To learn how to develop it most effectively, she joined an "Evolve" class, in which she and other classmates were all working on a public-service project. They met every month for nearly a year, and Lisa hosts an annual reunion.

Lisa has taken her message of "living alone, living connected" on the road, including a TEDx Mahtmodi talk. She created a webinar on networking for introverts. She has also led workshops on that theme for job seekers, recognizing that the unemployed are looking for more than just jobs. Closer to home, she joined the board of her townhouse development and also set up an online neighborhood network using nextdoor.com.

She took a three-day class on hosting that wasn't about where to put the fork and the knife but how to ask thought-provoking questions. That has helped with the workshops she directs and the Connection through Conversation Meetup group she continues to host every month. Lisa finds it gratifying when the same people come month after month, and the conversations become personal and even profound. If those are the only times the participants are in touch, though, then the relationships have not met Lisa's criterion for real friendship—that only happens when people "make an effort to stay in touch 'just because.'"[15]

Lisa's Plan B Connections site has been live since 2010. At a minimum, it lets people struggling with loneliness know that "someone's trying to do something about it." Lisa is not a minimalist, though. She admits that her real goal is "a national movement where everyone has someone they can rely on."

In the meantime, Lisa is looking for the next big thing in her own life. She thinks that self-help books that tout the significance of family and super close friends are often useless when it comes to suggesting work-arounds—what you do when you don't have those kinds of people in your life. Lisa believes that the single people living the happiest and most fulfilling lives all have some passion they can pursue on their own. She's searching for hers.

The Seduction of Solitude

It is a significant issue—whether people who truly live alone, residentially, find and nurture the social convoys who will be with them as they navigate their lives. But in the time-together/time-alone equation that every human tries to solve, the time-alone factor is probably more significant for people who have made a positive choice to live alone than it is for any other category of people. In spirit, they are the descendants of Henry David Thoreau, who said, "I love to be alone. I never found the companion that was so companionable as solitude."[16]

Tom appreciates his own time in his own space for what it does for him psychologically, emotionally, and intellectually.

> Spending time with yourself—it's really peaceful. That's not to say I
> don't find other people enjoyable . . . But I find it a lot easier, once

I'm alone, to relax, recharge, and think a bit; re-energize, come up with ideas, recover from all the stresses of the day. I do that best alone. I like the majority of my time to be alone so I can do that.

"I love being by myself," Sarah tells me. "I like my privacy. I like control over my time. I love the aesthetics of where I live and my space and my personal space and my cat."

In *One Square Inch of Silence*, Gordon Hempton and John Grossman said:

Good things come from a quiet place. Study, prayer, music, transformation, worship, communion. The words *peace* and *quiet* are all but synonymous, often spoken in the same breath. A quiet place is the think tank of the soul—the spawning ground of truth and beauty.[17]

Many solo dwellers luxuriate in the quiet of their own space from the moment they awake. Jane describes her ritual: "I get up in the morning, I make my coffee, I go back to bed with my book and my cat."

Lisa Cook is often up by 5:00 AM: "I love writing in my journal in the morning or just looking out the window; and the light's starting to come to the sky; and I just stare at those trees . . . I just love that view."

My friend Bobbie, who now shares a beautiful home and lovely life with her husband, really misses the total quiet she enjoyed during those many years of living alone.

Research shows that when adults spend time alone, they are more often in their own homes than anywhere else. Ideally, though, they would rather be out in nature.[18] Sarah and Lisa like walking. Jane, Sarah, and Tom are drawn to gardening. Tom also spends time biking, hiking, and bird watching.

My academic colleagues have been slow to appreciate the profound rewards of spending time alone. When they hear "alone," their thoughts skip straight to "lonely," and then off they go, churning out thousands of studies about loneliness. When I last checked PsycINFO, the database of all psychology publications, there were more than seven thousand entries on loneliness. On the same day, the number of articles about solitude—which allows for the possibility of a positive experience—was more than seven hundred.

Among those have been a few beautifully crafted arguments. The back cover of Anthony Storr's 1988 book, *Solitude: A Return to Self*, poses this question: "In the supreme importance that we place on intimate relationships, have we overlooked the deep, sustaining power of solitude in human life?" Slowly, scholars are beginning to explain and explore that power.

Time alone, they have found, can be good for creativity, self-discovery, and self-enrichment. It can feel peaceful, relaxing, and freeing, fostering that daydreamy fantasy life that the overscheduled among us miss out on. When something shattering happens in our lives, and we need to rearrange the pieces of that mental picture that used to guide and sustain us, solitude can feel essential.[19]

Not everyone can use their time alone in such restorative and productive ways. Maybe it is a skill. Storr suggested as much when, after noting that our ability to form attachments "is considered evidence of emotional maturity," added: "Whether there may be other criteria of emotional maturity, like the capacity to be alone, is seldom taken into account."[20]

Dan, of the five-story building in the East Village, wants to talk about toilet seats. He tries to make the case that it is more polite to leave the seat up than to put it down. Susan, Bobbie, my sister, and I let ourselves be led down this conversational alley for a while but ultimately remain unconvinced. On the bigger point, though, Dan is totally persuasive: when you live by yourself, you rule. All of those decisions—about toilet seats, television shows, music, meals, money, bed times, bed making, and everything else—are all yours.

As Sarah of Santa Barbara notes:

> If I don't feel like doing the dishes, I don't have to do the dishes. And if they sit there for five days, so what. It's my house. And if I don't want anyone to see it, I don't invite anyone over.

Susan, who lived with her husband, an Italian chef, before they divorced, now lives alone and appreciates the option of coming home from work, putting on her pajamas, and guiltlessly eating popcorn for dinner. And my sister doesn't want anyone telling her whether Joey O can sleep in her bed at night.

On the internet, best-things-about-living-alone articles are rampant. I've skimmed many of them. A *Buzzfeed* version, "19 Reasons Living Alone Is the Best," with well over a half million views, is typical of the genre. It begins with "You can use the bathroom without closing the door"; proceeds through "You can do all the embarrassing and gross things you want without fear of judgment" and "No one is going to steal your goodies"; and then ends, predictably, with "You don't ever have to wear pants."[21]

I know these lists are meant to be light, breezy clickbait, but I'm repeatedly left with the impression that they are written by people who don't really love living alone. They have a defensiveness about them. It's not that the reasons mentioned aren't worth mentioning; it's just that they shouldn't be the only kinds of reasons that get touted. They are about the ways that solo dwellers escape interference and constraints.

The writers seem oblivious to the ways in which time alone enables the people who savor it to lead their best possible lives.

Listen to people who embrace the solo-living experience and you hear emotions and yearnings that are totally missing from the best-of lists. There's that sense of awe when, for the first time ever, they get a place of their own. There's a personal history of protecting their own space, even if they are also pursuing close relationships. Notice, too, what happens when they are deprived of a place of their own—they can't stop thinking about it. These are people for whom the choice of living alone is more than a preference; it's a need.

The first place that Tom had to himself had little to recommend it. It wasn't well maintained, and Tom would never want to live there again. But that very first taste of a place of his own—that was really something: "Having your own room, and even having your own bathroom . . . That was, like, incredible to me."

Looking back on her life, Jane can see that she has always had a hankering for her own time and space. She felt privacy-deprived when she was married; that was the loneliest time of her life. Back in high school, her boyfriends all had something in common: they lived in some other town. At this point, she told me, she "could probably have a wonderful relationship with a man—if we lived across the country from each other."

A participant in my online survey of lifespaces observed:

> I always felt happy living alone, but until I moved in with friends, I did not realize how important it was for me to live alone! I look forward to nothing as much as I look forward to snuggling up in my room, alone with a good book and my favorite music playing. And I have started daydreaming constantly about moving out and, once more, being on my own entirely.

In their interviews of 140 working-age (twenty-five to forty-four) Scottish adults living on their own, and in their review of the scholarly research on living alone, Lynn Jamieson and Roona Simpson were struck by the different meanings and experiences attached to solo living for different people. So much depends on factors such as health, wealth, personal preferences, interpersonal resources, ethnicity, sexuality, gender, geography (rural or urban or suburban; different parts of the world), culture, and biography (how you came to live alone). Overall, though, they found that most of the stereotypes of solo dwellers just aren't true. For example, most people who live alone are not isolated and lonely; they are not self-obsessed, hyperconsuming materialists; and most do not turn their homes into either pigsties or shrines to themselves.[22]

The people I interviewed who loved having their very own places—including those who were open to living with others in the future—created graceful homes that made them feel happy and others feel welcome. Tom's place is Spartan but comfortable, and filled with nods to the people and things important to him—his books, his bike, his cat, and pictures of his family and friends.

When Sarah was returning from the most recent of her international trips, an elderly woman sitting next to her was looking out the window as the plane began its descent. "Oh, I love coming back to Santa Barbara," she said. Sarah realized she felt the same way: "I can't think of anywhere I've lived that I've liked coming home to so much." About the place in the town she now calls her own, she adds, "I like the calmness of it . . . and it feels right." A survey respondent who lived alone said, "My home is my nest. I love coming home to a small, comfortable home with my dog."

I so appreciate the kinds of spaces other people can create, maybe because I have so little talent for that myself. Lisa's guest bath, for example, is filled with pretty photos, wall art, towels, and tiles that make the room visually interesting and inviting. Sarah has a fabulous sense of style; every room is a sensual treat. The colors (sometimes striking, sometimes mellow), the furniture that is both comfortable and elegant, the tasteful artwork, the beautiful built-in cabinets and bookshelves, and the fresh flowers in every room—all would make the editor of a shelter magazine smile.

Does Anyone Love Solitude More than Finns?

In the fall of 2013, I was invited to give a series of talks on single life and solo living at the Association for People Who Live Alone in the coastal town of Turku, Finland. In Finland, more than 40 percent of all households are one-person households, compared to 27 percent in the United States.[23]

What I had heard about the Finns before visiting was that they love their solitude. The forests along the shores of the Baltic Sea offer exquisite locations for rustic vacation cottages, and nearly one in ten Finns has one.[24] The American Trevor Corson, who wrote about the Finnish countryside for the *Atlantic*, reported that Finns "would happily spend weeks in the forest, never seeing a single neighbor." Among those who lived in the simplest cottages with no indoor plumbing, as well as those who enjoyed more sumptuousness, "the most desirable luxury was still the simple satisfaction of solitude." Rather than gathering for raucous cocktail hours, they soak up the warmth in their saunas, go for a long swim, or row out on the lake, on their own.[25]

I have just one day in Turku when I am not giving any talks, and I opt to spend it checking out four homes of people who live alone. Three are in downtown Turku and another is about ten minutes away. All are small, ranging from 335 to 651 square feet of interior space; all of the beds are twins. Yet none of the residents of those places complain. The spaces have their perks. My favorite is the sauna that Tomi Flemming, a thirty-seven-year-old technician and president of the Association for People Who Live Alone, has in his bathroom. Tomi also has a balcony, as does Lars, a retired military man. In Tomi's, the plants and magazines give the

space a homey feel. Lars outfitted his with a small chest of draw
a hook for some coats, in addition to a few sled-styled chairs. Ne
the men plan to spend all of their time at home. Tomi tells me th
thing Dan Scheffey did: the city is his living room. Lars points
camper sitting near the entrance to his apartment building—he
often. His next trip will be to Estonia.

At her downtown apartment, Sanna, a health professional, ser
bowls of reindeer cheese soup in her open and airy living room. Th
streams through the green and yellow leaves of the trees out bac
then through a wall of windows, creating playful patterns of light c
hardwood floors; on the rows of prints on the walls; and on the n
colors of the couches, chairs, and drapes. I could have sat there for a
long time.

Marja Lumio, an elegant mother of a grown daughter, has a pla
her own in the countryside along with her stylish downtown apartn
Many single people in Finland cannot afford one of those coveted cat
but they, like everyone else, can roam freely around the lakes and wo
Sanna goes for long walks with her husky nearly every day on what
calls "my island." By some counts, the Turku Archipelago includes m
than twenty thousand islands, so individual Finns really can spend v
amounts of time on islands with no one else around.[26]

Is Living Alone Different for Men than for Women?

Writings about single life—both popular and academic—tend to focu
overwhelmingly on women. Because marriage, traditionally, is sup
posed to be more important to women than to men—in theory, mor
central to their identities and their happiness—single life should b
especially problematic for women. Research begs to disagree about th
happiness presumption, but no matter.[27] Angst-filled writings abou
women living single continue to proliferate.

Fortunately, alongside the tired old tales of those "poor" single women is a counter-narrative. It is one of strength, fulfillment, and independence. That story is often told of single women who live alone.

By living alone instead of with a husband and children, women are liberated from traditional roles and expectations. They are no longer the short-order cook, the cleaner-upper, and the laundress for a house full of family. They are freed of the emotional work of shoring up egos and soothing bruised feelings. They don't have to account to someone else for the money they spend. They also learn how to do the kinds of things that husbands traditionally did—or they find someone else to hire or to help.

What is less often noticed is what men get out of living alone. Researchers Jamieson and Simpson have noticed, though. They point out that as more and more men (and women) live alone in their early adult years, they are learning all sorts of skills that used to be the bailiwick of the other gender. In married life, for example, women were traditionally the kinkeepers and the social schedulers. They kept in touch with family, kept up with friends, arranged social gatherings, and covered all of the other social and emotional tasks of the couple.

In their interviews with people living alone and in their review of the relevant writings, the authors found, as did I, that most men living alone today have good social skills. Tom Giesler, who is still close to a friend from fourth grade, and who has an easy relationship with his sister and his dad, is an exemplary twenty-first-century solo dweller. Dan Scheffey—who took the initiative to rescue a troubled relationship from years past, and who told a roomful of traditional and chosen family members how much they meant to him—has extraordinary social skills and sensibilities. Neither needs a wife to have a soul-soothing social life or meaningful human connections.

That is important in and of itself. But it is also significant for what it suggests about the future. Right now, if you study people who live alone, as people such as Jamieson and Simpson and Klinenberg have done, what you typically find is that most solo dwellers are doing fine. There is

an exception, though. When there are people who conform to the stereotype of the sad, lonely, and isolated person living alone, those people are
disproportionately older men—particularly those who are unemployed
or in poor health. Maybe today's young and middle-aged men, when
they get older, will do a lot better if they live alone. They will already
know how to have a good life while going solo.

Twenty-First-Century Individualism: Opportunity or Threat?

In twenty-first-century America, individuals are freer than they have
ever been before. They are no longer tied to predetermined life courses
in which marrying, having kids, and staying married are obligatory.

They can, if they wish, cycle in and out of different dwellings, towns,
jobs, and relationships. As sociologist Ulrich Beck put it:

> Marriage can be subtracted from sexuality, and that, in turn, from
> parenthood; parenthood can be multiplied by divorce; and the
> whole thing can be divided by living together or apart, and raised
> to a higher power by the possibility of multiple residences and the
> ever-present potentiality of taking back decisions.[28]

Individuals—not couples or families, or other social groups—are
now the fundamental units of society. It is not that building blocks such
as couples or families are not still significant. They are. Married couples,
for example, can raise children together, and they can take advantage of
all of the deals that are cheaper by the couple—the government policies
that benefit only them and not people who are single.[29] They can talk as
if they are a single entity ("we really like modern art"), and other people
can smoosh together their two names as if they are one (DickAndJane).

And yet, today's married couples are not as enmeshed as they once
were. A study of couples in 2000 and twenty years earlier showed that

the spouses in 2000 were less likely to have their main meal together, work around the house together, go out for fun together, or have as many shared friends as did the couples from 1980.[30]

Contemporary couples often have their own mobile phones, not (just) one shared landline. They have their own laptops, their own online bookmarks tagging their own favorite sites and movies and books and blogs. Marketers know their separate preferences. Ask each person in a couple to name all of the people in his or her life—including the important ones and the not-as-important ones—and the two sets may well overlap significantly, but each person is at the center of his or her own unique social network. This networked individualism is the new social operating system in societies around the world.[31]

Single people who live alone, if they have adequate resources, have even more options for designing the lives they want to live. They can pursue their careers and their passions. They can avail themselves of copious amounts of contemplative solitude. They can create homes that reflect their values and their tastes. They can reimagine love and other relationships in the biggest, broadest senses of the words. Friends and nieces, for instance, rather than a spouse and offspring, can be the people who mean the world to them. They can set the priorities for their lives and then live by them.

In the United States, and in many other nations, individualistic values have triumphed. We value self-expression, self-development, autonomy, privacy, individuality, and perhaps most important of all, choice. In a bravura analysis of more than a million books published over two centuries, UCLA scholar Patricia Greenfield found that instances of the word *choose* climbed over time while uses of the word *obliged* declined. Between 1800 and 2000, the words *individual, self,* and *unique* showed up increasingly more often whereas the words *authority, obedience,* or *belonging* became less commonplace.[32]

The rise of individualism has, for many, been exhilarating. People who never did feel comfortable with marrying or parenting, or living in the suburbs, or handing over their lifelong loyalty to a single employer, for instance, are liberated from soul-crushing strictures and expectations. People who once believed that no one in the world shared their quirks or maladies discover others like them everywhere, and can share their lives online and off. Individuals of all stripes can design their own days, filling them with the people and places and spaces and pursuits that they find most engaging, most authentic, and most meaningful.

For others, though, the new developments are ominous and even terrifying. People who prefer certainty, predictability, and commitments that are bolted in place by powerful institutions and revered traditions feel insecure and adrift in the brave new world of individualism. Skeptics assessing the state of modern life fret that people are using their new-found freedoms to become self-obsessed and self-indulgent, flitting from one relationship, pursuit, or place to another, abdicating their responsibilities to their relatives and their communities, and threatening the very foundations of civic and family life. Sociologist Zygmunt Bauman coined the term *liquid love* to describe the fragility of contemporary human bonds and the never-ending efforts we marshal in our fraught and futile attempts to create some permanence.[33]

Contemporary anxieties about our weakening ties and compromised values have many precedents. Each new wave of large-scale social change, such as the rise of urbanization or the introduction of new technologies such as cars, telephones, televisions, and computers, stokes our fears and unleashes a tsunami of scolding screeds.[34]

What I wanted to know when I started this project was what people were doing with the cornucopia of choices and possibilities that define modern life. What I found was that people who could have chosen to live in all sorts of ways sometimes chose family. They created households with two or three or even four generations. Or they returned to their home-towns—or never left. Or they raised children on their own but named twelve godparents; or combined households with other solo parents and their children. Or they created new versions of old-fashioned villages, knocking down fences that once separated their yards; or gathering in cul-de-sacs or pocket communities, or founding cohousing communities.

The ever-single and the single-again-after-divorce-or-widowhood looked around at the other single people and formed a household of friends who all lived under the same roof. Sometimes couples or families joined in too; or they opened their homes to the people who touched their hearts—people might have been kids who had aged out of foster care or fellow immigrants.

The apotheosis of the modern individualistic society is the single person with no kids truly living alone, residentially. Untethered to a spouse or kids or even a roommate, and free to flee to beckoning opportunities on shinier shores, these people should be most likely to confirm the worst fears of the purveyors of doom.

I met people in that demographic. (I'm one of them myself.) I saw them creating comfortable homes where they settled in for the long haul, savoring long stretches of productive or relaxing solitude, welcoming visits from family and friends, looking after aging friends and relatives who needed help, and hosting salons in their living rooms. I learned about their regular get-togethers with their parents, siblings, and friends; their service on boards and their involvement in civic organizations; and their trips that ended with the loving anticipation of being back home again.

In the stories we tell each other about the workings of society, it is the married people and the traditional families who are holding us all together. Single people—especially those who live alone—are the isolates, holed up in their apartments, lonely and friendless. Yet when social scientists do systematic research, they find something quite different: singles look more like Dan Scheffey than the caricatures. Results of several studies—some of them based on representative national surveys—show that it is the single people, and not the married ones, who are creating and sustaining the ties that bind us.[35] Single people are more likely than married people to do what it takes to keep grown siblings together. They also spend more time helping, encouraging, and socializing with neighbors and friends. Singles are more likely to live with relatives than married people are, and they do more than their share of caring for aging relatives and others in need. Asked the question "Do you currently or have you ever regularly looked after someone, for at least three months, who is sick, disabled, or elderly?," it was the single people, more often than the married, who said yes.[36] Single people also visit their parents more and exchange help with them more, even when their parents are still relatively young and healthy.

You can see the dynamic unfolding if you follow people over the course of their adult lives. In the best example so far, a pair of researchers enlisted a nationally representative sample of more than twenty-seven hundred Americans to tell them about their lives over the course of six years.[37] All were single and under fifty, and not cohabiting when the study started. Most were in fairly regular contact with family and friends. For those who married, though, things changed. As married people, they had less contact with their parents and spent less time with their friends than when they were single. It wasn't just a honeymoon effect: three years after their weddings, they were still less connected to family and friends; and by the end of the study, they still had not resumed the relationships they had had before.

Children cannot explain the difference. The finding that single people—especially those who have always been single—are more connected to family and friends than married people holds up for people who have children and people who don't. It is true for men and women, whites and nonwhites, poor people and rich people.[38]

Compared with people who live with others, single people and solo dwellers are also more engaged in the life of the cities and towns where they live. They take more music and art classes, participate in more public events and civic groups, go out to dinner more often, and pursue more informal social activities.[39]

I was impressed by the solo dwellers I interviewed, but not everyone's personal story is an inspiring one. There are miserable and lonely and narcissistic people who live alone just as there are miserable and lonely and narcissistic people who live with spouses, kids, and other relatives or friends. Even people who feel totally contented and connected—who happily take advantage of constant-access opportunities of the internet, social media, and mobile devices—acknowledge that they face challenges. A bigger and more diverse social network is the twenty-first-century interpersonal prize; the time and talents it takes to juggle all the threads are some of the costs.[40]

The trade-off between the security of a set path through life with a small, dense set of enduring relationships and the freedom of an ever-growing cache of opportunities is one for the ages. It is not a unique dilemma of modern life. What is often lost in the debates is that opportunities are not obligations. I met people, young and old, without televisions or Facebook accounts. And just because you can live alone, far away from the place where you were born, does not mean that you can no longer choose to live with family and across the street from lifelong friends in the town where you grew up.

Finding Your Lifespace: How Do You Know What's Right for You?

I like to ask the people I interview what they think it takes to live the way they do. Jane says, "I think it would be very hard to be satisfied living alone unless you found yourself interesting." To Sarah, living alone and loving it is for people with a sense of adventure. To live alone and be happy, she thinks, you need "a certain self-confidence and sense of self . . . If you don't have that, I think living alone is really difficult. Because everything is done out of fear versus a kind of wonderment or excitement."

So, how do you know what's right for you? Think about each of the different ways you've lived and how you might answer some of my favorite questions that I put to the people I interviewed:

♠ Did you get the amount of privacy and alone time that you
  wanted?
♠ What about time spent with other people: was it about what you
  wanted, or were you wishing for more or less of it?
♠ What was the best experience you had while living that way?
  Any experiences that made you wish you were living some other
  way?
♠ When you had been away for a while, how did it feel to come
  back?

Now, consider all of your lifespaces at once and answer these
questions:

♠ Of all the different ways you have lived, what felt like the best fit
  for you?
♠ What was the happiest time in your life?
♠ How would you live if you could magically live any way at all?
  Pretend money is no object, and neither is anything else.

I hope that the many different stories you have encountered in this
book have suggested that the universe of potential lifespaces is bigger
than you realized; and that even if money is an obstacle in your life and
not the only one, there are still opportunities to find the place, the space,
and the people that make your life the best it can be. Maybe you'll even
become one of the next lifespace pioneers, coming up with something
so creative that even today's dreamy innovators could never have imagined it.

REVOLUTIONS IN LIVING, NOW AND IN THE FUTURE

Across America, and around the world, in cities and suburbs and small towns, the people have started a revolution in the ways we live now. The revolutionaries respect no political boundaries; they are not about to be relegated to any particular demographic boxes. They are young and old, rich and poor, married and single, parents and people who are not parents, religious and agnostic, all races and ethnicities, and just about every other category in and around—and beyond—these.

It is, in a way, a grassroots movement, except that most of the people who are living in the innovative ways that are changing the face of the nation do not see themselves as agents of change or as part of something bigger than themselves; they are just people navigating their lives. They are people who came to a place of great pain and worked their way through it by doing something that they never thought they would—and no one else did either. They are people who always dreamed of living in a particular way, in some far-off gauzy future, and then one day, decided to stop fantasizing and start living the dream. They are people who dared to become the future by living in ways that seem startling even to a nation high on creativity. And they are people whose acts of bravery were to embrace old-fashioned lifespaces fully, joyfully, and unapologetically.

How Are These Changes Revolutionary?

The pioneers of twenty-first-century lifespaces have earned their revolutionary status by unbundling the components of our relationships and our lives that were once so tightly packaged that no one had ever fathomed that they could be pulled apart. Others repackaged the pieces of our lives in equally unimaginable ways.

The pioneers looked up at the pedestals where married heterosexual couples and their children reigned and let them stay there. But not by themselves. They had to move over and make room for new kinds of couples and families, and for individuals with their networks of friends and family and neighbors and mentors.

At a time of stunning economic inequality, the lifespace pioneers showed us how equality could be the new model for how to live our interpersonal lives. The norms they lived by looked more like the norms of friendship than of the sex-role complementarity of traditional marriages or the hierarchical structures of traditional families. Even within marriages and families, friendship sensibilities often dominate.

While reaching out to more people and to more diverse people than ever before, the lifespace pioneers also staked unprecedented claims to their own spaces. They wanted solitude and privacy in addition to their meaningful connections.

People living in new ways and embracing the old have offered meanings of home that are expansive and personal and touching. Some ground their identities in the meanings they ascribe to *home*—identities that can be clear, singular, and strong or strikingly multidimensional. Lifespace pioneers have shown us that even those people most often mischaracterized as adrift in the world—single people, with no kids, living truly alone, residentially—can create warm and comfortable places they call home.

The Many Meanings of Home

Home has never meant just one thing. Scholars from a variety of disciplines have tried to figure it out, and have found that home can be a place, a space, a feeling, a set of practices, or "an active state of being in the world." The concept has been related to "house, family, haven, self, gender, and journeying."[1] Yet in the Western world, among traditionalists, the link to family became particularly resonant: "Without the family, a home is 'only a house'," they thought. The "family" they have in mind is most often "the white, middle-class, heterosexual nuclear family."[2]

My interviewees didn't get the memo. Very few of them were members of white, middle-class, heterosexual nuclear families. Some live totally alone, residentially—no spouse, no kids, and no one else either. If a home without a family is "only a house," they should feel bereft about their dwellings—or at best, indifferent.[3]

Sarah, who was married before but now lives on her own in her bungalow in Santa Barbara, California, says, "I can't think of anywhere I've lived that I've liked coming home to so much . . . It feels right."

The apartment where Tom lives alone in a suburb of Chicago "feels like home. It's comfortable, it's predictable, it's a place you know."

Maria, the woman who has opened her home to twenty-one people over the years—many of whom were total strangers before she welcomed them into her life—notes:

> At night, whenever I pull in the driveway, I just like think, *Oh, man. I get to go in there.* I think about it sometimes during the day. People who come here will say the same thing: "Man, we love your house." There's something about being here.

For Jane, who lives alone in North Carolina, love was not enough. When she lived in the Northeast, she said, "I loved my job. I loved my friends. I loved my house. But I knew I wasn't going to stay here. Whereas it feels like I could stay here [in North Carolina] forever."

Home, to many of the people I interviewed, is a good, comfortable feeling about the place where they live, and a sense that their place is going to be theirs for a while. Lisa Cook, who lives alone in Minnesota, says, "Home means the place where the plane lands [and] you're saying to yourself, 'Okay I'm home,' and you're not questioning like, 'why do I live here still'?" She adds, "I have made so many moves trying to find this concept of home and trying to grow my roots that this is more than a house to me… I think this is just a really important part of who I am right now. And this identity of being on the board [of her townhouse association] and being a community builder and everything, I don't think that I would want to give that up."

Maartje, the Dutch journalist who lives on her own in Amsterdam, admits that she was once a bit too enthralled with social media: "At a certain point, I spent so much time on Facebook that the virtual space seemed more important to me than the physical space." That's changing now, and she's thinking more deeply about how to make her house a home. One model is her parents', "where they have people over, and then they have this coffee table with conversation pieces, books . . . It's a place to show others."

People such as Rebecca Lewis (who lives in a four-generational household) and Maria Hall find it heartwarming when other people admire their homes and enjoy visiting them, but I got little sense from anyone that the display aspects of their places are the most significant. Instead, their homes help them live their best and fullest and most authentic lives. Len, Lauren, and Sally's multigenerational home reflects the music, the reading, and the contemplation that they all so enjoy. Anja's spirituality and artistic sensibilities suffuse her home (the duplex she shared with Tricia) inside and out. In her home, Maria created special spaces for each of the important parts of herself and for the people who live with her. They include the woman cave, the Jimmy Carter room, the busy kitchen and dining rooms, the music and performance room, the elegant sitting room, the nice guest room, and her own cloud-themed bedroom.

Andrew's contemplation on the meaning of home best fits the multiplicity of places, spaces, relationships, and experiences that fill our twenty-first-century lives. Andrew lives apart from his long-term partner, Brian. Home, he says, as we talk in his bright, open, airy room overlooking an abundance of trees, is the place where we are sitting. It is also his place in Florida that warms him for a spell during the brutal Minnesota winters. To Andrew, being with friends feels like home. So does being alone. Home is any place, any experience that feeds his soul "in some positive way."

The Friendship Model of Twenty-First-Century Relationships

An ideology of marriage and coupling that is celebrated in popular culture is intensive coupling. Couples who invest in it really do see each other as The One.

> [They] look to each other for companionship, intimacy, caring, friendship, advice, the sharing of the tasks and finances of household and family, and just about everything else. They are the repositories for each other's hopes and dreams. They are each other's soulmates and sole mates.[4]

A friendship model is about the ones instead of The One. A friendship relationship is usually specialized rather than comprehensive. We can have friends who are great for socializing, others who feed our passions, some who are always there in a pinch, and a few who always know what to say and how to listen. Ideally, friends are not envious of the other friends in our lives; they know that friendship is not supposed to be possessive.

As young adults step into their first marriages at older and older ages (or not at all), as the rate of divorce remains high, and as women continue to outlive men, more and more Americans are finding that they cannot draw a spouse in the center of their social circles—they don't have one. As more and more individuals live their entire adult lives without ever raising kids, they are finding other people to be there for them in later life—and earlier in their life too. As family size continues to dwindle, individuals are growing up with fewer siblings—if any. That, too, changes the potential look of the social convoys that accompany contemporary Americans over the course of their lives.

With little cultural celebration or even recognition, friendships have emerged as the essential twenty-first-century relationship. They are—as Liz Spencer and Ray Pahl said in the subtitle of their book, *Rethinking Friendship*—our *Hidden Solidarities Today*.[5] National surveys of Americans ranging in age from twenty-five to seventy-four have shown that adults have an average of ten people they see or talk to at least once a week, and a few more online-only friends.[6]

The values exemplified by friendship also grew ascendant, as they are the values of modern life. As essayist William Deresiewicz noted:

Modernity believes in *equality*, and friendships, unlike traditional relationships, are egalitarian. Modernity believes in *individualism*. Friendships serve no public purpose and exist independent of all other bonds. Modernity believes in *choice*. Friendships, unlike blood ties, are elective; indeed, the rise of friendship coincided with the shift away from arranged marriage. Modernity believes in *self-expression*. Friends, because we choose them, give us back an image of ourselves. Modernity believes in *freedom*. Even modern marriage entails contractual obligations, but friendship involves no fixed commitments. The modern temper runs toward unrestricted *fluidity* and *flexibility*, the endless play of *possibility*, and so is perfectly suited to the informal, improvisational nature of friendship. We can be friends with whomever we want, however we want, for as long as we want.[7] [Emphasis is mine.]

We do not have quite as much free choice in friendship as Deresiewicz suggested. We cannot select friends the way we choose T-shirts—the people we want as friends have to want us back (even on Facebook). He was right, though, that friends become a part of our lives in ways that are different than for biological or adoptive family members, or the in-laws who get added to our networks not because we invited them directly but as familial plus-ones. Friends like each other; they want to hear from each other and see each other just because the mere presence of friends is so pleasurable. It is that fondness that is the beating heart of friendship.

When today's generation of lifespace innovators decide to share a house, they choose their housemates not just on the basis of who can pay the bills or who they feel obligated to include. They are looking for people who are, or who have the potential to be, friends. So it is, too, for those who want to live in places of their own within real communities. It is not enough that their fellow community members share their vision of the good life; they also want to like the people they hope to see around all the time.

Much has been said about the role of economic woes in pushing many young adults back into the homes of their parents, and appropriately so. But the most underappreciated factor in the viability of that way of living is that young adults and their parents have more in common and just plain like each other more than the generations before them did. When today's children grow up, they and their parents often choose each other as friends.[8]

Friendship is ideological. It is, at its core, a relationship built on fairness and equality, rather than hierarchy or dependency or obligation or tradition. The generations who live together as grown-ups do not so much look up or down at each other as they look across and see someone more like an equal. In marriages, too, friendship norms have become increasingly powerful, as partners prefer to see each other as, well, *partners*, and not as the one who does the guy stuff and the other who does the gal stuff.

People living in innovative ways today often try to build equality into their lifespaces, and they report that their arrangements work best when such norms prevail. Cohousers make consensus the basis of their decision making. In the Villages that help seniors stay in their own homes, the seniors are the ones receiving the help, and yet, they sometimes step forward to give help too. Carmel Sullivan has found that CoAbode works better when the single moms find a house together than when one moves into the other one's place. In her sharing experiences and those of others, she found that mothers feel good about leaving their kids with the other mother while they run errands or take a class, because they take their turns watching the other mom's kids. Lucy Whitworth's one misgiving about the community she created is that as the property owner, everyone pays rent to her. In her ideal lifespace, everyone would have been there at the outset, financial resources in hand, to select and renovate and pay for the dwellings and the land.

There is strength in having a network of friends, and that power is multiplied by modern communication technologies. As cohousers told me, when they need something, all they need to do is send an email or a text, and soon, a friendly response (or two or three) will be sitting in their inbox. Requests can be for just about anything, from a lime to a ride to the store, to a hand in fixing a leak. When needs are more serious or more sustained, friendship circles can be invaluable. That's what Diane Dew discovered when she had two broken arms, and what Lucy Whitworth experienced when her forty-nine angels organized to help her through her recovery from cancer. Brigades of friends are godsends to the helpers as well as the person needing the help. When there are lots of helping hands, individual helpers can contribute what they are comfortable giving, when they are free to give it. No one is saddled with the role of the sole caregiver for long periods of time; and the accompanying psychological and physical costs so often suffered even by those whose caring comes from a place of profound love.

Mindful Living

There is no script for parenting a child with another adult who is not your romantic partner and never has been. There is no script for single parents and their kids who want to share a home with others in the same situation. There have been groups of unrelated adults living under the same roof for a very long time, but not with the same aspirations for making a home and sharing a life that people like Marianne Kilkenny cherish.

Lifespace pioneers have dealt with the challenge of scriptlessness by writing their own scripts. The arrangements of their lives are the prized products of much thoughtfulness and deliberation. They are living their lives mindfully. Adults who come together only as parents (and not romantic partners) discuss more different topics more deeply than most conventional couples ever do. Single mothers who sign up for CoAbode fill out lengthy questionnaires. Paul and the others in Marice's home are talking through their understandings of how they will live together; their house rules are a work in progress. When Diane Dew sought to become a member of the Mariposa Grove cohousing community, she answered twelve pages of questions. Many cohousing communities ask prospective members to spend a substantial amount of time in the community first, so the new people and the old can feel confident about the fit.

Little by little, the wisdom of the lifespace pioneers is becoming systematized and shared. Those who have mindfully shared a home, or have deliberately lived apart from the romantic partner they love, or have created contemporary versions of multigenerational living, or have spearheaded ways of living the new old age, are writing books about their experiences, which sometimes include tips and quiz questions and worksheets.[9] Conferences on cohousing and other intentional communities include panels and workshops on consensus decision-making and other aspects of community life. Websites such as Cohousing.org (the Cohousing Association of the United States), IC.org (the Fellowship for Intentional Community), NationalSharedHousing.org (for people wishing to share a home and a life), CoAbode.com (for single-parent families who want to live with other single-parent families), and Family ByDesign.com (for parenting partnerships) all include generous sections of resources, often with thoughtful discussions. Future generations will be able to continue to live mindfully in a variety of lifespaces, while benefitting from the wisdom of their predecessors.

Seeking Solitude and Privacy in an Age of Exposure and Sharing

The rise of people living alone is the most obvious demonstration of the growing allure of having time and space to yourself. Psychologically, a craving for some solitude and privacy—for control over access to your place and your space—may develop early in children who grow up with rooms of their own. In *Going Solo*, Klinenberg reported that university administrators have been inundated with student requests for private rooms.[10] When new dorms are built, single rooms or private rooms arranged around a living room often replace the shared rooms of the past. So compelling is a place of your own that some couples have insisted on living apart even while staying committed to their relationship for the long haul.

The renewed interest in multigenerational and extended-family living, in sharing a house with people who are not family, and in living within a deliberate community all seem to suggest an embrace of time together over time alone. Yet even within these arrangements, everyday life is not all about togetherness. Julie Phelps first started thinking longingly about multigenerational living on those days when she used to wander through

Chinatown in San Francisco, where she saw many Asian families who "shopped together, spent leisure time together, and shared homes." Now she lives contentedly in Massachusetts with her son, daughter-in-law, and grandson but is happy that her bedroom is on the opposite end of the floor from the younger generations. In fact, if she had all the money in the world, she would still live with them—but in her own wing of the house, with a kitchenette and sitting room and its own entrance. Brianna, from the four-generational Lewis household, seems less interested in time to herself than anyone I interviewed, yet she, like every other adult who was not married, has a room of her own and likes it that way. Marianne Kilkenny told the *New York Times*, "I am no longer fiercely independent. I now can be interdependent, and this is by choice."[11] But she, too, has a suite of her own, and thinks it's important to be able to close the door and know that no one will walk in without knocking.

A room of your own is not always enough, though. Lauren, who finds her multigenerational household so very satisfying, makes time for herself every day by taking a walk or a long, leisurely bath. Maria Hall, the woman who, over the years, has welcomed nearly two dozen people to share her home, still has that shed out back that has been her haven for decades. Before that, she had the "Prayer Room" that was her special secluded spot near a river.

In cohousing communities, pocket neighborhoods, and other deliberate communities, interpersonal connections are paramount but homes are private. Spatial design sometimes adds an extra layer of protection from surveillance—like when the backs of homes look out at open spaces, with no other homes in sight.

Even the most communal of living arrangements—actual communes—have made concessions to contemporary longings for a room of one's own. For instance, at Twin Oaks, initially inspired by B. F. Skinner's *Walden Two* and one of the most enduring of the communes from the '60s and '70s, the group houses include private rooms for the residents.[12] All sorts of living arrangements are growing in popularity, but I can't find any indications that old-style communes, in which people share just about everything, are making a comeback.

Into the Future

Social change sometimes begins with the personal experiences of just one or two individuals. In 1999, for example, Carmel Sullivan was raising a son on her own. She thought she might like to live with another single mother and her kids. So she posted a notice with a local rental service and immediately got eighteen responses. Fourteen years later, the CoAbode website she created to help other pairs of single mothers find each other and make plans to live together had profiles from seventy thousand women from all over North America.

In 1980, Durrett and McCamant were in Denmark to study architecture, but the most powerful lesson they learned came not from any class but from a neighborhood Durrett passed every day on his way to the train station. The people there seemed to have their own little village, where they were always chatting with each other in the spaces in between their homes. Years later, the twosome would bring the concept of cohousing to the United States and start their own architectural firm, the Cohousing Company. By 2014, there were more than one hundred completed cohousing communities and another hundred-plus in some stage of development in thirty-six states.

In the mid-'70s, Jim Greenup's grandmother and his widowed mother each moved into one of the units of an attached duplex. When his grandmother died, his uncle moved into her space. His relatives were improvising—the duplex was not suited for seniors with mobility issues. Now Jim is a developer and offers single-story houses with "accessory dwelling units" (mother-in-law apartments), as well as houses with two master bedrooms and two master baths—all with the kinds of design features that make senior living comfortable and convenient.[13]

Twenty-first-century builders across the country, with or without their own personal stories, are looking at the decades of demographic rumblings and realizing that not everyone is going to want a big, nuclear family house in the suburbs. They watch homeowners convert their sunrooms and garages into spaces for their young-adult children or aging parents and understand that there is a market for dwellings designed to be adaptable to changing households. So they are building them. They are finding buyers who want two complete master suites—with bathrooms and maybe even a kitchen. A few even want more than two. Valerie Grant wants one master bedroom suite for her mother, one for her young daughter, one for herself, and a fourth for guests.[14] Occasionally, married couples will fess up about their actual plans for dual suites—they each want a bedroom of their own.

Developers are also hearing about people's wishes for privacy; and so they locate suites on different floors or opposite ends of hallways. Sometimes the suites face different streets and have separate entrances.

The increasing desire of adults of all ages to have places of their own (and not just private suites) has also registered. Professionals in architecture and design are working on making more creative use of small spaces. Cities are experimenting with tiny apodments; and microhouses are popping up in small lots and in backyards. These small spaces are built to be adaptable to needs that change not over a lifetime but throughout the course of a season or even a day.

For innovations to work, laws and policies will need to be reimagined. Zoning laws enacted specifically to discourage the additions of mother-in-law apartments and the conversions of garages need to be rewritten to reflect the new American lifespaces. Policies built on narrow views of what counts as family need to be challenged. We all need to transcend our familiar ways of thinking about how to live, recognizing, for instance, that four sixtysomething women sharing a house do not constitute a there-goes-the-neighborhood threat!

As I write this, new Census Bureau figures are showing a slowing of the rate at which new multigenerational households are forming.[15] The *New York Times* writer Paula Span suggested that the increase in such living arrangements, especially during the recession, was just a "trendlet" and could continue to ebb as economic woes recede even further into the past. "What's afoot here, to a large extent, is economic necessity, not personal choice."[16]

She's probably right that those whose primary motivation for doubling up was financial will beat a path to other ways of living. Along the way, though, something more significant just may happen: some who thought they were living with family because that's what they could afford will discover that they actually *like* it. They, together with those who knew all along that they wanted to live with other generations, will become examples for others. Then, multigenerational living will become not (just) a fall-back but an opportunity; not just an old-fashioned household but a new way of thinking about how to live now.

And so it is with other twenty-first-century lifespaces, such as dual-dwelling duos, or single mothers and their kids teaming up through CoAbode, or single people coming together to be parents but not a couple. Whether those arrangements increase in numbers is less meaningful than what they contribute to our collective imaginings of how to live now and in the future.

More than ever before, Americans can pursue the ways of living that work best for them. There is no one blueprint for the good life; we can create our own lifespaces. What matters is not what everyone else is doing or what other people think we should be doing, but whether we can find the places, the spaces, and the people that fit who we really are and allow us to live our best lives.

ACKNOWLEDGMENTS

First of all, thanks to all of the people who let me into their homes and their lives. That was such a gracious and generous thing to do, and I deeply appreciate it. Those who agreed to be thanked by their full name: Lisa Cook, Lisa DePaulo, Diane Dew, Maartje Duin, Lynne Elizabeth, Tomi Flemming, Tom Giesler, Paul Godbout, Julie Guenther, Dorothy M. Hackett, Lucy Hale, Pryor Hale, Maria Hall, Karen Hester, Arlia S. Hoffman, Tricia Hoffman, Susan Hurt, Robert A. Jones, Gary Kelsey, Marianne Kilkenny, Vicki Larson, Therese Lee, Brianna Lewis, Rebecca "Mimi" Lewis, Marja Lumio, Nan Lund, April McCaffery, Diana Moghrabi, Kristin Noreen, Lars Rantanen, Dan Scheffey, Joan M. Shelly, Darren Spedale, Bobbie Spellman, Sarah Stokes, Carmel Sullivan, Marinus Van de Kamp, Lucy Whitworth, Leanna Wolfe, Betsy Woodard, and Anja Woltman. A few more wanted to be identified by first name only: Danica, David, Lindsay, and Marice. Thanks, too, to all the people who did not want to be named at all.

More than four hundred people described their lifespaces in my online survey. I learned a lot from them and I thank them for that.

The people I interviewed all got to see the first draft of what I wrote about them, and I thank them for taking a look and giving me feedback. I am so sorry that much of what was in those first drafts got cut, and I am even more sorry that some of the stories did not make it into the final version of the book. I hope I will still get a chance to publish the more complete stories as well as the missing stories in other places, either on my blogs or elsewhere. If that happens, I'll mention it on my website, BellaDePaulo.com.

Also left on the cutting-room floor were accounts of other innovative lifespaces. They included, for example, an inspired lifespace for the homeless—Community First Village—in Austin, Texas; a remarkable community in Greenbelt, Maryland, that was birthed at the time of so many of Franklin D. Roosevelt's other ambitious projects to move the nation beyond the Great Depression, and which still lives on, more than seventy-five years later; the architectural and interpersonal achievement that is Victoria Garden Mews, a place for family and friends, and all the ponds and gardens and pathways in downtown Santa Barbara; also in Santa Barbara, the new Alma del Pueblo (Soul of the City) Spanish-styled residences, built in the spirit of so many new urban designs that value walkability and sustainability. The elegant buildings are near a public market; public transportation; and a cornucopia of shops, restaurants, and cultural venues. I hope I'll get to publish the accounts of these lifespaces sometime too.

There were seven people who helped me in so many different ways that they deserve another mention. They include people who welcomed me to stay in their homes, put me in touch with other interviewees (and sometimes even set up the interviews), drove me all over, wined and dined me, and knew what to say or do whenever they saw my baffled face. Some helped in even more ways than that. Thank you, Lisa Cook, Lisa DePaulo, Pryor Hale, Tricia Hoffman, Susan Hurt, Kristin Noreen, and Joan Shelly.

Nancy Collins and Kay Trimberger read parts of the manuscript; and Christina Campbell, Susan Hurt, and Rebecca Zwick read the entire thing, back when it was tens of thousands of words longer than the published version. They all provided insightful feedback, and I am grateful for it.

Harriet Phinney helped me understand the Vietnamese single mothers who "ask for a child"; thank you. When I was just starting this project, Eileen Boris told me that I should read Dolores Hayden's work; now, I think everyone else should too. Cynthia Cohen, someone I've never met, offered to help me recruit people to interview as soon as she learned about this project. My nephew Mike DePaulo was my savior every time I had a problem with my computer; his patience with the technologically challenged is amazing. Nancy Collins, Susan Hurt, Karen Taylor, Per Wehn, and Rebecca Zwick probably heard more about this project for the past three years than they ever wanted to; I so appreciated their encouragement. Robin Gilmour and Alicia Rosenthal have also been wonderfully supportive. My nephew Brian DePaulo asked me how it was going all the time; that was so thoughtful of him.

One of my friends noticed that only two of my three siblings are mentioned in the book (Lisa and Pete, plus Pete's partner, Joan) and asked in jest what my other sib would think of that. Well, Joseph DePaulo and his wife, Kelly, and his kids, Kevin, Danny, and Natalie, are a nuclear family living in a single-family house in the suburbs. What can I say? I adore them.

In the opening pages, when I described how I came to write this book, I left out something important: my agent, Melissa Flashman, was passionate about this project. If she had not been so sure it was something I should pursue, I never would have done so.

Thank you, Emily Han, my editor at Beyond Words, for your enthusiasm and guidance throughout this project. Thanks to my development editor, Henry Covey, for thinking so deeply about this book and giving me such detailed feedback. I am also grateful to the whole team at Beyond Words, including the managing editor, Lindsay Brown; production editors Emmalisa Sparrow and Leah Brown; the marketing

ACKNOWLEDGMENTS

lead, Whitney Diffenderfer; the publicist, Jackie Hooper; the typographer, Bill Brunson; the copyeditor, Kristin Thiel; and the proofreader, Jennifer Weaver-Neist. Special thanks to Devon Smith for the design of the book—I love all the creative elements, such as the rooftops and keys at the beginning of the chapters, the houses that serve as bullet points, and the imaginative family and friend configurations used as text breaks. Thank you, too, to Beyond Words publisher, Richard Cohn, and Atria publisher, Judith Curr.

NOTES

Not Going Nuclear: So Many Ways to Live and Love

1. Williams, "Friends of a Certain Age."

1. How We Live Now:
Finding Our Place, Our Space, and Our People

1. Louie, "Making Family."
2. U.S. Census Bureau, Table MS-2.
3. Yen, "U.S. Growth of Distant Suburbs."
4. Roth, *American Architecture*.
5. Howard, "A Confederacy of Bachelors."
6. Martin et al., "Births: Final Data for 2012."
7. Stoll, "It's a Hub."
8. "Older Americans 2012."
9. "Beyond 50.05 Survey."
10. Kalata, "Looking at Act II," 13.
11. Linn, "Mt. Lebanon Women."
12. Abrahms, "Share Common Ground"; Chapin, *Pocket Neighborhoods*.
13. Fry and Passel, "In Post-Recession," 5.

14. Beirne, "I Moved Back Home."
15. Burton, "It's Small."
16. Beirne, "I Moved Back Home."
17. Huber, "Are We Too Close."
18. Leopold, "The Legacy."
19. Parker, "The Boomerang Generation," 1.
20. Mintz, "The Kids Are Moving."
21. Atlee, "Deep Green on a Budget."
22. Peck, "Living Together," 42.
23. Bengtson, "Beyond the Nuclear Family," 6.
24. U.S. Census Bureau News, "Facts for Features," 2.
25. U.S. Census Bureau, "More Adults Living in Shared Households." The most recent data available on adults sharing households are from 2011.
26. Strohm et al., "'Living Apart Together.'"
27. Green, "With This Cottage."
28. Lara, "One for the Price."
29. Ibid.
30. Hayden, *Redesigning the American Dream*, 19–24, 99.
31. In "*Redesigning the American Dream*," Hayden described three models of "home translated into the built form" (p. 6) as the haven strategy, the industrial strategy, and the neighborhood strategy.
32. Arieff, "The American Dream."
33. Marsden, *Social Trends*.
34. Short, Goldscheider, and Torr, "Less Help for Mother."
35. Arieff, "Saving the Suburbs."
36. Green, "The Semi-Detached Solution."
37. Durrett, *The Senior Cohousing Handbook*, 1. Durrett told the same story at the conference.
38. McCamant and Durrett, *Creating Cohousing*.
39. Umberger, "Post-Recession, Expect a Shift."
40. Donaldson, "The New American Super-Family"; "Coldwell Banker Releases."
41. Green, "Under One Roof, Building for Extended Families."
42. Adler and Chernikoff, "Economy Drives U.S. Families Together."
43. Green, "Under One Roof, Building for Extended Families."
44. El Nasser, "Cozy Pocket Neighborhoods Have Sprawl on the Move."
45. Yee, "In Winning Design."
46. Hoffman, "Shrink to Fit."
47. "Build Small / Live Large," International Living Future Institute.
48. Manzella, *Common Purse*.
49. Palgi and Reinharz, *One Hundred Years*.

50. Twin Oaks Community website, http://www.twinoaks.org.

51. Manzella, *Common Purse.*

52. Lotsa Helping Hands website, http://www.lotsahelpinghands.com.

53. Thompson and Weissmann, "The Cheapest Generation," 48.

54. Putnam, *Bowling Alone.*

55. Deresiewicz, "The End of Solitude."

56. Oishi and Schimmack, "Residential Mobility," 989.

57. Clark, "The Roommate Revolution."

2. One Big, Happy Family: Relatives Sharing and Caring

1. Swarns, "An In-Law."

2. Parnes, "'First Grandma.'"

3. Winfrey, "Oprah Talks."

4. Parnes, "'First Grandma.'"

5. Ruggles, "The Decline," 115.

6. Rosenfeld, *The Age of Independence*, 192.

7. Ruggles, "The Transformation," 110.

8. Ibid., 112.

9. Ibid., 124.

10. Rosenfeld, "Young Adulthood," 38, 46.

11. Ruggles, "The Transformation," 118.

12. Taylor et al., "The Return," 7. Numbers are percentages of all adults, not all households.

13. Ruggles, "The Transformation," 124–27.

14. Taylor et al., "Fighting Poverty," 1.

15. Bethell, "Family Matters," 2.

16. Taylor et al., "The Return," 1.

17. Bethell, "Family Matters," 2.

18. Caumont, "13 Data Milestones."

19. Fry and Passel, "In Post-Recession," 10.

20. Thompson, "A Record-High Number."

21. Payne and Copp, "Young Adults," 3.

22. Parker, "The Boomerang Generation," 1.

23. U.S. Census Bureau, Table MS-2.

24. U.S. Census Bureau, Table A-1.

25. Donatone, "Why Millennials"; Donovan and Guida, "Millennials Strike Back."

26. Segrin et al., "Parent and Child Traits," 569.

27. Arnett and Schwab, "Poll of Parents," 8.

28. Arnett and Schwab, "Poll of Emerging Adults," 9; "Poll of Parents," 5.
29. Fingerman and Furstenberg, "You Can."
30. Ibid.
31. Fingerman et al., "Helicopter Parents," 880, 890.
32. Fingerman and Furstenberg, "You Can."
33. Wright, "Millennials."
34. Fingerman and Furstenberg, "You Can."
35. Payne and Copp, "Young Adults," 3.
36. Parker, "The Boomerang Generation," 1.
37. Hoder, "Why the Nest."
38. Taylor et al., "The Big Generation Gap," 2
39. Shyong, "Making Room."
40. Leopold, "Legacy," 399.
41. Grinspan, "Anxious Youth."
42. Winograd and Hais, "Millennial Generation."
43. Newman, *The Accordion Family*, xvii, xix, 122.
44. DePaulo and Morris, "Singles in Society," 71.
45. Cohn and Morin, "American Mobility," 1.
46. U.S. Census Bureau, "About 36 Million," "Census Bureau Reports," "Mover Rate."
47. Noah, "Stay Put."
48. Fischer, "Ever-More Rooted," 194.
49. Cohn and Morin, "American Mobility," 14.
50. DePaulo, *Singled Out*, 169–84.
51. Deleire and Kalil, "Good Things Come," 405.
52. Ibid.
53. Ibid.
54. Augustine and Raley, "Multigenerational Households," 434.
55. Gerstel, "Rethinking Families," 3.
56. Ibid., 5.
57. Park, "Single Parenthood," 863.

3. One Big, Happy Friendship: Housemates Go Long and Deep

1. Medlicott, *The Ladies of Covington*; Reyes, "The Covington Chronicles," 53.
2. Chudacoff, *The Age of the Bachelor*; Crain, "Brother, Can You Spare a Room?"; Gamber, *The Boardinghouse*.
3. Hobbs and Stoops, "Demographic Trends in the 20th Century," 10.
4. Klemesrud, "Gray Panther Founder."

5. Folkart, "Maggie Kuhn, 89."
6. Ibid.
7. Klemesrud, "Gray Panther Founder."
8. Thomas Jr., "Maggie Kuhn, 89."
9. Klemesrud, "Gray Panther Founder."
10. National Shared Housing Resource Center website, http://nationalsharedhousing.org.
11. Hobbs and Stoops, "Demographic Trends in the 20th Century."
12. Golden Girl Homes website, "Gatherings, Workshops and Fun Events."
13. Brown and Lin, "The Gray Divorce Revolution."
14. Kalata, "Looking at Act II," 13.
15. Pluhar, *Sharing Housing*, xiii.
16. Heath, "Peer-Shared Households," 4.
17. Ibid.
18. Ibid.
19. Ibid.
20. Ibid.
21. Ibid., 17.

4. Living in a Community: From Neighbors to Friends

1. Leinberger, "The Next Slum."
2. Ibid.
3. Gallagher, *End of Suburbs*, 9.
4. Ibid., 6.
5. Ibid., 51–52.
6. Benfield, "Revitalizing the Suburb"; Gallagher, *End of Suburbs*, 25–26, 113, 116, 120; Leinberger, "Next Slum"; Walljasper, "How to Design."
7. "Congress for New Urbanism," Charter of the New Urbanism.
8. Arieff, "Is Your House."
9. Fromm, "American Cohousing"; Gilbert, "The Modern Homemaker"; McCamant and Durrett, *Creating Cohousing*; Sanguinetti, "Cohousing"; Yee, "Come Together"; The Cohousing Association of the United States website, http://cohousing.org.
10. Ibid.
11. Ibid.
12. Scanzoni, *Designing Families*, 95–96.
13. Carstensen et al., "Taking Time Seriously," 165.
14. Charles Durrett, in conversation with author, February 2, 2015.
15. Begijnhof, Amsterdam, "Begijnhof & Kapel"; Amsterdam.info, "The Begijnhof in Amsterdam."

16. Lee, "Anatomy of a Fareej," 14; Montgomery, *Happy City*, 143.

17. Gish, "Bungalow Court Housing," 376.

18. Ibid., 378.

19. Ibid., 367.

20. Ibid., 373.

21. Ibid., 384.

22. Chapin, *Pocket Neighborhoods*, 8.

23. Abrahms, "Sharing Common Ground," 17–19.

24. Badger, "The Case for Cul-de-Sacs."

25. Hochschild, "The Cul-de-Sac Effect."

26. Badger, "The Case for Cul-de-Sacs."

27. Kurutz, "Square Feet."

28. Ibid.

29. Williams, *The Big Tiny*.

30. Burton, "It's Small," 21; Seliger, "In the Backyard."

31. Eheart and Hopping, "Generations of Hope," 675–82; Eheart et al., "Generations of Hope Communities," 47–52; Gurwitt, "Fostering Hope"; Yeagle, "This Is the Village"; Smith, *Hope Meadows*. I did not visit Hope Meadows.

32. Ibid.

33. Johnson, "For Distant Generations."

34. Netterfield and Netterfield, "Generations of Hope."

35. Gurwitt, "Fostering Hope."

36. Johnson, "For Distant Generations."

37. Smith, *Hope Meadows*, 107–14.

38. Eheart et al., "Generations of Hope Communities," 47–48.

39. Ibid., 49.

40. Eheart and Hopping, "Generations of Hope," 675–82; Earheart et al,. "Hope Communities," 47–52; Gurwitt, "Fostering Hope"; Yeagle, "This Is the Village"; Smith, *Hope Meadows*.

41. Eheart et al., "Generations of Hope Communities," 51.

42. Ibid.

43. Generations of Hope website, "Residents of the Month."

5. Not-So-Single Parents:
Finding New Kinds of Community

1. Most of Carmel Sullivan's story comes from my interview with her. I also drew from the essay she wrote, "Single Mothers Unite."

2. CoAbode website, "CoAbode Press Articles."

NOTES

3. The "Extended Interview Questionnaire" was provided to me by Carmel Sullivan.

4. Ellis, "An Interview with CoAbode's Founder Carmel Sullivan."

5. Ibid.

6. Edwards and Williams, "Adopting Change," 163–64.

7. Schnarr, "Nowhere Else to Go."

8. Ibid.

9. Gross, "Anti-Abortion Revival."

10. Edwards and Williams, "Adopting Change," 165–68; Gross, "Anti-Abortion Revival."

11. Pinsof, "The Death," 135.

12. Rosenfeld, *The Age of Independence*, 192.

13. Ventura, "Changing Patterns," 1.

14. Martin et al., "Births: Final Data for 2011," 9.

15. Collins, *Black Feminist Thought*; hooks, *Feminist Theory*.

16. hooks, *Feminist Theory*.

17. Hrdy, *Mother Nature, Mothers and Others*; Johnson, "Raising Darwin's Consciousness."

18. Konner, "It Does Take a Village."

19. Most of April McCaffery's story comes from my interview with her. I also drew from posts from her blog, *It's All About Balance*, especially "Celebrating Friend-Love," "The 40th Birthday Post," and "Celebrating 10 Years of Independence."

20. McCaffery, "Celebrating Friend-Love."

21. Corrigan, "Glendale Theater Troupe."

22. Hayden, *Redesigning the American Dream*, 27–28, 174, 207.

23. Hayden, *Redesigning the American Dream*, 108–10; Hayden, *The Grand Domestic Revolution*, 346–55.

24. Hayden, *Redesigning the American Dream*, 88–91, 103–4, 156–170.

25. Hayden, *Redesigning the American Dream*, 134–37; Hayden, "What Would a Non-Sexist City Be Like?," S178–80; Hosken, "Special Housing."

26. Hosken, "Special Housing."

27. Hayden, *Redesigning the American Dream*, 137–38; Sprague, *More than Housing*.

28. Burleigh, "Architect Looks at Complex Needs."

29. Sprague, *More than Housing*, 40.

30. Ibid.

31. Klinenberg, *Going Solo*, 215.

32. Hayden, *Redesigning the American Dream*, 113.

33. European Urban Knowledge Network, "Frauen—Werk—Stadt"; Foran, "How to Design"; Ludwig, *Housing in Vienna*, 36, 96.

34. Cohn, "A Tiny Village."

35. Ibid.

36. Harriet M. Phinney, email message to the author, October 18, 2013.

37. Family by Design website, "About Us: Darren Spedale," "About Us: What We Believe," "Concerns About Parenting Partnerships," "FAQ," "The First 10 Questions"; Kendra, "Q & A"; Rodgers, "Finding a Parenting Partner."
38. Kendra, "Q & A."
39. Fowler and Rusli, "Don't Talk to Strangers."
40. Ellin, "Making a Child."
41. "Surrogate Couple Explain," YouTube video posted November 27, 2012.
42. Ellin, "Making a Child."
43. Elms, "The Rise of Co-Parenting."
44. "First Fridays"; North, "Life Partners Who Aren't."
45. Elms, "The Rise of Co-Parenting."
46. Ellin, "Making a Child"; Elms, "The Rise of Co-Parenting."
47. North, "Life Partners Who Aren't."
48. Elms, "The Rise of Co-Parenting."
49. North, "Life Partners Who Aren't."
50. Elms, "The Rise of Co-Parenting."
51. Kendra, "Q & A."
52. Rodgers, "Finding a Parenting Partner."
53. DePaulo, *Singled Out*, 169–84.
54. Wang and Taylor, "For Millennials," 1.
55. McGreevy, "Brown Signs Bill."

6. The New Couples: So Happy Not Together

1. Baumeister and Bushman, *Social Psychology*, 16.
2. Brambila, "Together Apart."
3. Cherlin, "Demographic Trends," 410; Levin and Trost, "Living Apart Together," 283; Reimondos, Evans, and Gray, "Living-Apart-Together," 48; Strohm et al., "'Living Apart Together,'" 190.
4. Strohm et al., "'Living Apart Together,'" 191.
5. Gerstel and Gross, *Commuter Marriage*, 1–22.
6. Bruni, "Of Love and Fungus."
7. Levin, "Living Apart Together," 223; Levin and Trost, "Living Apart Together," 279; Roseneil, "On Not Living"; Trost, "The Social Institution," 512–13; Jamieson et al., "Friends, Neighbors"; Jamieson and Simpson, *Living Alone*, 70–73.
8. Hess and Catell, "Dual Dwelling Duos," 26.
9. Discussed in Jamieson and Simpson, *Living Alone*, 70–73.

10. de Jong Gierveld, "Remarriage," 241; Duncan and Phillips, "People Who Live," 122; Haskey, "Living Arrangements," 41; Milan and Peters, "Couples Living Apart," 3; Reimondos, Evans, and Gray, "Living-Apart-Together," 48.

11. Reimondos, Evans, and Gray, "Living-Apart-Together," 52.

12. Regnier-Loilier, Beaujouan, and Villeneuve-Gokalp, "Neither Single," 97.

13. Reimondos, Evans, and Gray, "Living-Apart-Together," 52.

14. Regnier-Loilier, Beaujouan, and Villeneuve-Gokalp, "Neither Single," 100.

15. Ibid., 28.

16. Karlsson and Borell, "A Home of Their Own," 77.

17. Karlsson and Borell, "A Home of Their Own," 77; Holmes, "An Equal Distance?," 197; Holmes, "Love Lives."

18. Karlsson and Borell, "A Home of Their Own," 79.

19. Jamieson and Simpson, *Living Alone*, 75; Levin, "Living Apart Together," 234–35.

20. Stoessel, *Living Happily*.

21. Bruni, "Of Love and Fungus."

22. Gerstel and Gross, *Commuter Marriage*, 52–78; Jiang and Hancock, "Absence Makes the Communication," 556; Stafford, "Geographical Distance," 275.

23. Cherlin, *The Marriage-Go-Round*, 8; DePaulo, *Singled Out*, 7–25.

24. Thornton and Young-DeMarco, "Four Decades," 1023.

25. Pinsof, "The Death," 149.

26. Smith, "Getting the Word Out."

27. Diliberto, "It's Charles Osgood."

28. Glick, "Fifty Years," 866.

29. Jayson, "Living Together."

30. Ibid.

31. Conley et al., "The Fewer the Merrier?," 3.

32. Strohm et al., "'Living Apart Together,'" 191.

33. Larson, "Married, Living Together."

34. Duncan and Phillips, "People Who Live," 119–32.

35. Ibid.

36. Musick and Bumpass, "Reexamining the Case," 10–12.

7. Lifespaces for the New Old Age: Institutions Begone!

1. Ball, *Livable Communities*, 130–37.

2. "History of Sun City."

3. Durrett, *Senior Cohousing*, 99–120, 209, 276, 285–89.

4. Abrahms, "Elder Cohousing."

5. Mandhana, "Shared Meals."

6. Durrett, *Senior Cohousing*, 122–23.

7. Ibid., 123–24.

8. Dowds, "Cohousing Pioneers."

9. Most of the material about Lucy Whitworth came from my personal interview with her. I also drew from Rubin, "Senior and Seriously Ill."

10. Keenan, "Home and Community," found that 86 percent of Americans forty-five and older agree with the statement, "What I'd really like to do is stay in my current residence for as long as possible."

11. Basler, "Declaration of Independents"; Brooks, "How One Group."

12. Greenfield et al., "National Overview," 4.

13. Ibid., 5.

14. Ibid., 6.

15. Scharlach and Graham, "Villages in the U.S."

16. Brooks, "How One Group."

17. Greenfield et al., "National Overview," 4.

18. "Aging Americans," Associated Press, November 12, 2011.

19. Greenfield et al., "Conceptual Framework," 281; Mandhana, "Growing Older."

20. Hansen and Scharlach, "Community Services," 74.

21. Basler, "Declaration of Independents."

22. Margonelli, "How the Trailer Park."

23. Leland, "The Neighbors."

24. U.S. Census Bureau, "Older Americans Month," 1.

25. "Boomers@65."

26. Ball, *Livable Communities*, 137–44.

27. Thomas, *What Are Old People For*, 232.

28. Conan, "Green House."

29. Ibid.

30. Thomas, *What Are Old People For*, 227.

31. Jaffe, "Move Over."

32. Thomas, *What Are Old People For*, 226.

33. Ibid., 136.

34. Carstensen, "A Hopeful Future," 24.

35. Thomas, *What Are Old People For*, 226.

36. Conan, "Green House," quoting Dr. William Thomas.

37. Thomas, *What Are Old People For*, 224, 234.

38. Ibid., 235.

39. Ibid., 234.

40. Ibid., 179–80.

41. Ibid., 181–84.

42. Ibid., 181.

43. Rachel Scher McLean, email message to the author, August 13, 2014.

44. Thomas, *What Are Old People For*, 232.

45. Ball, *Livable Communities*, 148.

46. Conan, "Green House"; Jaffe, "Move Over."

47. Kane et al., "Resident Outcomes," 836–37.

48. Conan, "Green House."

8. There's Nothing Sweeter than Solitude: Living Alone

1. The description of the building and the 2005 quotes are from Green, "Among Friends."

2. Jamieson and Simpson, *Living Alone*, 34–35.

3. Rybczynski, *Home*, 18.

4. Averill and Sundararajan, "Experiences of Solitude," 106.

5. Data from 1950 through 2000 are from Hobbs and Stoops, "Demographic Trends," A-49. Data from 2010 are from Lofquist et al., "Households and Families," 5. Data from 2013 are from "Facts for Features," 2.

6. U.S. Census Bureau, Table MS-2.

7. Klinenberg, *Going Solo*, 14.

8. Ibid., 16.

9. Jamieson and Simpson, *Living Alone*, 27.

10. Klinenberg, *Going Solo*, 31; Rosenfeld, *The Age of Independence*, 64–65.

11. DePaulo, *Singled Out*, 15–16.

12. Klinenberg, *Going Solo*, 48–49.

13. Ibid., 10.

14. Rainie and Wellman, *Networked*, 8–9.

15. Cook, "An 'AHA' Moment."

16. Thoreau, *Walden*, 88.

17. Hempton and Grossmann, *One Square Inch*, 12.

18. Long and Averill, "Solitude," 30.

19. Averill and Sundararajan, "Experiences," 96–97; Long and Averill, "Solitude," 23–29.

20. Storr, *Solitude*, 11.

21. Kruvant, "19 Reasons."

22. Jamieson and Simpson, *Living Alone*, 8, 120–21; 141–43; 182–84

23. Ibid., 34.

24. Corson, "Saunas."

25. Ibid.

26. Heikkila and Jamsa, *Turku*, 6.

27. DePaulo, *Marriage*, 28–62.

28. Beck, *Risk Society*, 116.

29. DePaulo, *Singlism*, 41–52.
30. Amato et al., *Alone Together*, 67.
31. Rainie and Wellman, *Networked*. The phrase "networked individualism" comes from the title of this book.
32. Greenfield, "Changing," 1726, 1728.
33. Bauman, *Liquid Love*.
34. Wang and Wellman, "Social Connectivity," 1149.
35. Gerstel, "Rethinking Families," 10; Gerstel and Sarkisian, "Marriage," 18; Sarkisian and Gerstel, "'Till Marriage," 360.
36. Henz, "Informal Caregiving," 411.
37. Musick and Bumpass, "Reexamining the Case," 13.
38. Gerstel, "Rethinking Families," 10–11.
39. Klinenberg, *Going Solo*, 64, 231.
40. Rainie and Wellman, *Networked*, 11.

Revolutions in Living, Now and in the Future

1. Mallett, "Understanding Home," 65.
2. Ibid., 74.
3. Ibid.
4. DePaulo, *Singled Out*, 4.
5. Spencer and Pahl, *Rethinking Friendship*.
6. Wang and Wellman, "Social Connectivity," 1162.
7. Deresiewicz, "Faux."
8. Arnett and Schwab, "Poll of Parents," 8.
9. Bush et al., *My House, Our House*; Cullinane, *Single Woman's Guide*; Kilkenny, *Your Quest*; Newman, *Under One Roof*; Pluhar, *Sharing Housing*; Span, *When the Time Comes*; Stoessel, *Living Happily*.
10. Klinenberg, *Going Solo*, 53.
11. Edleson, "Looking for."
12. Twin Oaks Community website, http://www.twinoaks.org.
13. Bowden, "Homes for Multiple Generations."
14. Trejos, "Suites All Around."
15. Fry, "In Post-Recession," 4.
16. Span, "Who's Moving."

BIBLIOGRAPHY

Abrahms, Sally. "Elder Cohousing." *AARP Bulletin*, January 31, 2011. http://www.aarp
.org/home-garden/housing/info-01-2011/elder_cohousing.html.

———. "Share Common Ground." *AARP Bulletin*, May 7, 2012. http://www.aarp
.org/home-family/livable-communities/info-05-2012/pocket-neighborhoods
-common-ground.html.

Abrams, Amanda. "Where We Live: Greenbelt, an Experiment That Worked." *Washington Post*, June 1, 2012. http://www.washingtonpost.com/realestate/where-we
-live-greenbelt-an-experiment-that-worked/2012/05/31/gJQA5cM16U_story
.html.

Adler, Lynn, and Helen Chernikoff. "Economy Drives U.S. Families Together Under
One Roof." *Reuters*, March 18, 2010. http://ru.reuters.com/article/idUKN18243109
20100318.

"Aging Americans Can Stay Home with Aid of 'Villages.'" Associated Press, November
12, 2011. http://www.foxnews.com/us/2011/11/12/aging-americans-can-stay-home
-with-aid-villages.

Amato, Paul R., Alan Booth, David R. Johnson, and Stacy J. Rogers. *Alone Together: How
Marriage in America Is Changing*. Cambridge, MA: Harvard University Press, 2007.

Amsterdam.info. "The Begijnhof in Amsterdam." Accessed June 14, 2014. http://www
.amsterdam.info/sights/begijnhof.

Architecture Guide, s.v. "Mothers' House, A. E. Van Eyck. Accessed November 18, 2013.
http://www.architectureguide.nl/project/list_projects_of_architect/arc_id/580/
prj_id/360.

Arieff, Allison. "Is Your House Making You Look Fat?" *New York Times*, February
18, 2008. http://opinionator.blogs.nytimes.com/2008/02/18/is-your-house-making
-you-look-fat.

———. "Saving the Suburbs, Part 2." *New York Times*, February 3, 2009. http://opinion
ator.blogs.nytimes.com/2009/02/03/saving-the-suburbs-part-2.

———. "The American Dream: Phase II." *New York Times*, June 18, 2012. http://opinion
ator.blogs.nytimes.com/2012/06/18/the-american-dream-phase-ii.

Arnett, Jeffrey Jensen, and Joseph Schwab. "The Clark University Poll of Emerging
Adults." Worchester, MA: Clark University, December 2012.

———. "The Clark University Poll of Parents of Emerging Adults." Worchester, MA:
Clark University, September 2013.

Atlee, Jennifer. "Deep Green on a Budget." *Yes! Magazine*, Summer 2012: 38–42.

Augustine, Jennifer March, and R. Kelly Raley. "Multigenerational Households and the
School Readiness of Children Born to Unmarried Mothers." *Journal of Family Issues*
34, no. 3 (2012): 431–59.

Averill, James R., and Louise Sundararajan. "Experiences of Solitude: Issues of Assess-
ment, Theory, and Culture." In *The Handbook of Solitude: Psychological Perspectives
on Social Isolation, Social Withdrawal, and Being Alone*, edited by Robert J. Coplan
and Julie C. Bowker, 90–108. West Sussex, UK: Wiley Blackwell, 2014.

Badger, Emily. "A Brief History of How Living Alone Came to Seem Totally Normal." *Atlantic Cities*, August 27, 2013. http://www.citylab.com/housing/2013/08
/brief-history-how-living-alone-came-seem-totally-normal/6689.

———. "The Case for Cul-de-Sacs." *Altantic*, October 17, 2013. http://www.citylab.com
/housing/2013/10/sociologists-defense-cul-de-sac/7262.

Badham, James. "Urban Vision." *Dining & Destinations*, Spring/Summer 2013.

Bahrampour, Tara. "U.S. Birthrate Plummets to Its Lowest Level Since 1920." *Washington Post*, November 29, 2012. http://www.washingtonpost.com/local/us-birth

-rate-plummets-to-its-lowest-since-1920/2012/11/29/ee7e8d16-3a3f-11e2-b01f
-5f55b193f58f_story.html.

————. "Through a Growing Number of Senior Villages in the D.C. Area, Aging in Place Becomes Easier." *Washington Post*, February 6, 2014. http://www.washingtonpost .com/local/through-a-growing-number-of-senior-villages-in-the-dc-area-aging-in -place-becomes-easier/2014/02/06/e51fc660-7fbf-11e3-9556-4a4bf7bcbd84_story .html.

Ball, M. Scott. *Livable Communities for Aging Populations*. Hoboken, NJ: Wiley, 2012.

Basler, Barbara. "Declaration of Independents." *AARP Bulletin*, December 2005. Accessed May 28, 2014. http://bulletin.aarp.org/yourworld/yourhome/articles/declaration _of_independents.html (page discontinued).

Bauman, Zygmunt. *Liquid Love*. Malden, MA: Polity, 2003.

Baumeister, Roy F., and Brad J. Bushman. *Social Psychology and Human Nature: Comprehensive Edition*. Belmont, CA: Wadsworth Cengage Learning, 2013.

Beck, Ulrich. *Risk Society: Toward a New Modernity*. New Delhi: Sage, 1992.

Begijnhof, Amsterdam. "Begijnhof & Kapel." Accessed June 14, 2014. http://www.begi jnhofamsterdam.nl.

Beirne, Aodhan. "I Moved Back Home, and I'm Glad I Did." *New York Times*, November 6, 2012. http://www.nytimes.com/2012/11/06/booming/moving-home-after-college -can-be-a-good-thing.html.

Benfield, Kaid. "Revitalizing the Suburb Without Giving Up the Car." *Atlantic Cities*, December 9, 2013. http://www.theatlanticcities.com/jobs-and-economy/2013/12 /revitalizing-suburb-without-giving-car/7815.

Bengtson, Vern L. "Beyond the Nuclear Family: The Increasing Importance of Multigenerational Bonds." *Journal of Marriage and Family* 63 (2001): 1–16.

Bethell, Tom. "Family Matters: Multigenerational Families in a Volatile Economy." Generations United website, 2011. http://www.gu.org/RESOURCES/Publications/Family MattersMultigenerationalFamilies.aspx.

"Beyond 50.05 Survey." AARP Survey. Washington, DC: AARP, April 2005.

"Boomers@65: Celebrating a Milestone Birthday." *AARP*, 2011. http://www.aarp.org /personal-growth/transitions/boomers_65.

BIBLIOGRAPHY

Borgia, Steve. "A Model Integrated Community for Chicago to Study." *Chicago Reader*, December 13, 2012. http://www.chicagoreader.com/Bleader/archives/2012/12/13/a-model-integrated-community-for-chicago-to-study.

Bowden, Marilyn. "Homes for Multiple Generations." Bankrate.com, September 14, 2006. Accessed August 10, 2014. http://www.bankrate.com/brm/news/real-estate/20060914d1.asp.

Brambila, Nicole C. "Together Apart: Commuter Marriages on the Rise." *USA Today*, February 20, 2012. http://usatoday30.usatoday.com/news/health/wellness/story/2012-02-20/Together-apart-Commuter-marriages-on-the-rise/53170648/1.

Brooks, Mary Jo. "How One Group of Seniors Bucked Convention and Avoided the Retirement Home." PBS, August 8, 2013. http://www.pbs.org/newshour/rundown/in-boston-how-one-neighborhood-went-about-aging-in-place.

Brown, Susan L., and I-Fen Lin. "The Gray Divorce Revolution: Rising Divorce Among Middle-Aged and Older Adults, 1990–2010." *Journal of Gerontology Series B: Psychological Sciences and Social Sciences* 67 (2012): 731–41.

Bruce, Heidi. "It's Supportive." *Yes!* Summer 2012: 45.

Bruni, Frank. "Of Love and Fungus." *New York Times*, July 20, 2013. http://www.nytimes.com/2013/07/21/opinion/sunday/bruni-of-love-and-fungus.html.

"Build Small / Live Large Housing Summit." International Living Future Institute website. Accessed November 28, 2012. http://living-future.org/cascadia/buildsmall.

Burleigh, Nina. "Architect Looks at Complex Needs of Poor, Single Moms." *Chicago Tribune*, April 19, 1992. http://articles.chicagotribune.com/1992-04-19/features/9202040975_1_housing-projects-public-housing-designs.

Burton, Lynsi. "It's Small." *Yes! Magazine*, Summer 2012: 21.

Burton, Summer Anne. "Austin's Utopian Homeless Village Is Becoming a Reality." BuzzFeed, May 7, 2014. http://www.buzzfeed.com/summeranne/austins-utopian-homeless-village-is-becoming-a-reality.

Bush, Karen M., Louise S. Machinist, and Jean McQuillin. *My House, Our House: Living Far Better for Far Less in a Cooperative Household*. Pittsburgh, PA: St. Lynn's Press, 2013.

Carstensen, Laura L. "A Hopeful Future." In *Independent for Life: Homes and Neighborhoods for an Aging America*, edited by Henry Cisneros, Margaret Dyer-Chamberlain, and Jane Hickie. Austin, TX: University of Texas Press, (2012): 21–31.

Carstensen, Laura L., Derek M. Isaacowitz, and Susan T. Charles. "Taking Time Seriously: A Theory of Socioemotional Selectivity." *American Psychologist* 54, no. 3 (1999): 165–81.

Caumont, Andrea. "13 Data Milestones for 2013." Fact Tank: News in Numbers. Pew Research Center, December 23, 2013.

Cech, Laura Barnhardt. "Walkability Increasingly Drives Developers and Real Estate Market." *Washington Post*, November 16, 2012.

Chaker, Anne Marie. "The Shared Backyard." *Wall Street Journal*, June 12, 2012. http://online.wsj.com/news/articles/SB10001424052702303768104577460691523913090.

Chapin, Ross. *Pocket Neighborhoods*. Newtown, CT: The Taunton Press, 2011.

"Congress for New Urbanism," Charter of the New Urbanism. Accessed February 2014. http://www.cnu.org/charter.

Cherlin, Andrew J. *The Marriage-Go-Round: The State of Marriage and the Family in America Today*. New York: Alfred A. Knopf, 2009.

———. "Demographic Trends in the United States: A Review of Research in the 2000s." *Journal of Marriage and Family* 72, no. 3 (2010): 403–19.

CoAbode website. "CoAbode Press Articles." Accessed January 5, 2015. http://www.coabode.org/pressarticles.php.

Cohn, D'Vera, and Rich Morin. "American Mobility: Who Moves? Who Stays Put? Where's Home?" Pew Research Center: A Social and Demographic Trends Report. December 29, 2008.

Cohn, Julie. "A Tiny Village Where Women Chose to Be Single Mothers." *New York Times*, February 14, 2013. http://www.nytimes.com/2013/02/15/world/asia/in-vietnam-some-chose-to-be-single-mothers.html?pagewanted=all&_r=0.

The Cohousing Association of the United States website. Accessed November 20, 2014. http://www.cohousing.org.

"Coldwell Banker Releases Baby Boomer Survey Results." Press release. October 18, 2011. http://www.powersiteblog.com/coldwell-banker-releases-baby-boomer-survey-results/#sthash.KTOBY2bE.dpbs.

Colin, Chris. "To Your Left, a Better Way of Life?" New York Times, June 11, 2009. http://www.nytimes.com/2009/06/11/garden/11cohousing.html?pagewanted=all.

Collins, Patricia Hill. *Black Feminist Thought: Knowledge, Consciousness, and the Politics of Empowerment*. 2nd ed. New York: Routledge, 2000.

Conan, Neal. "Green House Projects Let Elders Age in Homes." *Talk of the Nation*, NPR, April 2, 2009. http://www.npr.org/templates/story/story.php?storyId=102656673.

Conley, Terri D., Amy C. Moors, Jes L. Matsick, and Ali Ziegler. "The Fewer the Merrier? Assessing Stigma Surrounding Consensually Non-Monogamous Romantic Relationships." *Analyses of Social Issues and Public Policy* 13, no. 1 (2013): 1–30.

Cook, Lisa. "An 'AHA' Moment Regarding Connections." *Living Alone, Living Connected* (blog), April 13, 2014. http://twincitieslimbo.wordpress.com/2014/04/13/an-aha-moment-regarding-connections.

Corrigan, Kelly. "Glendale Theater Troupe Gets a Glorious Donation." *Glendale News Press*, July 31, 2013. http://articles.glendalenewspress.com/2013-07-31/entertainment/tn-gnp-me-theater-troupe-gets-a-glorious-donation-20130731_1_stepping-stone-players-hayhurst-hall-troupe.

Corson, Trevor. "Saunas and Silence." *Atlantic*, April 1, 2009. http://www.theatlantic.com/magazine/archive/2009/04/saunas-and-silence/307322.

Chudacoff, Howard P. *The Age of the Bachelor: Creating an American Subculture*. Princeton, NJ: Princeton University Press, 1999.

Clark, Leilani. "The Roommate Revolution: Why Living Alone Is Overrated." *Yes! Magazine*, September 19, 2011. Accessed August 12, 2014. http://www.yesmagazine.org/happiness/the-roommate-revolution-why-living-alone-is-overrated.

Crain, Caleb. "Brother, Can You Spare a Room?" *New York Times*, March 29, 2009. http://www.nytimes.com/2009/03/29/books/review/Crain-t.html.

Cullinane, Jan. *The Single Woman's Guide to Retirement*. Hoboken, New Jersey: John Wiley & Sons, 2012.

de Jong Gierveld, Jenny. "Remarriage, Unmarried Cohabitation, Living Apart Together: Partner Relationships Following Bereavement or Divorce." *Journal of Marriage and Family* 66, no. 1 (2004): 236–43.

Deleire, Thomas, and Ariel Kalil. "Good Things Come in Threes: Single-Parent Multigenerational Family Structure and Adolescent Adjustment." *Demography* 39, no. 2 (2002): 393–413.

DePaulo, Bella. *Marriage vs. Single Life: How Science and the Media Got It So Wrong*. Charleston, SC: DoubleDoor Books, 2015.

———. *Singled Out: How Singles Are Stereotyped, Stigmatized, and Ignored, and Still Live Happily Ever After*. New York: St. Martin's Press, 2006.

———. *Singlism: What It Is, Why It Matters, and How to Stop It*. Charleston, SC: Double-Door Books, 2011.

DePaulo, Bella M., and Wendy L. Morris. "Singles in Society and in Science." *Psychological Inquiry* 16, no. 1–2 (2005): 57–83.

Deresiewicz, William. "Faux Friendship." *The Chronicle of Higher Education*, December 6, 2009. http://chronicle.com/article/Faux-Friendship/49308.

———. "The End of Solitude." *The Chronicle of Higher Education*, January 30, 2009.

Diliberto, Gioia. "It's Charles Osgood All the Time, for All the News That's Fit to Rhyme." *People*, November 2, 1981. http://www.people.com/people/article/0,,20080598,00.html.

Donaldson, Doug. "The New American Super-Family." *Saturday Evening Post*, July/August 2012.

Donatone, Brooke. "Why Millennials Can't Grow Up." *Slate*, December 2, 2013. http://www.slate.com/articles/health_and_science/medical_examiner/2013/12/millennial_narcissism_helicopter_parents_are_college_students_bigger_problem.html.

Donovan, Tim, and William Guida. "Millennials Strike Back: No, We're Not Just Whiny Babies!" *Salon*, December 10, 2013. http://www.salon.com/2013/12/10/millennials_strike_back_no_were_not_just_whiny_babies.

Dowds, R. Philip, "Cohousing Pioneers: Second Round," 119, issue 20 (to Cohousing mailing list). December 24, 2013. Cited with permission of the author.

Duncan, Simon, and Miranda Phillips. "People Who Live Apart Together: How Different Are They?" *Sociological Review* 58, no. 1 (2010): 112–34.

Durrett, Charles. *The Senior Cohousing Handbook*. 2nd ed. British Columbia, Canada: New Society Publishers, 2009.

Edleson, Harriet. "Looking for a Housemate, Not a Mate, in Later Life." *New York Times*, July 11, 2014. http://www.nytimes.com/2014/07/12/your-money/looking-for-a-housemate-not-a-mate-in-later-life.html.

Edwards, Christine E., and Williams, Christine L. "Adopting Change: Birth Mothers in Maternity Homes Today." *Gender & Society* 14, no. 1 (2000): 160–83.

Eheart, Brenda Krause, and David Hopping. "Generations of Hope." *Children and Youth Services Review* 23, no. 9/10 (2001): 675–82.

Eheart, Brenda Krause, David Hopping, Martha Bauman Power, Elissa Thomann Mitchell, and David Racine. "Generations of Hope Communities: An Intergenerational

Neighborhood Model of Support and Service." *Children and Youth Services Review* 31, no. 1 (2009): 47–52.

El Nasser, Haya. "Cozy Pocket Neighborhoods Have Sprawl on the Move." *USA Today.* March 29, 2011. http://usatoday30.usatoday.com/news/nation/2011-03-30-pocket 30_ST_N.htm.

Ellin, Abby. "Making a Child, Minus the Couple." *New York Times*, February 8, 2013. http://www.nytimes.com/2013/02/10/fashion/seeking-to-reproduce-without-a -romantic-partnership.html.

Ellis, Audrey. "An Interview with CoAbode's Founder Carmel Sullivan." CoAbode website. Accessed January 5, 2015. http://www.coabode.org/interview.php, accessed November 14, 2013.

Elms, Emma. "The Rise of 'Co-Parenting': How Broody, Single Women Are Advertising Online for Men to Help Them Have and Raise Babies . . . But They Don't Want a Relationship." *Daily Mail*, August 17, 2013. http://www.dailymail.co.uk/home /you/article-2394446/With-biological-clocks-ticking-broody-adults-like-Rachel -finding-new-way-bring-baby-dreams-life.html.

European Urban Knowledge Network, s.v. "Frauen—Werk—Stadt." http://www .eukn.org/E_library/Social_Inclusion_Integration/Equality/Gender_Equality /Frauen_Werk_Stadt.

Family by Design website. "About Us: Darren Spedale." Accessed November 22, 2013. http://www.familybydesign.com/content/about-us/.

———. "About Us: What We Believe." Accessed November 22, 2012. http://www.family bydesign.com/content/about-us/what-we-believe/.

———. "Concerns About Parenting Partnerships." Accessed November 22, 2013. http://www.familybydesign.com/content/learn/intro-to-parenting-partnerships /concerns-about-parenting-partnerships (page discontinued).

———. "FAQ About Parenting Partnerships." Accessed November 22, 2012. http://www .familybydesign.com /content/about-us/faq-about-parenting-partnerships/.

———. "The First 10 Questions to Ask Yourself When Considering a Parenting Partnership." Accessed November 22, 2012. http://www.familybydesign.com/content/learn /intro-to-parenting-partnerships/the-first-10-questions-to-ask-yourself-when -considering-a-parenting-partnership/.

Fingerman, Karen L., Yen-Pi Cheng, Eric D. Wesselmann, Steven Zarit, Frank Furstenberg, and Kira S. Birditt. "Helicopter Parents and Landing Kids: Intense Parental

Support of Grown Children." *Journal of Marriage and Family*, 74, no. 4 (2012): 880–96.

Fingerman, Karen L., and Frank F. Furstenberg. "You Can Go Home Again." *New York Times*, May 30, 2012. http://www.nytimes.com/2012/05/31/opinion/the-parent -trap.html.

"First Fridays: Ivan Fatovic, Founder and CEO of Modamily," CassandraDaily (blog). June 1, 2012. http://www.cassandradaily.com/life/first-fridays-ivan-fatovic-founder -and-ceo-of-modamily.

Fischer, Claude S. "Ever-More Rooted Americans." *City & Community* 1, no. 2 (2002): 177–98.

Folkart, Burt A. "Maggie Kuhn, 89; Iconoclastic Founder of Gray Panthers." *Los Angeles Times*, April 23, 1995. http://articles.latimes.com/1995-04-23/news/mn -58042_1 _maggie-kuhn.

Foran, Clare. "How to Design a City for Women." *Atlantic Cities*, September 16, 2013. http:// www.theatlanticcities.com/commute/2013/09/how-design-city-women/6739.

Fowler, Geoffrey A., and Evelyn M. Rusli. "Don't Talk to Strangers—Unless You Plan to Share Your Mac-and-Cheese." *Wall Street Journal*. January 12, 2013. http://online .wsj.com/news/articles/SB10001424127887323689604578222662251857844.

Fox, Emily Jane. "Work from Home Soars 41% in 10 Years." *CNN Money*, October 4, 2012. http://money.cnn.com/2012/10/04/news/economy/work-from-home.

Fromm, Dorit. "American Cohousing: The First Five Years." *Journal of Architectural and Planning Research* 17, no. 2 (2000): 94–109.

Fry, Richard, and Jeffrey S. Passel. "In Post-Recession Era, Young Adults Drive Continu- ing Rise in Multi-Generational Living." Washington, DC: Pew Research Center's Social & Demographic Trends project, July 2014.

Gallagher, Leigh. *The End of the Suburbs: Where the American Dream Is Moving*. New York: Portfolio/Penguin, 2013.

Gamber, Wendy. *The Boardinghouse in Nineteenth-Century America*. Baltimore, MD: The Johns Hopkins University Press, 2007.

Generations of Hope website. "Residents of the Month—October, 2013." Accessed May 2, 2014. Page discontinued. For more about Generations of Hope, see http://www .generationsofhope.org/about.

Gerstel, Naomi. "Rethinking Families and Community: The Color, Class, and Centrality of Extended Kin Ties." *Sociological Forum* 26, no. 1 (2011): 1–20.

Gerstel, Naomi, and Harriet Gross. *Commuter Marriage*. New York: Guilford Press, 1984.

Gerstel, Naomi, and Natalia Sarkisian. "Marriage: The Good, the Bad, and the Greedy." *Contexts* 5, no. 4 (2006): 16–21.

Gilbert, Katie. "The Modern Homemaker." *Psychology Today*, March/April 2013.

Gish, Todd. "Bungalow Court Housing in Los Angeles, 1900–30: Top-Down Innovation? or Bottom-Up Reform?" *Southern California Quarterly* 91, no. 4 (Winter 2009–2010): 365–87.

Glick, Paul C. "Fifty Years of Family Demography: A Record of Social Change." *Journal of Marriage and Family* 50, no. 4 (1988): 861–73.

Golden Girl Homes website. "Gatherings, Workshops and Fun Events." Accessed November 20, 2014. http://www.goldengirlhomes.us/events.html.

Green, Penelope. "Among Friends: Buying and Rehabbing a Town House." *New York Times*, March 6, 2005. Accessed July 28, 2014. http://www.nytimes.com/2005/03/06/realestate/06habi.html.

———. "With This Cottage." New York Times, April 11, 2012.

———. "Under One Roof, Building for Extended Families." *New York Times*, November 29, 2012. http://www.nytimes.com/2012/11/30/us/building-homes-for-modern-multi generational-families.html.

———. "The Semi-Detached Solution." *New York Times*, January 9, 2013.

Greenfield, Emily A., Andrew E. Scharlach, Carrie L. Graham, Joan K. Davitt, and Amanda J. Lehning. "A National Overview of Villages: Results from a 2012 Organizational Survey." *Partnering for Change*. New Brunswick, NJ: Rutgers, the State University of New Jersey, December 1, 2012.

Greenfield, Emily A., Andrew E. Scharlach, Amanda J. Lehning, and Joan K. Davitt. "A Conceptual Framework for Examining the Promise of the NORC Program and Village Models to Promote Aging in Place." *Journal of Aging Studies* 26, no. 3 (2012): 273–84.

Greenfield, Patricia M. "The Changing Psychology of Culture from 1800 Through 2000." *Psychological Science* 24, no. 9 (2013): 1722–31.

Grinspan, Jon. "Anxious Youth, Then and Now." *New York Times*, December 31, 2013. http://www.nytimes.com/2014/01/01/opinion/anxious-youth-then-and-now.html.

BIBLIOGRAPHY

Gross, Jane. "Anti-Abortion Revival: Homes for the Unwed." *New York Times*, July 23, 1989. http://www.nytimes.com/1989/07/23/us/anti-abortion-revival-homes-for-the-unwed.html.

Gurwitt, Rob. "Fostering Hope." *Mother Jones*, March/April 2002. http://www.mother jones.com/politics/2002/03/fostering-hope.

Guth, Robert A. "In Secret Hideaway, Bill Gates Ponders Microsoft's Future." *Wall Street Journal*, March 28, 2005. Accessed August 10, 2014. http://online.wsj.com/news /articles/SB111196625830690477.

Hansen, Jennie Chin, and Andrew Scharlach. "Community Services." In *Independent for Life: Homes and Neighborhoods for an Aging America*, edited by Henry Cisneros, Margaret Dyer-Chamberlain, and Jane Hickie. Austin, TX: University of Texas Press, (2012): 71–83.

Haskey, John. "Living Arrangements in Contemporary Britain: Having a Partner Who Usually Lives Elsewhere and Living Apart Together (LAT)." *Population Trends* 122, Winter (2005): 35–45.

Hayden, Dolores. "What Would a Non-Sexist City Be Like? Speculations on Housing, Urban Design, and Human Work." *Signs* 5, no. 3 (1980, Spring): S170–87.

———. *The Grand Domestic Revolution: A History of Feminist Designs for American Homes, Neighborhoods, and Cities*. Cambridge, MA: The MIT Press, 1981.

———. *Redesigning the American Dream: Gender, Housing, and Family Life*. Revised and expanded edition. New York: Norton, 2002.

Heath, Sue. "Peer-Shared Households, Quasi-Communes and Neo-Tribes." *Current Sociology* 52, no. 2 (2004): 161–79.

Heikkila, Markku, and Esko Jamsa. *Turku: Enduring Beauty*. Kirjapaja, Helsinki: Kirjapaja, 2008.

Hempton, Gordon, and John Grossmann. *One Square Inch of Silence: One Man's Quest to Preserve Quiet*. New York: Atria Books, 2010.

Henz, Ursula. "Informal Caregiving at Working Age: Effects of Job Characteristics and Family Configuration." *Journal of Marriage and Family* 68, no. 2 (2006): 411–29.

Hess, Judye, and Padma Catell. "Dual Dwelling Duos: An Alternative for Long-Term Relationships." *Journal of Couples Therapy* 10, no. 3, 4 (2001): 25–31.

Hester, Karen. "Retrofit Cohousing: A Different Kind of Fixer-Upper." Accessed February 11, 2013. http://www.cohousing.org/cm/article/temescal.

"History of Sun City." Sun City Arizona web site. Accessed June 1, 2014, http://sunaz .com/history-of-suncity/.

Hobbs, Frank, and Nicole Stoops. "Demographic Trends in the 20th Century." U.S. Census Bureau, Census 2000 Special Reports, Series CENSR-4. Washington, DC: U.S. Government Printing Office, 2002.

Hochschild Jr., Thomas R. "The Cul-de-sac Effect: Relationship between Street Design and Residential Social Cohesion." *Journal of Urban Planning and Development* (2013). 10.1061/(ASCE)UP.1943-5444.0000192, 05014006.

Hoder, Randye. "Why the Nest Isn't So Empty Anymore." *New York Times.* August 21, 2013. http://parenting.blogs.nytimes.com/2013/08/21/why-the-nest-isnt-so-empty -anymore/.

Hoffman, Jan. "Shrink to Fit." *New York Times*, September 21, 2012.

Holmes, Mary. "An Equal Distance? Individualisation, Gender and Intimacy in Distance Relationships." *Sociological Review* 52, no. 2 (2004): 180–200.

———. "Love Lives at a Distance: Distance Relationships Over the Lifecourse." *Sociological Research Online* 11, no. 3 (2006).

hooks, bell. *Feminist Theory: From Margin to Center.* Cambridge, MA: South End Press, 1984.

Hosken, Fran P. "Special Housing for Single-Parent Families Takes Hold in London." *Christian Science Monitor*, April 23, 1981. http://www.csmonitor.com/1981/0423 /042320.html.

Howard, Hilary. "A Confederacy of Bachelors." *New York Times*, August 3, 2012. http:// www.nytimes.com/2012/08/05/nyregion/four-men-sharing-rent-and-friendship -for-18-years.html?pagewanted=all.

Hrdy, Sarah Blaffer. *Mother Nature: Maternal Instincts and How They Shape the Human Species.* New York: Ballantine Books, 1999.

———. *Mothers and Others: The Evolutionary Origins of Mutual Understanding.* Cambridge, MA: Harvard University Press/ Belknap Press, 2011.

Huber, Robert. "Are We Too Close to Our Kids?" *AARP Magazine*, December 2012 / January 2013.

Jaffe, Ina. "Move Over Nursing Homes—There's Something Different." NPR, July 24, 2013. http://www.npr.org/2013/07/24/196249703/move-over-nursing-homes-theres -something-different.

Jamieson, Lynn, David Morgan, Graham Crow, and Graham Allan. "Friends, Neighbors and Distant Partners: Extending or Decentering Family Relationships?" *Sociological Research Online* 11, no. 3 (2006).

Jamieson, Lynn, and Roona Simpson. *Living Alone: Globalization, Identity and Belonging.* Basingstoke, Hampshire, England: Palgrave Macmillan, 2013.

Jayson, Sharon. "Living Together Not Just for the Young, New Data Show." *USA Today*, October 17, 2012. Accessed December 27, 2013. http://www.usatoday.com/story /news/nation/2012/10/17/older-couples-cohabitation/1630681/.

Jiang, L. Crystal, and Jeffrey T. Hancock. "Absence Makes the Communication Grow Fonder: Geographic Separation, Interpersonal Media, and Intimacy in Dating Relationships." *Journal of Communication* 63, no. 3 (2013): 556–77.

Johnson, Dirk. "For Distant Generations in Illinois, Unrelated But Oh So Close." *New York Times*, September 15, 2008. http://www.nytimes.com/2008/09/16/us/16 rantoul.html?pagewanted=print.

Johnson, Michael Eric. "Raising Darwin's Consciousness: An Interview with Sarah Blaffer Hdry on *Mother Nature*." *Primate Diaries* (blog). March 16, 2012. http://blogs .scientificamerican.com/primate-diaries/2012/03/16/raising-darwins-conscious ness-an-interview-with-sarah-blaffer-hrdy-on-mother-nature/.

Kalata, Jean. "Looking at Act II of Women's Lives: Thriving and Striving from 45 On." Washington, DC: AARP Foundation, 2006.

Kane, Rosalie A., Terry Y. Lum, Lois J. Cutler, Howard B. Degenholtz, and Tzy-Chyi Yu. "Resident Outcomes in Small-House Nursing Homes: A Longitudinal Evaluation of the Initial Green House Program." *Journal of the American Geriatric Society* 55, no. 6 (2007): 832–39.

Karlsson, Sofie, and Klas Borell. "A Home of Their Own: Women's Boundary Work in LAT-Relationships." *Journal of Aging Studies* 19, no. 1 (2005): 73–84.

Keenan, Teresa A. "Home and Community Preferences of the 45+ Population." Washington, DC: AARP Research and Strategic Analysis, 2010.

Kendra [no last name listed]. "Q & A with Family by Design Founder Darren Spedale." *It's Conceivable*, July 24, 2013. Accessed November 22, 2013. http://itsconceivable now.com/2013/07/24/family-design-founder-darren-spedale/.

Keyes, Scott. "'Occupy' Group Houses Homeless Couple for Christmas—Plans to House More in 'Tiny Houses.'" *Think Progress*, December 27, 2013. Accessed

June 10, 2014. http://thinkprogress.org/economy/2013/12/27/3104771/occupy-madison-homeless/.

Kilkenny, Marianne. *Your Quest for Home: A Guidebook to Find the Ideal Community for Your Later Years*. San Bernadino, CA: Create Space, 2014.

Klemesrud, Judy. "Gray Panther Founder and a Family of Choice." *New York Times*, June 22, 1981.

Klinenberg, Eric. *Going Solo: The Extraordinary Rise and Surprising Appeal of Living Alone*. New York: Penguin Press, 2012.

———. "Living Alone Is the New Norm." *Time*, March 12, 2012.

Kolker, Claudia. "Leaving Home." *AARP Magazine*, June/July 2012.

Konner, Melvin. "It Does Take a Village." *New York Review of Books*, December 8, 2011. http://www.nybooks.com/articles/archives/2011/dec/08/it-does-take-village.

Kruvant, Mackenzie. "19 Reasons Living Alone is the Best." *Buzzfeed*. January 9, 2014. Accessed July 28, 2014, http://www.buzzfeed.com/mackenziekruvant/living-alone-is-the-best.

Kurutz, Steven. "Square Feet: 84. Possessions: 305." *New York Times*. April 16, 2014. http://www.nytimes.com/2014/04/17/garden/square-feet-84-possessions-305.html.

Landphair, Ted. "At 75, New Deal's 'Green Towns' Endure." *Voice of America*, June 22, 2012. Accessed May 2, 2014. http://www.voanews.com/content/at-75-new-deals-green-towns-endure/1215808.html.

Lara, Adair. "One for the Price of Two." *San Francisco Chronicle*. June 29, 2005.

Larson, Vicki. "Married, Living Together or Something Like That." *OMGchronicles* (blog). January 14, 2013. http://omgchronicles.vickilarson.com/2013/01/14/married-living-together-or-something-like-that/.

Lee, Vivian. "Anatomy of a Fareej: Sustainable Urban Design." *World Policy Journal* 27, no. 4 (2010): 14.

Leinberger, Christopher B. "The Next Slum?" *Atlantic*, March 1, 2008. Accessed February 9, 2014. http://www.theatlantic.com/magazine/archive/2008/03/the-next-slum/306653.

Leith, Katherine H. "Home is Where the Heart Is . . . or Is It? A Phenomenological Exploration of the Meaning of Home for Older Women in Congregate Housing." *Journal of Aging Studies* 20 (2006): 317–33.

Leland, John. "The Neighbors Who Don't Knock." *New York Times*, June 8, 2012. Accessed May 10, 2014. http://query.nytimes.com/gst/fullpage.html?res=9900EED 71530F933A25755C0A9649D8B63.

Leopold, Thomas. "The Legacy of Leaving Home: Long-Term Effects of Coresidence on Parent-Child Relationships." *Journal of Marriage and Family*, 74, no. 3 (2012): 399–412.

Levin, Irene. "Living Apart Together: A New Family Form." *Current Sociology* 52, no. 2 (2004): 223–40.

Levin, Irene, and Jan Trost. "Living Apart Together." *Community, Work, & Family* 2, no. 3 (1999): 279–94.

Linn, Virginia. "Mt. Lebanon Women Find a Cooperative Household a Good Fit." *Pittsburgh Post-Gazette*, July 14, 2012.

Lofquist, Daphne, Terry Lugaila, Martin O'Connell, and Sarah Feliz. "Households and Families: 2010." 2010 Census Briefs, U.S. Government Printing Office, Washington, D.C., April, 2012.

Long, Christopher R., and James R. Averill. "Solitude: An Exploration of the Benefits of Being Alone." *Journal for the Theory of Social Behaviour* 33, no. 1 (2003): 21–44.

Louie, Elaine. "Making Family Out of Friends." *New York Times*, September 26, 2012. http://www.nytimes.com/2012/09/27/greathomesanddestinations/friends-become -family-in-a-bushwick-loft.html.

Lotsa Helping Hands website. Accessed February 11, 2013. http://www.lotsahelping hands.com.

Ludwig, Michael. *Housing in Vienna: Innovative, Social and Ecological*. Catalog of an exhibit, Vienna, Austria, 2008.

Mallett, Shelley. "Understanding Home: A Critical Review of the Literature." *The Sociological Review*, 52, no. 1 (2004): 62–89.

Mandhana, Niharika. "Growing Older in an Urban Village." *New York Times*, August 15, 2011. Accessed May 28, 2014. http://newoldage.blogs.nytimes.com/2011/08/15 /growing-older-in-an-urban-village.

———. "Shared Meals, and Lives." *New York Times*, August 22, 2011. http://newoldage. blogs.nytimes.com/2011/08/22/shared-meals-and-lives/.

Manzella, Joseph C. *Common Purse, Uncommon Future*. Santa Barbara, CA: Praeger, 2010.

Margonelli, Lisa. "How the Trailer Park Could Save Us All." *Pacific Standard*, April 22, 2013. Accessed May 12, 2014. http://www.psmag.com/navigation/politics-and-law /how-the-trailer-park-could-save-us-all-55137/.

Marsden, Peter V. *Social Trends in American Life: Findings from the General Social Survey since 1972*. Princeton, NJ: Princeton University Press, 2012.

Marshall, Nancy L., Anne E. Noonan, Kathleen McCartney, Fern Marx, and Nancy Keefe, "It Takes an Urban Village." *Journal of Family Issues* 22 (2001): 163–82.

Martin, Joyce A., Brady E. Hamilton, Michelle J. K. Osterman, Sally C. Curtin, and T. J. Mathews. "Births: Final Data for 2012." *National Vital Statistics Reports* 62, no. 9 (2013): 1–87.

Martin, Joyce A., Brady E. Hamilton, Stephanie J. Ventura, Michelle J. K. Osterman, and T. J. Matthews. "Births: Final Data for 2011." *National Vital Statistics Report* 62, no. 1 (June 28, 2013): 2–9.

McCaffery, April. "Celebrating Friend-Love." *It's All About Balance* (blog). February 14, 2013. http://formerlyaprildawn.blogspot.com/2013/02/celebrating-friend-love.html.

———. "The 40th Birthday Post." *It's All About Balance* (blog). April 10, 2013. http://for merlyaprildawn.blogspot.com/2013/04/the-40th-birthday-post.html.

———. "Celebrating 10 Years of Independence." *It's All About Balance* (blog). July 4, 2013. http://formerlyaprildawn.blogspot.com/2013_07_01_archive.html.

McCamant, Kathryn, and Charles Durrett. *Creating Cohousing: Building Sustainable Communities*. British Columbia, Canada: New Society Publishers, 2011.

McGreevy, Patrick. "Brown Signs Bill Allowing Children More than Two Legal Parents." *Los Angeles Times*, October 4, 2013. http://articles.latimes.com/2013/oct/04/local/la-me -pc-cal-governor-signs-bill-allowing-children-more-than-two-legal-parents-2013 1004.

Medlicott, Joan. *The Ladies of Covington Send Their Love*. New York: St. Martin's, 2000.

Milan, Anne, and Alice Peters. "Couples Living Apart." *Canadian Social Trends* 2, no. 3 (2003): 279–94.

Mintz, Steven. "The Kids Are Moving Back in After College? Smart Career Move." *The Washington Post*, June 1, 2012. http://www.washingtonpost.com/opinions /the-kids-are-moving-back-in-after-college-smart-career-move/2012/06/01/gJQA MWla7U_story.html.

Montgomery, Charles. *Happy City: Transforming Our Lives through Urban Design*. New York: Farrar, Strauss and Giroux, 2013.

Musick, Kelly, and Larry Bumpass. "Reexamining the Case for Marriage: Union Formation and Changes in Well-Being." *Journal of Marriage and Family* 74, no. 1 (2012): 1–18.

National Shared Housing Resource Center website. Accessed February 5, 2013. http://nationalsharedhousing.org/.

Netterfield, Carol, and Netterfield, David. "Generations of Hope." YouTube video, 4:12. Posted by Illinois Times, August 4, 2010. https://www.youtube.com/watch?v=kZG_K9fltc8.

Newman, Katherine S. *The Accordion Family*. Boston, MA: Beacon Press, 2012.

Newman, Susan. *Under One Roof: All Grown Up and (Re)learning to Live Happily Ever After*. Guilford, CT: Lyons Press, 2010.

Noah, Timothy. "Stay Put, Young Man." *Washington Monthly*, November/ December 2013. http://www.washingtonmonthly.com/magazine/november_december_2013/features/stay_put_young_man047332.php.

North, Anna. "Life Partners Who Aren't—And Never Will Be— Lovers." *BuzzFeed*, November 8, 2012. http://www.buzzfeed.com/annanorth/life-partners-who-arent-and-never-will-be.

Oishi, Shigehiro, and Ulrich Schimmack. "Residential Mobility, Well-Being, and Mortality." *Journal of Personality and Social Psychology* 98 (2012): 980–94.

"Older Americans 2012: Key Indicators of Well-Being." Federal Interagency Forum on Aging-Related Statistics. Washington, DC: U.S. Government Printing Office, June 2012.

Oppenheimer, Mark. "It's a Wonderful Block." *New York Times*, October 5, 2008. http://www.nytimes.com/2008/10/05/realestate/keymagazine/105newhaven-t.html?pagewanted=print.

"Our View." YouTube video, 28:40. Posted by Santa Barbara Village, December 3, 2013. https://www.youtube.com/watch?v=9487TMyxHNM.

Palgi, Michal, and Shulamit Reinharz, eds. *One Hundred Years of Kibbutz Life*. New Brunswick, NJ: Transaction Publishers, 2011.

Park, Hyunjoon. "Single Parenthood and Children's Reading Performance in Asia." *Journal of Marriage and Family* 69, no. 3 (2007): 863–77.

Parker, Kim. "The Boomerang Generation: Feeling OK about Living with Mom and Dad." Pew Social and Demographic Trends, 2012.

Parnes, Amie. "'First Grandma' Embraces Life in D.C." *Politico*, September 12, 2011. http://www.politico.com/news/stories/0811/61719.html.

Payne, Krista K., and Jennifer Copp. "Young Adults in the Parental Home and the Great Recession." National Center for Family & Marriage Research, 2013. http://www.bgsu.edu/arts-and-sciences/ncfmr.html (page discontinued).

Peck, Kathy. "Living Together." *AARP Bulletin* (Letters), October 2012: 42.

Perrigan, Dana. "Houses United." *San Francisco Chronicle*, December 10, 2006. http://www.sfgate.com/bayarea/article/HOUSES-UNITED-For-those-who-live-in-cohousing-2543542.php.

Pinsof, William M. "The Death of 'Till Death Us Do Part': The Transformation of Pair-Bonding in the 20th Century." *Family Processes* 41, no. 2 (2002): 135–57.

Pluhar, Annamarie. *Sharing Housing: A Guidebook for Finding and Keeping Good Housemates.* Peterborough, NH: Homemate Publishing, 2011.

"Principles of Urbanism," *New Urbanism.* Accessed December 28, 2013. http://www.newurbanism.org/newurbanism/principles.html.

Putnam, Robert. *Bowling Alone: The Collapse and Revival of American Community.* New York: Simon & Schuster, 2000.

Rainie, Lee, and Barry Wellman. *Networked: The New Social Operating System.* Cambridge, MA: The MIT Press, 2012.

Rapoza, Kenneth. "One in Five Americans Work from Home, Numbers Seen Rising Over 60%." *Forbes*, February 18, 2013. http://www.forbes.com/sites/kenrapoza/2013/02/18/one-in-five-americans-work-from-home-numbers-seen-rising-over-60.

Regnier-Loilier, Arnaud, Eva Beaujouan, and Catherine Villeneuve-Gokalp. "Neither Single, Nor in a Couple: A Study of Living Apart Together in France." *Demographic Research* 21, no. 4 (2009): 75–108.

Reimondos, Anna, Ann Evans, and Edith Gray. "Living-Apart-Together (LAT) Relationships in Australia." *Family Matters* 87 (2011): 43–55.

Reyes, Karen Westerberg. "The Covington Chronicles." *AARP Magazine*, July/August 2007: 53.

Rodgers, Nicole. "Finding a Parenting Partner: A Q & A with FamilybyDesign Founder, Darren Spedale." *Role/Reboot*, March 4, 2013. http://www.rolereboot.org/family /details/2013-03-qa-with-family-by-design-founder-darren-spedale.

Roseneil, Sasha. "On Not Living with a Partner: Unpicking Coupledom and Cohabitation." *Sociological Research Online* 11, no. 3 (2006).

Rosenfeld, Michael J. *The Age of Independence: Interracial Unions, Same-Sex Unions, and the Changing American Family*. Cambridge, MA: Harvard University Press, 2007.

———. "Young Adulthood as a Factor in Social Change in the United States." *Population and Development Review* 32, no. 1 (2006): 27–51.

Roth, Leland M. *American Architecture: A History*. 2nd ed. Boulder, CO: Westview Press, 2003.

Rubin, Rita. "Single and Seriously Ill: Care Circles Fill in for Family." *Today Health*, August 29, 2011. http://www.today.com/id/44247864/ns/today-today_health/t/single-ser iously-ill-care-circles-fill-family.

Ruggles, Steven. "The Transformation of American Family Structure." *American Historical Review* 99, no. 1 (1994): 103–28.

———. "The Decline of Intergenerational Coresidence in the United States, 1850 to 2000." *American Sociological Review*, 72, no. 6 (2007): 964–89.

Rybczynski, Witold. *Home: A Short History of an Idea*. New York: Penguin Books, 1986.

———. *Last Harvest*. New York: Scribner, 2007.

Sanguinetti, Angela. "Cohousing: A Behavioral Approach, Transformational Practices, and the Retrofit Model." PhD diss., University of California, Irvine, 2013.

Sarkisian, Natalia, and Naomi Gerstel. "Till Marriage Do Us Part: Adult Children's Relationships with Their Parents." *Journal of Marriage and Family* 70, no. 2 (2008): 360–76.

Scanzoni, John. *Designing Families: The Search for Self and Community in the Information Age*. Thousand Oaks: Pine Forge Press, 2000.

Scharlach, Andrew, and Carrie Graham. "Villages in the US: Member Impacts." Presentation to the Santa Barbara Village, Santa Barbara, CA, May 2013.

Schnarr, Nancy. "Nowhere Else to Go—Homes for Unwed Mothers in Canada during the 20th Century." Accessed November 18, 2013. http://www.theclayandglass.ca /wp-content/uploads/2011/08/Unwed-Mothers-research-Nancy-Final.pdf-FOR -WEBSITE-PROVIDE-PDF-PG2.pdf

Segrin, Chris, Alesia Woszildo, Michelle Givertz, and Neil Montgomery. "Parent and Child Traits Associated with Overparenting." *Journal of Social and Clinical Psychology* 32, no. 6 (2013): 569–95.

Seliger, Susan. "In the Backyard, Grandma's New Apartment." *New York Times*, May 1, 2012. http://newoldage.blogs.nytimes.com/2012/05/01/in-the-backyard-grandmas -new-apartment.

Short, Susan E., Frances K. Goldscheider, and Berna M.Torr. "Less Help for Mother: The Decline in Coresidential Female Support for the Mothers of Young Children, 1880–2000." *Demography* 43 (2006): 617–29.

Shyong, Frank. "Making Room for the Unexpected, in More Ways than One." *Los Angeles Times*, January 1, 2014. http://articles.latimes.com/2014/jan/01/local/la -me-shyong-parents-moving-in-20140102.

Sifferlin, Alexandra. "Bill Gates Is the Richest Man in the World (Again)." *Time*, March 3, 2014. http://time.com/11389/bill-gates-worlds-richest-man.

Smith, Jack. "Getting the Word Out: The Time is Right for 'Posslq.'" *Los Angeles Times*, November 17, 1985. http://articles.latimes.com/1985-11-17/magazine/tm-6681_1 _word-posslq.

Smith, Wes. *Hope Meadows: Real-Life Stories of Healing and Caring from an Inspiring Community*. New York: Berkley Books, 2001.

Span, Paula. *When the Time Comes: Families with Aging Parents Share Their Struggles and Solutions*. New York: Grand Central Life and Style, 2009.

———. "Who's Moving in Now?" *New York Times*, August 4, 2014. http://newoldage .blogs.nytimes.com/2014/08/04/whos-moving-in-now.

Spencer, Liz, and Ray Pahl. *Rethinking Friendship: Hidden Solidarities Today*. Princeton, NJ: Princeton University Press, 2006.

Sprague, Joan Forrester. *More than Housing: Lifeboats for Women and Children*. Boston, MA: Butterworth Architecture, 1991.

Stafford, Laura. "Geographic Distance and Communication during Courtship." *Communication Research* 37, no. 2 (2010): 275–97.

Stoessel, Lise. *Living Happily Ever After Separately: How Separate Spaces Could Save Your Marriage*. Richmond, VA: Brandylane, 2012.

Stoll, Shannan. "It's a Hub." *Yes! Magazine*, Summer 2012: 42–43.

Storr, Anthony. *Solitude: A Return to the Self*. New York: Ballantine Books, 1988.

Strohm, Charles Q., Judith A. Seltzer, Susan D. Cochran, and Vickie M. Mays. "'Living Apart Together' Relationships in the United States." *Demographic Research* 21, no. 7 (2009): 177–214.

Sullivan, Carmel. "Single Mothers Unite." In *Chicken Soup for the Single Parent's Soul: Stories of Hope, Healing, and Humor*, edited by Jack Canfield, Mark Victor Hansen, Laurie Hartman, and Nancy Vogl, 31–34. Deerfield Beach, FL: HCI Books, 2005.

"Surrogate Couple Explain Their Unconventional Decision," YouTube video, 3:40. From an interview by Rosie O'Donnell excerpted from *The Rosie O'Donnell Show* and posted by Anderson Cooper on *Anderson Live*, November 27, 2012. http://www.youtube.com/watch?feature=player_embedded&v=ah2E4W280-Q.

Swarns, Rachel L. "An In-Law Is Finding Washington to Her Liking." *New York Times*, May 3, 2009. http://www.nytimes.com/2009/05/04/us/politics/04robinson.html.

Taylor, Paul, Kim Parker, Seth Motel, and Eileen Patten. "The Big Generation Gap at the Polls is Echoed in Attitudes on Budget Tradeoffs." Pew Research Center, December 20, 2012.

Taylor, Paul, Rakesh Kochhar, D'Vera Cohn, Jeffrey S. Passel, Gabriel Velasco, Seth Motel, Eileen Patten. "Fighting Poverty in a Tough Economy, Americans Move in with Their Relatives." Pew Research Center, October 3, 2011.

Taylor, Paul, Jeffrey Passel, Richard Fry, Richard Morin, Wendy Wang, Gabriel Velasco, and Daniel Dockterman. "The Return of the Multi-Generational Family Household." Pew Research Center, March 18, 2010.

Thomas Jr., Robert McG. "Maggie Kuhn, 89, the Founder of the Gray Panthers, Is Dead." *New York Times*, April 23, 1995. http://www.nytimes.com/1995/04/23/obituaries/maggie-kuhn-89-the-founder-of-the-gray-panthers-is-dead.html.

Thomas, William H. *What Are Old People For?* St. Louis, MO: VanderWyk & Burnham, 2007.

Thompson, Derek. "A Record-High Number of Young People Are Still Living with Their Parents: Why?" *Atlantic Cities*, August 30, 2013. http://www.theatlantic.com/business/archive/2013/08/a-record-high-number-of-young-people-are-still-living-with-their-parents-why/279159.

Thompson, Derek, and Jordan Weissmann. "The Cheapest Generation: Why Millennials Aren't Buying Cars or Houses, and What That Means for the Economy." *Atlantic*, September 2012.

Thoreau, Henry David. *Walden; or Life in the Woods*. Mineola, New York, 1995. (Originally published in 1854.)

Thornton, Arland, and Linda Young-DeMarco. "Four Decades of Trends in Attitudes Toward Family Issues in the United States: The 1960s Through the 1990s." *Journal of Marriage and Family* 63, no. 4 (2001): 1009–37.

Toker, Zeynep. "New Housing for New Households: Comparing Cohousing and New Urbanist Developments with Women in Mind." *Journal of Architectural and Planning Research* 27 (2010): 325–39.

Trejos, Nancy. "Suites All Around." *Washington Post*, June 30, 2007. http://www.washingtonpost.com/wp-dyn/content/article/2007/06/29/AR2007062900942.html.

Trost, Jan. "The Social Institution of Marriage." *Journal of Comparative Family Studies* 41, no. 4 (2010): 507–14.

Twin Oaks Community website. Accessed August 10, 2014. http://www.twinoaks.org.

Umberger, Mary. "Post-Recession, Expect a Shift in Building Trends." *Los Angeles Times Times*, April 17, 2011. http://articles.latimes.com/2011/apr/17/business/la-fi-umberger-20110417.

U.S. Census Bureau. "About 36 Million Americans Moved in the Last Year, Census Bureau Reports." November 18, 2013. http://www.census.gov/newsroom/releases/archives/mobility_of_the_population/cb13-192.html (page discontinued).

———. "Census Bureau Reports More Adults Living in Shared Households, More Receiving Food Stamps, Public Assistance Unchanged." November 28, 2012. https://www.census.gov/newsroom/releases/archives/american_community_survey_acs/cb12-224.html.

———. "Census Bureau Reports National Mover Rate Increases After a Record Low in 2011." December 10, 2012. http://www.census.gov/newsroom/releases/archives/mobility_of_the_population/cb12-240.html.

———. "Mover Rate Reaches Record Low, Census Bureau Reports." November 15, 2011. http://www.census.gov/newsroom/releases/archives/mobility_of_the_population/cb11-193.html.

———. "Older Americans Month: May 2014." Facts for Features. March 25, 2014. http://www.census.gov/content/dam/Census/newsroom/facts-for-features/2014/cb14-ff07_older_americans.pdf.

U.S. Census Bureau News, "Facts for Features: Unmarried and Single Americans Week, September 21–27, 2014." U.S. Department of Commerce, Washington, DC,

July 30, 2014. http://www.census.gov/content/dam/Census/newsroom/facts-for -features/2014/cb14ff-21_unmarried.pdf.

U.S. Census Bureau. Table A-1, "Years of School Completed by People 25 Years and Over, by Age and Sex: Selected Years." https://www.census.gov/hhes/socdemo/education /data/cps/historical/tabA-1.xls.

———. Table MS-2, "Estimated Median Age at First Marriage, by Sex: 1890 to the Present," Current Population Survey, March, and Annual Social and Economic Supplements, 2013. http://www.census.gov/population/socdemo/hh-fam/ms2.xls.

Ventura, Stephanie J. "Changing Patterns of Nonmarital Childbearing in the United States." *NCHS Data Brief*, no.18 (May 2009): 1–8.

Village-to-Village Network website. Accessed May 28, 2014. http://www.vtvnetwork.org /content.aspx?page_id=22&club_id=691012&module_id=65139.

Walljasper, Jay. "How to Design Our Neighborhoods for Happiness." *Yes! Magazine*, July 26, 2013. http://www.yesmagazine.org/happiness/how-to-design-our-neighbor hoods-for-happiness.

Wang, Hua, and Barry Wellman. "Social Connectivity in America: Changes in Adult Friendship Network Size from 2002 to 2007." *American Behavioral Scientist* 52, no. 8 (2010): 1148–69.

Wang, Wendy, and Paul Taylor. "For Millennials, Parenthood Trumps Marriage." Pew Research Center: Social and Demographic Trends, March 9, 2011.

Williams, Alex. "Friends of a Certain Age: Why Is It Hard to Make Friends Over 30?" *New York Times*, July 13, 2012. http://www.nytimes.com/2012/07/15/fashion/the -challenge-of-making-friends-as-an-adult.html?pagewanted=all.

Williams, Dee. *The Big Tiny: A Built-It-Myself Memoir*. New York: Blue Rider Press, 2014.

Winfrey, Oprah. "Oprah Talks to Michelle Obama." *O, The Oprah Magazine*, April 2009. http://www.oprah.com/omagazine/Michelle-Obamas-Oprah-Interview-O-Maga zine-Cover-with-Obama/4.

Winograd, Morley, and Michael D. Hais. "Millennial Generation Safe at Home." *New Geography*, April 15, 2012. http://www.newgeography.com/content/002774 -milennial-generation-safe-home.

Wright, Jennifer. "Millennials: The Worst, Most Entitled, Most Spoiled Generation in the History of the Humankind?" *Alternet*, June 1, 2013. http://www.alternet.org /culture/millennials-generation-y?paging=off&current_page=1#bookmark.

BIBLIOGRAPHY

Yeagle, Patrick. "This Is the Village It Takes." *Illinois Times*, August 5, 2010. http://illinois times.com/article-7603-this-is-the-village-it-takes.html.

Yee, Kate Madden. "Come Together: Cohousing and the Art of Neighborhood." *The Monthly*, November 2013. http://www.themonthly.com/feature1311.html.

Yee, Vivian. "In Winning Design, City Hopes to Address a Cramped Future." *New York Times*, January 22, 2013. http://cityroom.blogs.nytimes.com/2013/01/22/city -unveils-winner-of-tiny-apartment-competition.

Yen, Hope. "U.S. Growth of Distant Suburbs Falls to Historic Low." Associated Press, April 5, 2012.

6/5/15